Creative Design Decisions

Creative
Design
Decisions

*A Systematic Approach to
Problem Solving in Architecture*

Stephen J. Kirk

Kent F. Spreckelmeyer

Illustrated by Steve Padget

 VAN NOSTRAND REINHOLD COMPANY
New York

To Fount Smothers.

Designed by Joy Taylor

Van Nostrand Reinhold Company Inc.
115 Fifth Avenue
New York, New York 10003

Van Nostrand Reinhold Company Limited
Molly Millars Lane
Wokingham, Berkshire RG11 2PY, England

Van Nostrand Reinhold
480 La Trobe Street
Melbourne, Victoria 3000, Australia

Macmillan of Canada
Division of Canada Publishing Corporation
164 Commander Boulevard
Agincourt, Ontario M1S 3C7, Canada

16 15 14 13 12 11 10 9 8 7 6 5 4 3 2 1

Library of Congress Cataloging-in-Publication Data
Kirk, Stephen J.
   Creative design decisions.
   Bibliography: p.
   Includes index.
   1. Architecture—Decision making. 2. Architectural
design. I. Spreckelmeyer, Kent F., 1950–
II. Title.
NA2540.K5 1988   720'.68   87-8199
ISBN 0-442-24643-9

Contents

Preface

DECISION MAKING IN DESIGN

The process of design requires a continuous flow of information among the architect, the building owner, the contractor, the people who will ultimately use the building, and any number of design specialists, analysts, and consultants. The process involves the generation and selection of alternatives that satisfy owner and user needs. The criteria used to generate and evaluate these alternatives are usually defined—implicitly or explicitly—by the project owner. At times these criteria are established by regulation, as by life-safety codes or accessibility requirements, and at other times the designer defines the criteria in isolation from any owner guidelines or direction. Only rarely are the people who use environments consulted during the design process, especially if the project involves a large and complex building program.

Until recently, design decisions have been made informally, usually at predetermined points in the building-delivery schedule (fig. P-1). This decision making is becoming more formalized as owners look for processes that consider well-defined design objectives—costs, energy use, aesthetics, function, circulation—and many points of view: those of the owner, designer, user, builder, building manager, and community. This book proposes such a process and provides the reader with a more formal structure for making design decisions. This process also encourages the designer to consider energy use, cost, and the building users' needs as integral parts of the design process. Architects, engineers, and other design professionals can thus make more informed design decisions. The purposes of the book are to enhance the decision-making skills of design professionals; to clarify and simulate the consequences of a wide range of design dimensions, including cost, energy use, aesthetics, and behavioral factors; and to provide a framework for decision making that will allow a large number of people to participate in the process.

Should it be built?———What kind is required?———How much to construct?———How is it being used?

FIGURE P-1.   Traditional decision points in the design process.

NEED FOR FORMAL PROCESS

Why has this need for more formality in design arisen? There are a number of reasons. Foremost among them is the increasing complexity of defining design problems. As William Peña has suggested, architects are traditionally trained as problem solvers, not as design analysts. However, David Meeker, former executive vice-president of the American Institute of Architects, has questioned whether design professionals are prepared to meet the challenges inherent in an information age. "Are [architects] satisfied with their expertise in energy-conscious design? Are communities aware of [design professionals'] interests and concerns in shaping the built environment and the joint role in ensuring design excellence?" (Meeker, *Construction News*, April 24, 1981). There is also a wide separation between the people who use a facility and those who own it. This means that design professionals must consider a number of points of view, as opposed to the traditional scenario in which the patron both commissioned the design (as owner) and utilized the facility upon construction completion. Contemporary facilities are often designed for client organizations where not only are the users and owners different and separate, but some are even unknown to or remain unseen by the designers themselves. For example, decisions in hospital design are often made by clients and designers with little or no input from those most affected by those decisions—the physicians, staff, and patients.

Just as the concept of the client is broadening, so too is the design team expanding. In the past, a single designer, usually the architect, could analyze a client's needs and develop a satisfactory solution. Today, with the increased complexity of building types and the technical support systems for these facilities, many specialists are required to solve a client's problems. These new disciplines, along with the established ones, are finding themselves as team players in a game that has neither formalized rules nor a systematic approach to a conclusion.

During the last decade a fourth, and possibly the most critical, reason appeared, prompting clients to ask for a more formalized decision-making process in design: the need to conserve resources. Resources are defined here as economic wealth (capital costs and life-cycle costs) and land, the ambient environment, energy, and the people associated with these resources.

The final reason that clients want a more formal approach to decision making is that it is now feasible for the designer to store, retrieve, and manipulate large quantities of data quickly and inexpensively. Recent trends in computer-aided design techniques have allowed designer resources and energy to shift from the construction documents stage of design to earlier stages of a project and so consider a wider range of design alternatives. Society in general has a heightened level of sophistication because of the information revolution, and it is important that designers integrate this technology into the creation of humane and efficient environments.

Most of the formalized decision-making techniques in design, such as life-cycle costing and value engineering, have entered the design process as methods to solve very specific and specialized aspects of design problems. As the complexity of design problems has grown, so have the number and range of consulting services. Certainly traditional decision-making processes are not sufficient to allow the designer to select an automated material-handling system, determine the payback period and life-cycle cost implications for a proposed hospital wing, or predict how people might respond to a novel and complex building form. Only specialized tools can address these issues. This book presents many of the tools—and a problem-solving approach—to help the designer answer such questions.

PURPOSE AND SCOPE OF THIS BOOK

This book presents a number of analytic techniques that architects, engineers, planners, and other design professionals can apply within their own practices. These techniques are summarized below.

Technique	*Use*
Function analysis	Assists in operationally defining the goals to be achieved in design and defines the problem to be solved
Group creativity	Expands the available alternatives to solve a problem and enlarges the pool of people in the creative process
Life-cycle costing	Precisely measures the economic consequence of design alternatives
Decision analysis	Measures multiple objectives—both financial and nonmonetary—of design problems
Post-occupancy evaluation	Measures how people in the building perform with defined functions
Communication	Facilitates clear and understandable data accumulation and information dissemination

This text also aims to organize the process of design into a more clearly defined and problem-defining and problem-solving procedure that facilitates the use of the analytic techniques through the design and construction cycle. This procedure is summarized in the following steps.

Problem-solving Step	*Purpose*
Inform	Gather and analyze appropriate information to understand and define the problem clearly
Speculate	Generate design alternatives that address the problem
Evaluate	Evaluate various alternatives based on economic and nonmonetary considerations
Synthesize	Combine the most promising aspects of the alternatives into new design solutions
Recommend	Communicate the most promising alternative(s) that satisfy the problem

The third objective of this book is to provide a number of sample applications of the analytic techniques. These examples will clarify how a more formalized decision-making process can be implemented in design projects. This text should be viewed as a sourcebook and guide to decision makers. Each technique chapter is referenced with an extensive bibliography to allow the decision maker to gain a detailed knowledge of the methods introduced in the book.

Finally, this book offers a design process that accommodates both imagination and critical evaluation in a problem-solving approach to design. Architects are expected to be both innovators and evaluators. Intuition, creativity, and imagination have traditionally been considered primary tools of the designer. This book searches out processes and techniques that combine analytic tools with the creative aspects of design.

The book opens with the historical background of decision-making processes in design, which sets the stage for a specific problem-solving methodology. This methodology can be applied during a project's feasibility, design, construction, and occupancy stages. Analytic techniques such as function analysis, group creativity methods, life-cycle costing, decision analysis, post-occupancy evaluation, and communication methods are then presented to help architects, engineers, and planners implement this methodology in their own practices. To reinforce the problem-solving methodology and illustrate the analytic techniques, several project applications are presented. These projects vary considerably in size and complexity and include a data-processing center and a corporate headquarters. Each illustrates the application of the problem-solving techniques during the phases of the facility cycle from project feasibility through occupancy. These examples demonstrate how a formalized process of decision making can provide a larger degree of design input from the owners, designers, users, and occupants of built environments. Many criteria—including cost, energy, aesthetics, function, and expandability—can be defined and analyzed during the design process. The conclusion summarizes the benefits of this approach to problem solving in architecture, and looks at how it might be formally integrated into the design profession.

Acknowledgments

The production of this book, like the design process, was a team effort. The authors would like to acknowledge the contributions of those people who lent their expertise and special knowledge. The manuscript and countless revisions were typed and proofed by Cindy Muckey, the word-processing supervisor in the School of Architecture and Urban Design at the University of Kansas. Mary Erickson edited and corrected the final drafts of the text and provided suggestions concerning the organization of the material in each chapter. Robert W. Marans also provided helpful editorial comments. Most of the charts and worksheets were produced by the graphics department at the Detroit offices of Smith, Hinchman & Grylls, Inc. The original artwork and illustrations for the entire text were done by Steve Padget.

A major contribution to the material found in the case-study examples came from Frank Jennings of Automatic Data Processing, Inc. and Lee Murray of the Tulsa architectural firm of Murray Jones Murray. A special thanks goes to these individuals and organizations for providing the authors the opportunity to implement the decision-making techniques outlined in the book in their own practices. They spent many hours helping to develop these techniques and utilizing them in a number of design projects.

The authors are also indebted to their host organizations for technical, bibliographic, and financial support. Mr. Kirk's firm—Smith, Hinchman & Grylls, Inc.—has been a leading proponent of value engineering services in the design professions and enabled him to develop many of the life-cycle costing and function analysis techniques outlined in this book. The School of Architecture and Urban Design at the University of Kansas has encouraged and supported Dr. Spreckelmeyer in the development and implementation of the post-occupancy evaluation and decision-analysis tools described in the case studies. The university also provided the authors with excellent bibliographic and research services.

CHAPTER 1

The Evolution of
Design Decisions in
Architecture

ARCHITECTS must assume the central decision-making role in the design and building process, except for specific types of design projects—such as public works, product development, and manufacturing processes—that are the responsibility of engineers and industrial designers. While this book may be relevant to design needs in these areas, its primary focus is building applications. This is the role that architects historically have envisioned for themselves, one that was at the root of the emergence of the architectural profession during the late nineteenth and early twentieth centuries. Ideally, architects are the generalists of the building process, orchestrating the technical specialists and establishing the vision of what the built environment will mean to those who use and experience it. The architect as "master builder" describes the role of the designer throughout the history of monuments, palaces, and cathedrals. In the history of the built environment, however, only a small proportion of our environment has been shaped by a formal design process. Traditionally associated with the elite stratum of society, architects have helped construct buildings that served the rich and powerful. The remainder of the environment has been shaped either by laypersons or by builders, contractors, and real-estate developers. In recent years, much attention has been given to the process of informal design—"architecture without architects"—because of its pervasiveness in the human experience.[1]

Today, it appears that the designer is becoming less the generalist and key decision maker in architecture and more a team player in a complex management process. In any substantial design project, the decision-making process lies in the hands of an array of design

2

participants—project managers, construction managers, principal architects, job captains, consultants, client representatives, and cost analysts. Who makes the key decisions in this process and who is responsible to whom? If architects are to provide the central focus for decision making in design, it is important to understand the skills they should possess and the philosophy of design they may be required to espouse. A brief history of how the design professions have evolved begins the search for such philosophical understandings.[2]

THE ARCHITECTURAL PROFESSION

The rise of architecture as a licensed profession in Western Europe and North America during the nineteenth century encouraged the establishment of efficiently run design offices. Most licensing laws in Great Britain and the United States were based on the premise that the architect must assume a public and legal responsibility for design decisions.[3] The act of design was distinguished from the act of building, and the architect—under the auspices of various professional organizations—carved out a specialized area of knowledge. Fees were standardized and codes of professional conduct were established to define and regulate the architect's conduct in the building process. To a large extent, the practice of architecture became associated with an office rather than an individual. Instead of viewing the activity of initiating and producing building plans as a unified process, the establishment of architecture as a licensed profession created a segmented view of that process. The complex buildings that emerged from the industrial revolution required far more specialized knowledge than could be possessed by one person. The modern architecture office, therefore, was a response to professional and societal pressures for increased competence and technical knowledge.[4]

Clients were changing too. The construction of banks, stock and commodity exchanges, factories, and transportation centers was being managed less by a single individual and more by building committees and boards of directors. They made collective decisions in selecting designers, reviewing architectural competitions, and looking after the interests of the users of the facility. Designers were required to submit designs in open competition with their colleagues. This additional pressure increased the urgency of establishing well-organized offices in order to maintain control over the production of design work and to maximize the productivity of the work force employed by the architect.

A third major change was the introduction of the general contractor in the 1800s. The general contractor was a businessperson who was concerned primarily with the financial aspects of the design project. The introduction of the general contractor into the building process kept the master mason and other building tradespersons from participating in the decision-making process with designers and displaced the client's and designer's direct contact with the building crafts.

As more specialists, more client committees, and a host of subcontractors became involved in the design process, there arose the need for more formal communications. Specialized drawings were required at various stages of the design cycle. Drawing requirements increased dramatically with the development of complex building components, more challenging mechanical, electrical, vertical circulation, and structural systems, and new specialized trades. Presentation drawings also changed, becoming more pictorial. This came about partially because well-educated patrons, who had often possessed high levels of design skills themselves, were being replaced with building committees composed of businesspersons and merchants who had to be graphically led through a design by a designer.

The final trend in this era of increased specialization was the compartmentalization of professional tasks and the introduction of new building types and building systems. These changes meant that both the size of the typical design office and the variety of disciplines responsible for decision making had to expand. The architect was becoming just another player on the team while fighting to remain the generalist who coordinated the entire project. Design decision making was becoming more complicated, while more and more of the central control of the design process was slipping through the architect's fingers.[5]

THE OFFICE VERSUS THE INDIVIDUAL

The architect's change in image from master builder to practitioner occurred over a relatively short period of time. Soon after the founding of the American Institute of Architects in 1857, there followed the establishment of major design firms that continue—at least corporately—to this day. The training of architects during the early years of the profession reflected this transformation. L'Ecole des Beaux-Arts in Paris became the center of architectural education and was built around the studio as the laboratory for problem solving in design. Key elements of studio instruction in the Beaux-Arts system were the interaction between the studio master and the individual student as well as the exchange of ideas among students themselves. Although individualism and competition were accepted as part of this manner of instruction, the Beaux-Arts system supported the concepts of group creativity and design collaboration.[6]

Among the first Beaux-Arts-trained American architects were Richard Morris Hunt and H. H. Richardson, two of the most influential architects in the United States during the second half of the nineteenth century. The first American atelier—a studio combining training with practice—was begun by Hunt in New York in 1857; Richardson went into practice nine years later. Both offices encouraged collaboration to come up with a range of design solutions to a single problem. This allowed a large portion of the office to participate and created an atmosphere of cooperation and collective teamwork in the office. Hunt and Richardson both utilized the rational approach to design encouraged by the Beaux-Arts, and they each established a creative atmosphere that nurtured designers (Kostof 1977, 309–12).

This style of collaborative and personalized structure in design offices lasted only a short time. America was growing rapidly, and the large scale of building projects demanded large design organizations. In 1879 C. F. McKim and Stanford White, who had trained with Richardson, established the New York office of McKim, Mead and White. This was to become one of the first of the larger design offices, with a staff of eighty-nine by 1909. With increased size came a new type of office organization. When the office was small, all the principals and staff had shared responsibilities, as was characteristic of the offices of Hunt and of Richardson. As McKim, Mead and White grew larger, McKim became involved in business, development, and marketing; William Mead was responsible for project management and production; and White took over important design decisions. It became clear that, besides assuming specialized functions, the principals would have to delegate authority as part of this new office organization (Kostof 1977, 313–14). The large firm set the tone of architectural practice at the beginning of the twentieth century.

D. H. Burnham of Chicago expressed the tendency of design firms to increase the amount of specialization and size of projects: "My idea is to work up to a big business, to handle big things, deal with big businessmen, and to build a big organization, for you can't handle big things unless you have an organization" (Kostof 1977, 315). After H. H. Richardson's death, the principle of team participation in the Richardson office was transmuted into the practice of separate responsibilities. Along with the switch from team effort to separation of responsibilities and the dividing of decision making into various disciplines, a new attitude emerged regarding the ideals of the design profession. The practice of design had become business, with architects making money and meeting payrolls by practicing the business of architecture.

To achieve efficiency in the design office, decision making had to be separated from production. Individuals took specialized control of design projects and coordinated different design tasks. This separation further decreased the involvement of the individual and created a new kind of employee—the "project manager," who supervised the work process itself (Kostof 1977, 318). The architect was reduced from master problem solver to office specialist, participating in the project on the same level as the structural, mechanical, and service specialists.

THE MODERN MOVEMENT

Thus, by the beginning of the twentieth century, the office structure of architectural firms had assumed much the same appearance that it has today. Even in small firms, the specialization of work tasks and office functions is a common feature of design decision-making processes. A number of architects in the first half of this century, however, found this segmented approach to design decisions unsatisfactory. Frank Lloyd Wright, Le Corbusier, Alvar Aalto, and Walter Gropius defined the design process in terms much more related to the technological and social conditions of the modern era, rather than responding primarily to economic pressures to survive as a business. Wright and Aalto envisioned natural or organic responses to social needs in an industrial world. Le Corbusier's rational approach to design using austerity and strict geometric orders reflected a desire for economy and repetition in construction processes. Gropius wanted to bring together machine technology and modern de-

FIGURE 1-1. The project team.

sign theory; he approached all design problems from a unified perspective. He considered it crucial, for example, that all designers share a common education and approach problems as generalists, each working as a team member in solving problems. The Bauhaus was established to show how similar methods can solve all design problems. Teams composed of different design disciplines were assembled in his studios to find common solutions to a wide variety of design projects (Kostof 1977, 322).

This form of cooperation and joint responsibility was a dramatic change from the parceling out of responsibilities in Burnham's office. Gropius considered the concept of cooperative decision making "particularly promising, and very appropriate to the spirit of our age; especially when these groups include engineers and economists" (Kostof 1977, 323). This collaboration was to culminate in the unified process of decision making and design cooperation among a team of designers. "If [the architect] will build up a closely cooperating team together with the engineer, the scientist, and the builder, then design, construction, and economy may again become an entity—a fusion of art, science and business" (Kostof 1977, 323). The architect, in the mind of Gropius, would again assume the role as the central organizer and synthesizer of this diverse and creative team of designers (Kostof 1977, 324).

CREATIVITY IN DESIGN

As the business of architecture and the associated structure of efficient design offices grew, the decision-making process became increasingly remote from the occupants and users of the facility. The purpose of "function" in architecture was somehow dismissed from the concerns of the architect. Because of the separation of the designer and the building occupant, little chance seemed to exist for the architect to once again discover—firsthand—the needs of the user. A new decision-making process should allow the participation of all the people who will be affected by a final architectural product. The design process of Alvar Aalto began to define such an approach. Aalto conceived of a design process that was more a collaboration of creative individuals than a disparate collection of isolated specialists and disconnected client representatives:

> To him the art of building was an art only in the sense that medicine and cooking are arts. He conceived it as a humanistic activity based on technical knowledge which can only be pursued successfully by people with a capacity for creative synthesis. [Ruusuvuori 1978, 13]

Aalto sums up his own decision-making process thus:

> When I personally have to solve some architectural problem, I am constantly—almost without exception, indeed—faced with an obstacle difficult to surmount, a kind of "three in the morning feeling." The reason seems to be the complicated, heavy burden represented by the fact that architectural planning operates with innumerable elements which often conflict. Social, human, economic and technical demands combined with psychological questions affecting both the individual and the group, together with the movements of human masses and individuals, and internal frictions—all these form a complex tangle which cannot be unravelled in a rational or mechanical way. The immense number of different demands and component problems constitute a barrier from behind which it is difficult for the architectural basic idea to emerge. I then proceed as follows—though not intentionally. I forget the entire mass of problems for a while, after the atmosphere of

the job and the innumerable different requirements have sunk into my subconscious. I then move on to a method of working which is very much like abstract art. I just draw by instinct, not architectural synthesis, but what are sometimes childlike compositions, and in this way, on this abstract basis, the main idea gradually takes shape, a kind of universal substance which helps me bring the innumerable contradictory component problems into harmony. [Ruusuvuori 1978, 22–25]

From this short description of a design process, several important points emerge, suggesting a generalized model of decision making. First, a design problem is composed of many—as well as conflicting—points of view, objectives, functional requirements, and individuals. Second, a period of absorbing this diffuse and immense amount of data takes place and the designer must reach a point of appreciation—not necessarily understanding—of the entire problem. Next, the designer reaches deep within a creative reservoir to generate a large number of ideas and potential solutions. Finally, some form of synthesis or process of discrimination occurs that allows these ideas to be brought into balance to address the original problem statement. The distinction Aalto made between "creativity" and "synthesis" is crucial, especially in the light of Burnham's assumption that designs can emerge from the synthetic process of piecing together the disjointed efforts of technical and graphic specialists.

Aalto and Wright shared this philosophy of creativity, and their works are marked by a wide variety of design alternatives and variations of architectural form. Both used industrial processes to produce economical solutions that offered variety as well as the human dimension that was central to their architecture. Aalto comments on these issues:

> The right economy of building is to see how many good things we can provide at low cost. But we should never forget that we are building for man. All economics have the same problem—the relationship between the quality of the product and its price. If we leave quality out, then the whole economy is senseless in any field, including architecture. [Ruusuvuori 1978, 147]

REDEFINITION OF THE CLIENT

Both Aalto and Gropius recognized the element missing in the architecture of the industrialized office—the user of the building. It would take years, however, before the user would be represented in the design process. At the same time that Aalto was expressing a philosophy of design based on individual creativity and a human focus, modern design offices grew larger and more specialized. The largest of these offices, employing hundreds of architects, designers, engineers, and technical consultants, were organized into teams to offer their clients a complete set of design services. Rather than teamwork in Gropius's sense, however, work typically was accomplished linearly from design to production to construction. Generally, each team of workers came from the same discipline. The projects thus did not benefit from the different views and insights of a variegated team. The final product tended to replicate the office's previous products, upholding the original standard of design quality but exhibiting none of the inspiration that arises from differing points of view or a range of design skills (Kostof 1977, 329). This is quite a contrast to Aalto's view that "every commission is different and so solutions to problems cannot be stereotyped" (Ruusuvuori 1978, 167).

One of the most disturbing features of the Modern Movement in architecture was the institutionalization and standardization of the building user in the design process, revealed dramatically in the Pruitt-Igoe high-rise housing project in St. Louis. This modern solution to urban housing needs was fairly common in the 1950s and 1960s, and scores of such "projects" sprang up in the centers of American cities.[7] Seventeen years after the construction of Pruitt-Igoe—years of crime as well as of environmental neglect in the "projects"—the administrators finally asked residents for their suggestions. The users' response was "Blow it up!" and in July 1972, the city demolished a large portion of the structures in Pruitt-Igoe. A crisis in architecture was evident.[8]

POSTMODERNISM

During the late 1960s and throughout the 1970s, architects once again turned their concerns to originality of form. A new design expression surfaced, in large measure responding to the uniformity and standardization of the Modern Movement. This approach was first articulated by Robert Venturi in his book *Complexity and Contradiction in Architecture* (1966). It was a major departure from how architecture had been practiced during much of the twentieth century. Venturi spoke of an architecture that broke with the simplicity

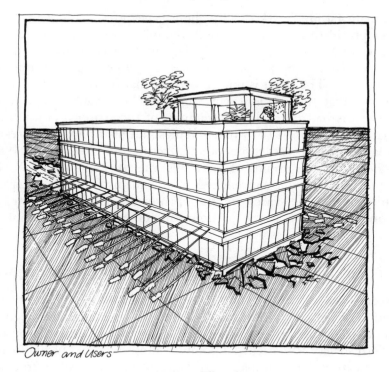

Owner and Users

FIGURE 1-2. The client.

of form and straightforward solutions embodied by the Modern Movement. He called for an architecture of "messy vitality." Venturi was concerned with "form" as a single design objective. He was beginning to define this new means of expression by purposely choosing the distorted rather than the straightforward. He introduced new ideas that sparked the imaginations of the architect to use "black and white and sometimes gray" instead of "black and white," to choose richness of meaning over clarity of meaning (Venturi 1966, 22–23).

Others began following Venturi's lead. The firm SITE did a series of designs for the Best Products hardware company that embodied many principles outlined by Venturi. A showroom in Sacramento, California, contains a fourteen-foot-tall, forty-five-ton chunk of brickwork that appears to peal away from the building at opening time. A jumble of broken bricks fall away from the front of Best's Houston showroom, a playful gesture its designers called "an indeterminate facade." Asked why these types of designs were used, Best's president replied, "We built the unusual showrooms because they were *fun*, but also because they made a contribution to the company by getting people to notice us and getting them into the stores. . . . The point is not necessarily that people love the buildings but that they *notice* them." Before SITE came along, Best's showrooms had been classic examples of the stripped-down functional-box design. SITE'S James Wines said his firm was interested in making the "lowest forms of architecture into art" (Patton 1981, 77–79). By the beginning of the 1980s, the effects of Venturi's philosophy had become entrenched in the mainstream of American architecture.[9] The search for the unconventional design form had begun to reappear as the predominant objective in the problem-solving process of design.

PROPOSAL FOR A DECISION PROCESS IN DESIGN

It seems likely that an appropriate and sensible approach to the solution of design problems will draw a bit on all the architectural practices and attempt to solve all the problems discussed above. Modern society has reached a point of complexity and technological sophistication that will make it difficult, if not impossible, to abandon the ideas of the specialist and the corporate design office. Even if the predictions of Alvin Toffler and E. F. Schumacher are correct, the need for designers to interact and operate in large teams will probably remain.[10] Designers of all sorts—architects, product designers, mechanical engineers, and management experts—seem to work best when their individual ideas and contributions to a team effort are utilized *intact*, not as isolated pieces of a grand and remote puzzle. Designers are by nature synthesizers and expect to see the uniqueness of their ideas expressed as part of a whole. Clients and building users expect, and should demand, that originality and creativity be primary ingredients of an architectural service. Aalto was right to recognize that central to the practice of architecture must be the childlike spark of intuition, that this exuberance makes architecture a humane and human-centered pursuit. What lessons can architects learn from this to improve their decision-making capabilities?

First, we must address the problem of making the creative act of problem solving pivotal in design. Recent studies have shown that the lack of creative problem-solving skills prevails in contemporary society. The steady decline in secondary school and college test scores, the proportional rise in functional illiteracy, and the growing difficulty of filling jobs requiring problem-solving abilities are symptoms of this situation. A number of psychologists contend, however, that problem solving can be learned. A central concept in the acquisition of this skill is the ability for a problem solver to seek out the unorthodox, searching for ways to circumvent the problem when it seems too difficult to solve head-on. Several methods have been devised to improve problem-solving abilities. For instance, switching from one idea to another avoids the risk of getting bogged down with a single problem. The ability to criticize one's own work and ideas is a sign of creative involvement in the problem. Devising symbols and models for the component parts of a problem is a way of simplifying complex problems. This last technique plays a critical role in modern problem-solving, since studies have shown that although an educated person's vocabulary may exceed fifty thousand words and phrases, no one can remember more than about seven unrelated things at a time (Browne 1980). Dealing with many unrelated things at once requires a formalized, systematic approach to problem solving. The key to devising an effective system of problem solving "seems to depend on three things: accumulating many facts, storing them in an efficient memory network, and being able to perceive relationships between the facts in one part of a network and another" (Browne 1980).

In fact, many fields have similar approaches to problem solving. Comparing seemingly unrelated fields reveals a common problem-solving approach (fig. 1-3). In all of these fields, a complex system is to be structured or analyzed in order to achieve some predetermined set of goals or objectives. These fields are distinct from one another in the decision maker's view of the problem, the time frame to be considered, and the scale of the problem to be solved. By making the analytical framework or problem-solving process explicit, involvement of a wide range of decision makers, including citizen and building-user groups, is possible (Amara 1981).

In the view of Buckminster Fuller, a positive approach to the solution of environmental problems lies in the ways that designers make the most out of a limited supply of physical resources. This requires a cooperative effort on the part of designers and the use of a variety of problem-solving techniques. Fuller expressed a confidence that most architects and designers are just beginning to understand:

Field of Planning	*Choices*	*Knowledge*	*Preferences*
Systems engineering Operations research Systems analysis Value engineering*	Requirements	Alternatives/systems	Evaluation
Decision analysis	Decisions	System structure/ uncertainty	Value/time/risk/ preferences
Policy analysis	Goals/strate- gies	Processes/indicators	Attainment/values
Futures field	Images	Forecasts/premodels/ scenarios	Group participation/ preferences

* added by authors
Source: Roy Amara, "The Futures Field, Which Direction Now?" *The Futurist*, June 1981, p. 44.

FIGURE 1-3. Analytical frameworks for decision making.

Within the twentieth century this invisible revolution of continually learning how to do more with the same or more with less resources (metallurgically, electronically, chemically, mechanically, structurally, aerodynamically, and hydrodynamically) has in only three-quarters of the twentieth century brought 60 percent of humanity into enjoying a vastly more effective, healthier, and more realistically informative means of coping with life's changes. [Hubbard 1981, 36]

Perhaps this is the direction of the future for architecture. A rational problem-solving approach to architecture of the future that includes both creativity and the capacity to analyze and discriminate may be the response necessary to meet the challenges voiced by Fuller.

Throughout the history of the built environment, patrons have looked to architects as problem solvers and communicators of design knowledge. An incomplete compilation of the current decision makers in architecture is outlined in figure 1-4. Striking in this summary are the range and number of decision makers in the design process. The decision-making process has progressed from one based on the judgments of a single designer to the complexity of modern design in which the goals and aspirations of the owner and designer—not to mention the user—are often subordinate to the financier, code enforcer, or materials supplier. The gradual addition of economic, technological, and social variables to the design equation has meant that the design process has become fragmented into

Client

Owners
Managers
Occupants
Users

Architect

Principal
Project manager
Job captain
Designers
Draftspersons
Specification writers
Job supervisors
Construction manager
Marketing experts

Building Officials

Fire marshal
Zoning board
Building department
System inspectors
Assessor
Funding agencies
Environmental groups

Builder

General contractor
Subcontractors, suppliers
Job superintendent
Tradespersons
Unions

Developers

Financiers
Lenders
Legal advisors
Insurance experts
Leasing agents
Realtors

Consultants

Engineering services
Interior designers
Industrial designers
Lighting and acoustic
  experts
Behavioral scientists
Cost analysts
Schedulers
Landscape architect
Value engineer

FIGURE 1-4. Decision makers in the design process.

myriad subspecialties, each controlled by systems experts. It has also meant that the transmission of values and information from someone who needs a building to the person who is able to design a solution is often masked in the contemporary building process. The increase in the number of people involved in the decision-making process and the number of conflicting goals that a building program must satisfy has widened the communication gap between the users and designers of built environments.

The dilemma of modern design, therefore, is the need to provide expertise that can respond to the generalized perspective of the building process as a whole. A common solution to this dilemma has been to highlight only a limited number of the objectives contained in building programs. "Energy-conscious," "cost-effective," "functionally efficient," and "whimsical" buildings have emerged as descriptors of design solutions that address a single environmental objective, often to the detriment of other programmatic demands of building users and owners. In a sense, modern designers have reverted to the more ancient design processes in that they have come to represent very narrow concerns and limited pressure groups. The design process of the future must put the architect at the center of the decision-making process, capable of responding to diverse points of view and multiple design objectives.

CONCLUSION

The approach to decision making outlined in this book allows the various actors in the design process to participate fully in solving environmental problems. Although this decision-making process has been developed over a long period of time in a variety of design contexts and is supported by a number of theories, the basic elements are quite straightforward. The first component of the decision-making process is the systematic definition of all the factors that will affect the programming, design, construction, and occupancy of a building solution. These factors have been referred to in the past as goals, objectives, design attributes, and performance criteria. What they really represent to the architect are the economic, social, technical, and aesthetic dimensions of a design problem that will form the basis for determining whether any particular design solution satisfies the needs of the owners, users, occupants, and community affected by that solution. During the design process, these concerns should be represented and analyzed by those with the most to lose or gain by the architect's decisions. The economic factors can best be addressed by a person trained in the life-cycle cost implications of building systems, while the functional and operational aspects of a building program need to be articulated by the people who will actually occupy the completed facility. This implies a widening of the definition of "client" in the design process. The decision-making process presented here assumes that modern design problems consist of conflicting objectives and that design solutions must satisfy the competing interests of large numbers of people.

As was seen from the above critique of the modern architectural office, a primary focus of the profession since the late nineteenth century has been the trend toward specialization and compartmentalization of design tasks. What the authors propose in this respect is the recognition that design problems will continue to be composed of many distinct facets and that techniques of analysis must be incorporated into architectural practice which address these various elements from particular points of view. The strength of the specialized design office has been the ability to solve well-defined and narrow environmental problems. This ability, however, is only the first step in a complete approach to problem solving in architecture.

Second, it is assumed that design problems can be solved by a wide assortment of alternatives. These alternatives may involve a new building or may require reorganization of an existing facility. The designer must find a way to analyze large amounts of design information and combine these data into new and unique forms. As we have seen in the preceding discussion, the options available to designers have grown steadily, and that indeed is one of the greatest challenges designers face today.

The necessity for architects to increase their capacities to generate creative solutions to design problems has been—and should continue to be—the central focus of architectural education. The design philosophy of Aalto reviewed in this chapter acts as an exemplar of this creative capacity and suggests ways in which this aspect of design can be incorporated into a general model of architectural decision making.

Finally, a system of evaluation must be established to help the architect select the alternatives that best address the goals of the building owner, user, and designer. This system should provide a framework in which all the actors of the design process can participate and feel that they have contributed to the creative process of synthesizing a final design solution. The framework that is suggested in this text has its roots in the general model of scientific inquiry but is tempered by the knowledge that design is as much related to discovery and reflection as to proof and validation. The evaluation process that is presented, therefore, should be viewed as a guide to remind the architect of how various alternatives relate to a given set of objectives and not as a rigid, prescriptive formula for producing the "optimum" solution.[11]

The decision process in design thus encompasses three basic components consisting of objectives, alternatives, and evaluation.

An important component of this process is a set of decision-making techniques that help balance design objectives with a range of solution alternatives. This model of decision making is cyclical and repetitive in that it can be used in each phase of the design process as well as throughout the life of a building project. While the mechanics of the decision-making process remain unchanged throughout design, objectives of the various user groups and design consultants will change and be compared to an expanding and increasingly concrete and detailed set of feasible alternatives. The process centralizes the decision-making activity of design within a compact and rational framework, and decentralizes the opportunity for a wide variety of points of view and design solutions to come into play.

NOTES

1. One of the purposes of this book is to offer guidelines on broadening the decision-making process in architecture and expanding the building user's role in that process. See Rudofsky (1964) for a discussion of how informal design processes have found expression in the built environment.

2. Much of the material concerning the early development of the architectural profession can be found in Spiro Kostof's book *The Architect* (1977) and in *The Image of the Architect* (1983) by Andrew Saint.

3. See Saint (1983, chapters 3 and 4) for a discussion of the rise of professionalism in architecture in Britain and the United States.

4. For a detailed analysis of the effects of these pressures on architectural practice, the reader should refer to Judith Blau's book *Architects and Firms: A Sociological Perspective on Architectural Practice* (1984).

5. See Kostof (1977, 190–204) for a thorough discussion of the factors that led to the establishment of the modern design office.

6. Reference is made to Joan Draper's chapter in Kostof (1977), which details the methods and practices of L'Ecole des Beaux Arts.

7. One of the most compelling analyses of this neglect can be found in Jane Jacob's book *The Death and Life of Great American Cities*.

8. Refer to Wolfe (1981, 80–82) for an amusing description of a sad situation.

9. Charles Jencks (1984) is cited as a source for the historical foundations of this movement in architecture.

10. Refer to Toffler (1980) and Schumacher (1973) for an insightful account of how the information revolution has affected the design process.

11. Refer to Schön (1983) for an excellent critique of how the design process can best be defined by normative rather than prescriptive models.

CHAPTER 2

The Design

Process

THE DECISION-MAKING process presented here is defined as a general model of choice behavior that can be applied at any point in the design process. This chapter discusses the relationship between this process and the facility cycle; it introduces various techniques (discussed in detail in chapters 4 through 9) that may be used in the design process. The advantages and disadvantages of a management approach to problem solving in the design professions are reviewed. Areas of interest to practitioners—resource planning, office organization and team structure, and level of effort for project documentation—are discussed.

FACILITY CYCLE

Architects and engineers historically have been involved in translating well-defined client needs and desires into a design solution that is communicated to a contractor through drawings and specifications. But the total life span and usefulness of a facility involve considerations that are much broader than those addressed in this traditional view of design, and so the cycle is broken into the four stages: feasibility, design, construction, and occupancy (fig. 2-1). These four stages actually constitute a continuum since at any given point in the life of a building, its owner, users, and designers may be setting the stage for a continuation of the cycle.

Figure 2-2 summarizes each of the four facility cycle stages, their context and end product. The product of one stage becomes the context for or conditions on decision making for the next stage. This is true even for the products of occupancy, which in turn become the context for the feasibility of a new or renovated facility.

20

FIGURE 2-1. The facility cycle.

Project Feasibility Phase

The project feasibility phase is the starting point of the cycle. It is an investigation to determine the need for a facility and its potential for economic and functional success. For example, a developer may want to construct housing units on a given piece of land. An economic analysis is conducted to determine the total project costs of design, construction, and operation in order to tell the developer the amount of money that must be invested, the time frame for the investment, the cost of money, and the costs of keeping the facility operational.[1]

The feasibility phase continues into project planning if the initial economic and functional analyses indicate success. Planning further develops a fiscal plan to ensure that specific physical and spatial requirements can be met and also to begin the search for programmatic information that will go into a design solution. Planning involves deciding in advance what to do, how to do it, when to do it,

Facility Stage	Context	Product
Feasibility 	The activities to be performed or the goods to be produced by the users of the facility	Decision to build and statement of the design problem to be solved and results expected
Design 	The problem defined and data collected to allow a designer to solve the problem	Acceptance by the client of a design solution and communication of that solution and expected quality to the contractor
Construction 	Construction documents clearly communicating the architectural solution and quality expected	Acceptance of the completed facility by the client and designer
Occupancy 	Environment suitable for the needs of the users to perform their intended activities	Activities performed or goods produced by a facility's users

FIGURE 2-2. Facility cycle stages—context and products.

and who is to do it. Parameters are determined, including financial data on possible building sites, configurations and sizes of alternate building solutions, and other owner and user criteria. Establishment of the project's scope, an analysis of the physical characteristics and limitations of the site, an evaluation of services and amenities required by the occupants of the facility, and an assessment of environmental impact are concerns of this phase. Planning sets the criteria that will establish the total scope of the facility to be designed. Plans and construction specifications will be prepared on the basis of this feasibility study.

Project Design Phase

The project design evolves from information generated during the feasibility phase and eventually hardens into a set of instructions to the people who will build the facility. The design stage finalizes the selection of construction materials, the building configuration, the building image, comfort levels, space utilization, process flows and circulation, mechanical and electrical systems, the control and operation of the facility, and site development. The design phase interprets the goals and objectives formulated during the feasibility stage and shows how they can be carried out. It also instructs the builder to establish a firm project budget. It sets standards for facility operation and maintenance, and it establishes the quality of the aesthetics, ease of maintenance, and the degree of comfort and safety of the architectural solution.[2]

Project Construction Phase

The proposed decision-making process that is outlined in this book can also play an important part in the construction phase of the project. Many private and governmental agencies include incentive and penalty clauses in their construction contracts. Contractors thus share in savings that result from improvements in a facility's performance from reducing initial or future costs, such as energy and maintenance.[3] For example, the contractor may propose a different type of material for a roof, material that provides the same level of insulation and can be installed at a significant savings in time or money. The contractor can benefit based on a percentage of initial or future reductions in estimated future annual owning and operating costs.

Occupancy Phase

Increases in energy and other ownership costs have resulted in more emphasis on reducing the burden of energy, maintenance, alteration, staffing, tax, and other operating costs. These costs have historically increased throughout the life of a building project, and they fluctuate from year to year, depending on inflation rates and the escalating costs of fuel and other materials. While operation and maintenance costs escalate, construction costs are fixed. In many cases, investments in retrofitting initial construction early in a project's occupancy will save operation and maintenance costs throughout the project's life. It is best to anticipate operation and maintenance aspects of a facility during the design stage so that a facility can be changed or altered before construction and occupancy occur.[4]

DECISION-MAKING TECHNIQUES

Many publications describe decision-making techniques that can be useful in the practice of architecture. This book demonstrates to the

Technique	Purpose	Tools
Function analysis	Defines the goal to be achieved in a design	Function, cost, worth Graphical function analysis Function analysis system technique (FAST)
Group creativity	Expands the number of alternatives to solve a problem	Brainstorming Delphi Manipulation Pattern analysis
Life-cycle costing	Allows precise measurement of economic consequences of various design alternatives	Present worth method Annualized method Return-on-investment Saving-to-investment ratio Payback period
Decision analysis	Allows measurement of both economic and nonmonetary consequences of various alternatives	Defining design objectives Objectives scaling Weighting of objectives Alternative evaluation
Post-occupancy evaluation	Discovery of how people and things behave in environments	Observation Interviewing Questionnaires Objective environmental data collection Data analysis
Communication	Facilitation of clear and understandable data accumulation and information dissemination	Group dynamics Modeling Computer-aided design Mathematical analysis

FIGURE 2-3. Decision-making techniques.

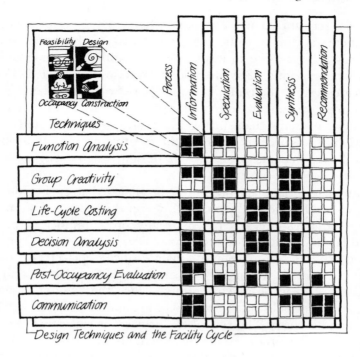

FIGURE 2-4. Decision techniques and the facility cycle.

designer how these tools can be integrated into the various stages of the facility cycle. The techniques outlined here are thought by the authors to be the most useful methods currently available to designers and clients. Figure 2-3 lists the techniques and the purpose and tools associated with each. Figure 2-4 illustrates when during the four facility-cycle phases the techniques are most commonly used.

MANAGEMENT CONSIDERATIONS

Proper management of the decision-making process is a key element. The decision maker must decide how a problem is to be studied, which team members should participate, the length of the decision-making process; he or she also must ensure documentation of the process and encourage implementation of the design team's recommendations.

Timely planning and control of the effort level for the overall project and individual design studies are critical management functions. During the conceptual design phase, for example, the project goals are scrutinized to determine where major performance improvements are likely to be achieved. Based on this broad survey, resources are set aside to ensure the availability of personnel and funds when specific decision-making exercises are needed. During schematic design, the building components with the greatest potential for improvement are selected for study. Normally this is a higher percentage of items than during the final design stage, and a large allocation of resources is based on the fact that greater opportunities for producing benefits occur early in design, when changes are easiest to effect.

Sufficient money and staff must be allocated at the beginning of a project if effective evaluation is to go on throughout design. Estimating these resources is based usually on a number of project-related factors: initial investment cost, size, building type, complexity, and projected annual energy, maintenance, replacement, and tax costs. The initial investment cost can be significant in determining the levels of decision-making efforts, since the amount of money available for special studies tends to be greater for projects with large initial or unit costs. The size of the project, as expressed in square footage or BTUs produced or consumed, also influences the level of study effort. Because of the effects of scale, even a small unit-cost savings can result in a great dollar savings in large and complex buildings. In addition, the magnitude of energy and other operating costs may justify intensive study at the early design stages. Size often correlates directly with initial costs, although construction costs are not in themselves always an accurate indicator of how decisions should be made during the design process. Two buildings may both have first costs of $10 million, but one may contain half as much space as the other or one may consume twice as much energy. The design processes for the two buildings may also vastly differ depending on building type and complexity. Complex facilities normally incorporate high-cost features that have long-term economic and functional consequences. Complex facilities—such as research and development buildings and hospitals—may warrant a much higher level of review effort than relatively simple facilities.

For project owners and organizations with limited experience in design management, the allocation of dollars to decision making begins with setting upper and lower fee limits. A reasonable upper limit is 1 percent of the project cost. The lower boundary might be one-tenth of 1 percent of the project cost or not less than $5,000.

Choice of the funding level within this range is based on the project-related factors mentioned above. The design of a $10 million building, for example, may call for high energy costs and a new telecommunications system. The project architect might then select a funding level for decision making that is well above the middle of the funding range.[5]

Project managers and client organizations with some experience in building evaluation usually develop and continually update a set of criteria that take into account the project-related elements discussed above. Such a set of criteria is shown in figure 2-5. It should be noted that neither the discussion of funding nor figure 2-5 takes into account all possible study areas, such as those concerned with energy use or solar design.

The conventional approach to resource allocation in a design project is to start with relatively few consultants and design participants and to add participants as the design becomes more complex and detailed. A major jump in resource requirements usually occurs during the construction documents stage. With architecture's increased use of the computer, this jump may be curtailed in that fewer resources are spent on automated drafting and computer-aided design techniques than in the past. This technology allows a much larger portion of resources to be used earlier in a project, when key design decisions must be carefully considered. A wider range of ideas is generated, alternatives are more thoroughly evaluated, and results are better synthesized. Figure 2-6 illustrates this shift in allocation of project resources.[6]

As a rule, the focus of decision making is on those areas of the design problem that are likely to produce the most significant results or the most important consequences for the design as a whole. Although some facets of the problem may appear to be quite small in terms of budget or scale, they may in fact have tremendous impact on the eventual success or failure of the design. The selection of a specific coloration or reflectivity value on the paving surface at the south face of a building, for example, may have long-term consequences on the building's energy performance. The designer has traditionally faced this decision in the latter stages of design; a more logical decision-making process might address this issue earlier. In order to develop a strategy for selecting specific aspects of a problem to which to apply rigorous decision-making techniques, a list of study areas should be prepared and priorities assigned to those areas

Areas of Study	Conceptual	Schematic	Design Development
General project	Design concepts	Schematic floor plans	Floor plans
Budget	Program interpretation	Schematic sections	Sections
Layout	Site/facility massing	Approach to systems integration	Typical details
Criteria and standards	Access, circulation	Floor-to-floor height	Integrated systems
	Project budget	Functional space relationships	Space circulation
	Design intentions		Specifications
	Net to gross ratios		
Structural	Performance requirements	Schematic basement plan	Basement floor plan
Foundation	Structural bay sizing	Selection of foundation system	Key foundation
Substructure	Framing systems exploration	Structural system selection	Elements, details
Superstructure	Subsurface conditions	Framing plan outline	Floor and roof framing plans
	Underground concepts	Sizing of elements	Sizing of major elements
	Initial framing review		Outline specifications
	Structural load criteria		
Architectural	Approach to elevations	Concept elaboration	Elevations
Exterior closure	View to/from building	Selection of wall systems	Key elevation details
Roofing	Roof type and pitch	Schematic elevations	Key roofing details
Interior construction	Interior design	Selection of roof systems	Initial finish schedules
Elevators	Configuration of key rooms	Room design	Interior construction elements
Equipment	Organization of circulation scheme	Selection of partitions	Integration of structural framing
	Need and types of vertical circulation	Circulation sizing	Key interior elevations
	Impact of key equipment on facility and site	Basic elevator and vertical transportation concepts	Outline specification for equipment items
	Passive solar usage	Impact of key equipment on room design	

Mechanical HVAC Plumbing Fire Protection	Basic energy concepts Impact of mechanical concepts on facility Initial systems selection Space allocation Performance requirements for plumbing, HVAC, fire protection	Mechanical systems selection Refinement of service and distribution concepts Input to schematic plans Energy conservation	Detailed system selection Initial system drawings and key details Distribution and riser diagrams Outline specifications for system elements
Electrical Service and distribution Lighting and power	Basic power supply Approaches to use of natural and artificial lighting Performance requirements for lighting Need for special electrical systems	Window/skylight design and sizing Selection of lighting and electrical systems General service, power, and distribution concepts	Detailed systems selection Distribution diagrams Key space Lighting layouts Outline specification for electrical elements
Site Preparation Utilities Landscaping	Site selection Site development criteria Site forms and massing Requirements for access Views to/from facility Utility supply Site drainage	Design concept elaboration Initial site plan Schematic planting, grading, paving plans	Site plan Planting plan Typical site details Outline specification for site materials

FIGURE 2-5. Study areas. (Reprinted, by permission, from A. J. Dell'Isola and S. J. Kirk, *Life Cycle Costing for Design Professionals* [New York: McGraw-Hill, 1981] 92)

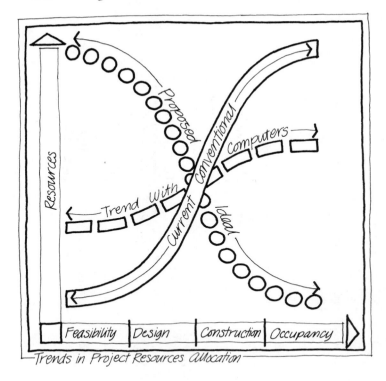

Feasibility | Design | Construction | Occupancy

Trends in Project Resources Allocation

FIGURE 2-6. Project resource allocation.

thought to have the greatest potential impact on building performance, user satisfaction, and cost control. There is no one way to come up with such a list and to establish priorities within it, but some guidelines are available.

Most design elements—including costs—are distributed unevenly throughout a project. The life-cycle costs of different design features vary widely, and the bulk of these costs tends to be concentrated in a small number of areas. The factors often considered in developing a list of potential study areas are energy utilization, maintenance and replacement costs, initial cost, small unit costs that a large project magnifies to large total costs, and user and functional requirements. High energy, maintenance, and replacement costs often depend on the specific characteristics of HVAC and lighting systems, operating equipment, and architectural finishes. These recurring costs can have considerable long-term economic impact and deserve special attention. The scope of a project, in either size or initial cost, may decree the study of areas that otherwise would be omitted from consideration. In a large project, a small cost differential per square foot for floor covering, wall finishes, or repetitive details can add up to substantial total savings. This holds true for specialized on-site construction components as well as for the prefabricated and standardized building units. The study of special user requirements, relating to building configuration, orientation, interior layout, or equipment locations, may reveal only marginal initial economic impact, but the careful consideration of these factors can dramatically improve the overall satisfaction level of building users and the degree to which the building satisfies programmatic requirements. Finally, the results of a specific feature of a design problem can sometimes be applied in future design projects.

OFFICE ORGANIZATION AND DECISION-MAKING TEAMS

The design function is the focus of architectural practice and is the flash point of design decision making. Changes in the design process lead to a change in how design is practiced. Research and evaluation skills are introduced to complement a designer's creative capabilities. Research skills, for instance, promote the updating of knowledge within the profession, as well as the development of new techniques for a specific practice. Evaluation ensures that a designer's decisions are consistent with project goals and with information produced by the research arm of the practice. These elements work together to support the design focus of architectural practice.

Specialized knowledge of cost estimating, life-cycle costing, energy, and programming are necessary in most design projects. Ideally, each member of the decision-making team would possess general knowledge of the design as a whole and expertise in a specific area of the design process.

Team Members

Project design and decision-making teams operate under the premise that two minds are better than one and that each mind is stimulated by participation in a group effort. Because not all individuals are alike in ability to communicate, perception of ideas, or ability to put ideas to work, the team benefits from individual differences. These

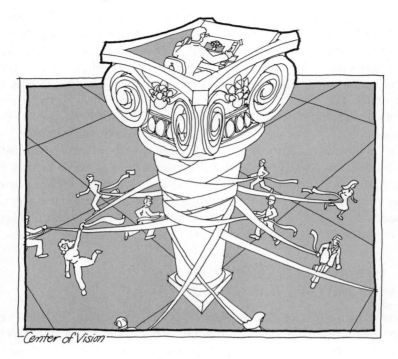

Center of Vision

FIGURE 2-7. The architect as the central decision maker.

types can be categorized as idea people, communicators, and organizers.

Idea people generate concepts and creative solutions to problems. Idea people can conceive of innovative combinations of materials, new plan types, improved circulation patterns, new processes, greater environmental flexibility, and efficient energy utilizations. Idea people provide the team with a vision of how a problem can be solved in a variety of ways. Communicators provide a concise picture of the consequences of design solutions. They are able to focus attention on specific design recommendations and to use media such as graphics, the spoken word, and three-dimensional images. Organizers turn ideas and concepts into reality. In architecture they develop and analyze ideas in order to produce final design and construction documents. Organizers are oriented toward management and analysis, and bring order and direction to the complex process of designing environments.[7]

Multidisciplinary Teams

The structure of a decision-making team depends on what is being studied, the time and resources available, and the degree of formality with which the study is to be conducted. A multidisciplinary team is essential for the methodology outlined here (fig. 2-9). The exchange of ideas and knowledge from other disciplines encourages an objective analysis of design problems and is essential for the architect's understanding of complex, unique environmental settings.

Anomalies frequently arise in a design project, and it is often the architect who must generate solutions to these unusual design situations. If the architect is seen as the only person who is capable of innovating, solutions suggested by users or clients may be overlooked or ignored. Many firms operate through design divisions; the structural work is performed by the structural division, the electrical work by the electrical division, the design work by the architectural

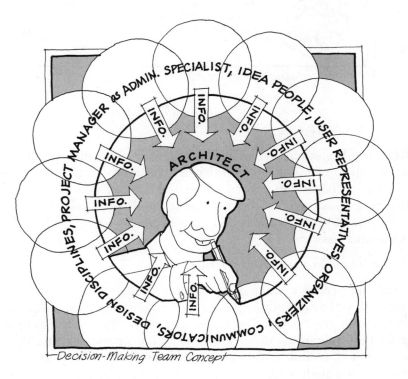

FIGURE 2-8. Decision-making team concept.

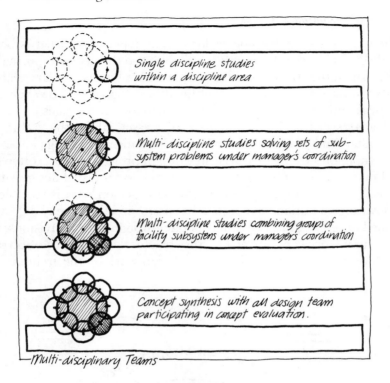

Single discipline studies within a discipline area

Multi-discipline studies solving sets of sub-system problems under manager's coordination

Multi-discipline studies combining groups of facility subsystems under manager's coordination

Concept synthesis with all design team participating in concept evaluation.

Multi-disciplinary Teams

FIGURE 2-9. Multidisciplinary teams.

division. Often these divisions do not effectively communicate with one another, yielding isolation that is counterproductive to decision making in the design process. Equal and timely participation by members of a design team will enhance the design, and all members will come to see the project from a collective—rather than an indi-vidualistic—perspective.

Documentation of Decision-making

Clear and precise documentation of the decision-making process is essential to the communication of information from feasibility stud-ies through the final design stages and on to the construction and occupancy of the building. Documentation provides a mechanism for review of technical, functional, and cost data and for application of this information to future projects. It also provides a kind of "operator's manual" for the occupants of the completed environment in that it reminds the users how the building was conceptualized and how it should be used. Documentation of all design decisions is becoming necessary because of the legal consequences of building as well. The need to record each step of the design process has been brought into focus because of the enormous increase in liability claims against designers, building clients, and contractors during the past twenty years.

The amount of effort devoted to documentation is generally established on a project-by-project basis. Of prime concern are the clarity and completeness of the documentation and its cost in relation to the professional fee associated with the decision-making effort. Normally, documentation comprises 10 to 25 percent of this fee. It may be established at less than 10 percent of the budget, however, if only an informal report is required. This is especially true if maximum use is made of self-documenting data sheets and checklists. Generally, more documentation is needed for projects with high initial and long-term operating costs and projects with a large number of specialized building components. More than the usual amount of documentation may be required when design decisions represent a departure from common practice or when a high degree of uncertainty must be resolved in analyzing design alternatives.

The documentation for a particular design problem may range from carefully organized, illustrated, and typeset materials detailing most aspects of the design, to handwritten notes, quick sketches, and computations covering only key decisions. The use of standardized, self-documenting data collection and calculation sheets and standard report forms can substantially reduce the effort and cost of documentation. A number of these forms and procedures are outlined in chapters 4 through 9 and should be considered an integral part of the decision-making exercises.

NOTES

1. The feasibility phase is closely related to architectural programming. Reference is made to Palmer (1981) for a complete discussion of this part of the design process.

2. This phase is comparable to the traditional architectural design process, consisting of conceptual design, schematic design, design development, construction documents, and bidding.

3. Although generally not thought to be a major responsibility of the designer,

the construction phase has recently taken on added importance with the introduction of construction management as a designated architectural service (DeVido, 1984).

4. See chapter 8 for a detailed discussion of the importance of building occupancy to the design process.

5. Material in this chapter has been abstracted from work conducted by Stephen Kirk for the U.S. Army Corps of Engineers.

6. See Mitchell (1977) for a discussion of how computer-aided design techniques can reduce the level of effort in the production phases of design and allow the architect more freedom in distributing resources throughout the design process.

7. See chapter 8 by Spreckelmeyer in Bechtel, Marans, and Michelson (1987) for a description of how these characteristics affect the ways in which architectural programmers approach design problems.

CHAPTER 3

A Model for Decision Making in Design

THE FRAMEWORK for the decision-making process in design has its roots in a number of design philosophies and associated professions—the sciences, engineering, and business. This chapter restates these theories and ideas in a way that can lead to the enhancement of the traditional design process and help the designer build strength as an environmental problem solver. The logic for the decision-making process and a methodology for implementing that logic are illustrated through a simple design problem. The methodology is tied to a number of specific analytic techniques that are described in detail in chapters 4 through 9.

A DECISION-MAKING MODEL

The model of decision making defined in this chapter is patterned on the scientific method: the orderly progression from problem definition, generation of alternatives that address the problem, testing of alternatives against a set of well-defined criteria, and selecting the alternative that best solves the problem. The scientific method assumes that problems can be analyzed by first observing a phenomenon and establishing a succinct hypothesis of how that phenomenon will react to a specific set of constraints or external rules. This process of problem solving begins with general assumptions about the nature of a problem and, through a series of evaluative and analytic tests, ends with a concrete method for solving that problem.[1]

As outlined in chapter 1, a number of architectural theorists have presented a similar process of problem solving in the recent past. Although these theorists have not always directly used the analogy

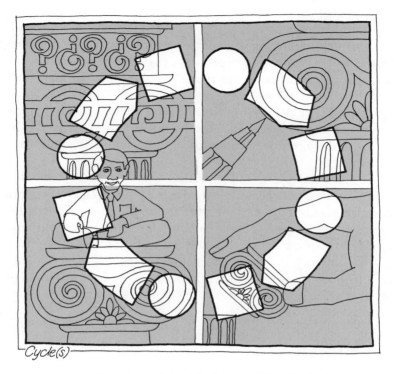

Cycle(s)

FIGURE 3-1. A model of decision making in design.

of the scientific method, the basic ingredients of this method can be ascertained in the writings of Alvar Aalto, Walter Gropius, and Buckminster Fuller. William Peña has acknowledged this approach to decision making in predesign activities. His five-step process of architectural programming has become a standard guide to defining—or, as he says, "seeking out"—architectural problems, and his use of the terms "goals," "facts," "concepts," "needs," and "problem statement" parallels the scientific method.[2]

The model presented here, however, diverges somewhat from Peña's approach. Whereas he argues that architects use his approach to define and analyze problems, the authors would argue that it is equally useful to search out and evaluate solutions to those problems. Peña's approach to decision making is seen primarily as a predesign activity, one that should not be confused with the creative act of design itself. While acknowledging that much design can never be fully organized by a model as simplistic as the one we present, the authors do believe that the framework and rigor that characterize Peña's approach to problem seeking are essential in the complex process of understanding and creating built environments. Essentially the model outlined here proposes that design is an iterative and cyclical process and that the framework for making decisions should reflect that cyclical, repetitive character. Unlike Peña's model, the one proposed here does not become invalid after the analytic process of programming is complete, but is instead used to deal with a different and more concrete set of design parameters and alternatives.[3]

The decision-making model outlined here assumes that a design problem can be analyzed and defined at varying levels of abstraction, then synthesized in a way that adds to the designer's knowledge of successive—and hence more concrete—levels of understanding. It assumes that the model can be applied in all phases of the facility cycle. The model is, therefore, defined as a two-dimensional approach to problem solving: one that describes the methodology of decision making and another that specifies its applications to architectural problems.

METHODOLOGY

Methodology involves three separate activities in decision making: where in time or space an environmental problem is found, the transmutation of that problem into a solution, and the nature or form of that solution. A problem exists within a specific *context* of abstract ideas and human values, information, and economic, social, and cultural norms. A *process* of rational decision making is applied within this context to arrive at an understanding of the nature of the problem. A *product* or set of instructions to solve the problem issues from this process in the form of strategies, plans, specifications, or buildings.

The context of a design problem is its setting. The designer's primary activity here is to define functional, economic, and social constraints on the problem: economic and social limitations of the client group, cultural norms that guide the client's organization and inform the public about the building, and legal codes. A review of the context of a design problem will establish the kind of information the architect must consider and the range of design solutions that are feasible. In the early stages of architectural programming, for example, the context of the problem is no doubt very general in nature, and the issues facing the decision maker will be centered on abstract conceptual solutions and broad planning strategies. In the later stages of design development, however, the context will have become much more focused and will address narrow questions of cost, size, spatial configuration, and scale.

After the information has been defined and analyzed, ideas are generated and speculations suggest how this information might be arranged so as to solve a design problem. Evaluation tests how various alternatives satisfy the constraints and contextual limitations of the problem. The synthesis of a design combines the ideas and observations that became apparent during evaluation into a single, refined design concept. Finally, a solution is selected and recommended by the decision maker.

The last phase of methodology is communication of the solution to those who must act on this information at the next stage of the design process. The product of this phase will constitute the information pool and the context for problem solving at the next level of decision making. The product of one stage of decision making thus initiates action in the following phase of design. Programming concepts and planning strategies, for example, are the bedrock of schematic design decisions and spatial configuration, which in turn give rise to refined design solutions. This iterative process continues until eventually the occupied environment becomes the context for making programmatic decisions about how that environment might change or be modified by a new facility.

A critical feature of this model of decision making, again, is its cyclical and expanding character. Not only is the methodology used at each point in the facility cycle, but it is also a repetitive sequence of decision-making events. A recommendation should not be accepted in this methodology simply because the five steps have been

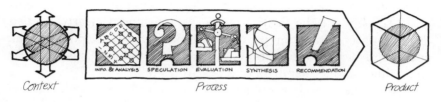

FIGURE 3-2. Decision-making methodology.

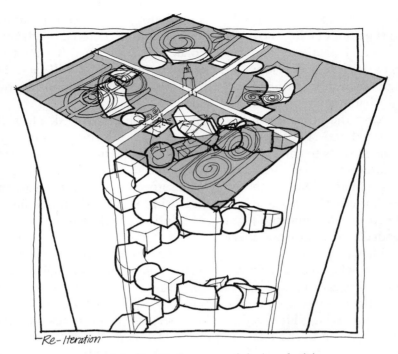

Re-Iteration

FIGURE 3-3. Cyclical nature of design decisions.

completed. That recommendation must be checked against the initial contextual constraints to see how it satisfies the problem's original definition. There is, therefore, the need to approach the methodology not as a linear progression from problem to solution, but as a fluid and flexible guide by which a designer or a design team can measure progress from general to specific understandings of user needs and client objectives.

APPLICATIONS IN DESIGN

Decisions are made constantly and information analyzed continuously throughout the facility cycle. Establishing a clearly defined decision process in design provides a common reference point for the analysis of design information and facilitates the exchange of ideas and values among members of a design team.

The earlier a design problem is systematically analyzed, the easier it will be for changes to be made at relatively minor cost and time loss. If a design team—composed of the owner, designers, programmers, building users, and technical consultants—is assembled during the feasibility stage of the facility cycle, major decisions concerning overall design strategy can be resolved before expensive and time-consuming design efforts have been expended. Inappropriate decisions taken during the early phases of the design process may have devastating consequences on a project's design development or occupancy phase.

Typical decisions made during a feasibility study include:

- Facility construction versus other economic investment
- New versus existing location
- New facility versus renovation of existing structure
- Total site development versus future expansion
- Resource conservation versus resource expenditure
- High-rise versus low-rise construction
- High-profile building image versus sedate, quiet image

To begin preparing a feasibility study, the decision maker must first be aware of the design parameters that have formed in the mind of the client—the reason that an environmental problem is assumed to exist. This awareness not only determines if action will be taken but also establishes the design strategy and philosophy that will color subsequent phases of the design process.

The design phase's second major set of decisions answers the question, "What physical solutions might satisfy the strategies and design philosophies that were articulated during the feasibility analysis?" Looking at the project as a whole and considering the site, surrounding community, social setting, and internal functions, the decision maker begins to explore the formal and functional potentials of alternative designs and trade-offs that occur as different solutions are proposed. Using the methodology, the designer begins to formulate and filter the better design concepts for later development, always keeping in mind the context established during the earlier feasibility stage.

In the construction phase, the design team executes a specific design solution and realizes in final form a client's environmental objectives. Procurement of materials and coordination of labor skills, along with project scheduling and resource allocation, are tasks associated with this phase. New professional services such as construction management are becoming critical to decision making in the building industry. Controlling the construction budget and executing the schedule, while maintaining building quality, make this phase of the facility cycle an important aspect of the design process and one that should remain under the firm control of the project architect.

During occupancy of the completed building, the owner can test, in real life, the design goals and strategies established during the earliest phases of the project. Although not traditionally associated with the formal process of design, the occupancy phase of the facility has taken on added importance as buildings have become more complex and as the need to adjust environmental conditions to building users has increased. Clients are also becoming more sophisticated in their perception of how their facilities are used, views that can help establish design guidelines and standards of performance for future building programs.

This decision-making process is most effective when design decisions must be made by groups, rather than when the owner and designer are solitary individuals. When decisions are made by a multidisciplinary design team, the methodology becomes a point of reference to which all team members can relate. The iterative nature of this process means that the methodology remains the same while the detail of design decisions becomes more refined. The process is applied as often as necessary during each phase of the facility cycle in order to solve project problems. The critical ingredient of the methodology is a central decision maker who guides events and orchestrates actions of the larger design team: that decision maker is the architect.[4]

DESIGN EXAMPLE

Although the problem-solving methodology is applicable in each of the four phases of the facility cycle, a simple illustration of its use will be outlined for the design phase since this is the area most familiar to architects. (Chapter 10 offers an example that goes through all four stages of the facility cycle.) The study context is first explained. The problem-solving process is then delineated, and the information requirements and analysis, speculation of ideas, evaluation of alternatives, synthesis of design, and recommendation of a solution are detailed. Finally, the design decisions and documentation of the process are illustrated.[5]

Context

Example: design a large corporate headquarters. The proposed building is to house 500 people in the first phase of construction and must be designed to expand to accommodate 2,000 occupants within twenty years. The building will be located on an open site adjacent to the existing headquarters facility and involves a space budget of 185,000 gross square feet and a capital cost budget of $35 million. A series of design concepts for this project was completed at a decision-making workshop organized by the project architect early in 1981. At the time these concepts were produced, a number of decision-making exercises had been performed during the programming and early schematic phases. During the early schematic phase, for example, six programmatic concepts were analyzed in relation to five well-defined project goals. From this analysis, the design team chose two design strategies that seemed to address the client goals of life-cycle cost, internal building comfort and external image, building function, and building growth. Study areas of the schematic design phase began with general diagrams of facility activities and circulation patterns and evolved into physical forms that defined specific building elements. (This early decision-making process is outlined in chapter 7.)

The context of the design problem during the latter stages of concept design might be summarized as follows:

1. The design team understood the general goals and budget limitations of the client group and defined five specific project objectives: cost, building image, space requirements, expandability, and circulation patterns.
2. The team investigated a range of programmatic solutions and, based on an analysis of project objectives, two concept schemes were selected for further refinement.
3. General space and project budgets were established and approved by the client group.
4. The project moved from the planning phase to the early design phase concerned with specific architectural features of the proposed building.

Elements to be investigated during the latter stages of schematic design, therefore, will be those that now begin to deal with specific building systems. In this example, the design team chose to study architectural solutions to exterior closure, structural framing, mechanical systems, lighting, and power distribution. By identifying issues to be investigated at a given stage of the problem, the design team begins to establish the character of information that is produced at the completion of that phase in the particular decision-making process. From the context described above, the design team chooses to elaborate and refine the architectural aspects of both the "Tower" and "Street" concepts in figure 3-4, so that the products of this phase of decision making will be accurate statements of the physical nature of those two alternatives. Detailed building sections and exterior elevations, for example, will replace the schematic site plans found in figure 3-4.

Twelve people make up the decision-making team during this phase of design. Although members of the client organization who will eventually occupy the new building participated in the pro-

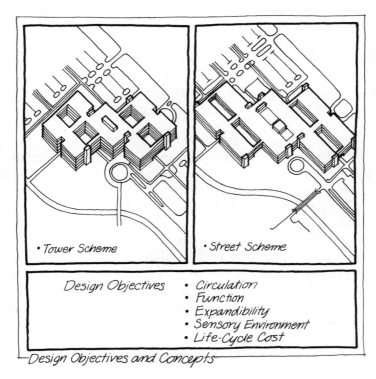

FIGURE 3-4. Design objectives and concepts.

gramming phase and were key decision makers in analyzing early schematic alternatives, this phase of design is concerned primarily with technical matters. In order to study the problems associated with various building systems, the team contains architects, engineers, and cost analysts from the project architect's office and representatives from the client's own design department. Based on the various levels of design expertise, the twelve participants are divided into two teams: one to deal with mechanical and electrical systems, the other, the design team, to study enclosure and structural systems.

Information Analysis

The design team's first task is to search out information concerning various building systems. The team needs to learn how the systems will go together and which components will be necessary in order to construct the completed environment. The design team searches out data from similar building projects and peruses manufacturers' literature. The team is to eliminate extraneous information and to concentrate only on the pertinent data. Therefore, a major task is to rank the value of available information.

A technique useful during this information phase is function analysis, focusing attention on the purposes of a particular building element or building activity. Function analysis takes a large-scale building element and divides it into discrete component parts. At the end of the analysis the design team has a better idea of how each building system fits into a logical and hierarchical framework for the building as a whole. In this case the design team uses function analysis to help it define exterior closure, mechanical, and electrical systems. For example, in the case of an exterior closure system, the design team first asks questions that deal with how a particular closure design should insulate and weatherproof. It should protect the interior of the building from heat and cold as well as act as an exterior finish and protection for a building skin. The design team uses a system of verbs and nouns in a function analysis to define the various functions of a system closure. The various parts of a closure system are broken down into approximately a dozen subunits in which the function is described both by an active verb and by a modifying noun (fig. 3-5).

When the design team agrees that an exterior closure system needs to provide a specific degree of insulation, then it knows that

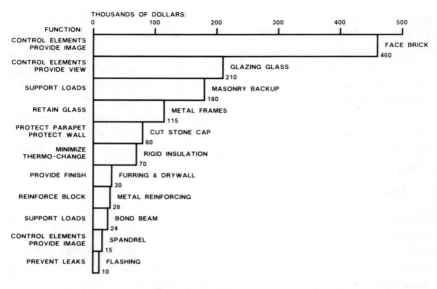

FIGURE 3-5. Function analysis: exterior closure.

various insulation components and materials must be investigated carefully to find the one that provides the quality appropriate to a given construction system. This technique helps the design team sift through a large amount of manufacturers' literature to find building elements that will suit a particular design. The team also carries out similar exercises in structural framing systems; the second team investigates heating, ventilating and air conditioning systems, power distribution layouts, and lighting systems. When the function analyses are completed, each member of the design team searches out technical data in a particular area of expertise on the various subcomponents necessary to assemble any given building system.

A modified post-occupancy evaluation (of other facilities) is useful during the information and analysis stage. Investigation of building components is often more effective if existing buildings are examined with an eye toward the functioning of these components in actual use. Post-occupancy evaluation shows how a given system has performed in similar situations over time. In the case of the exterior closure system analyses, post-occupancy evaluation techniques are used to verify assumptions made during function analyses and to temper definitions of systems components with knowledge gleaned from existing buildings.

The decision-making techniques that are important to designers in the information and analysis stage are those that help define the purposes of building components and those that illustrate how buildings and particular systems have performed in the past. The techniques used during this part of the methodology should be ones that help designers collect and classify large amounts of information as well as those techniques that help designers to sift information.

Speculation

During the speculation phase, the design team explores how information can be combined to yield physical solutions to the already-defined functions and activities. The purposes are to generate design alternatives and to creatively seek out solutions from as many sources as possible. Whereas the information and analysis phase was concerned with precise definitions and data reduction, in the speculation phase the design team expands the range of design options and builds on the designer's integrative skills. The Delphi technique (a form of brainstorming) was used in the case study to generate alternative designs. This technique encouraged open speculation and uninhibited exchange of ideas among the team members. During the speculation phase, no idea was seen by the design team as unfeasible or too unusual to be considered. The design team concerned with building closure system came up with approximately twenty-five ideas regarding closure systems (see fig. 3-6). From this initial Delphi session, the team outlined a number of component designs.

Once a set of building closure designs was proposed, a second Delphi session engendered opinions about the strengths and weaknesses of each alternative. The purpose of the second session was to give each design team member a chance to respond either positively or negatively to the design proposals and to clarify the various solutions. Similar Delphi sessions and alternative idea exercises were conducted for the structural, mechanical, and electrical components.

At the end of the speculation phase, the design team collected information concerning each building subsystem and formulated a range of solutions for the larger decision-making group to consider. No attempt was made at this point to constrain ideas pertinent to the building design. The next step was to weigh the various proposals in light of the original design objectives.

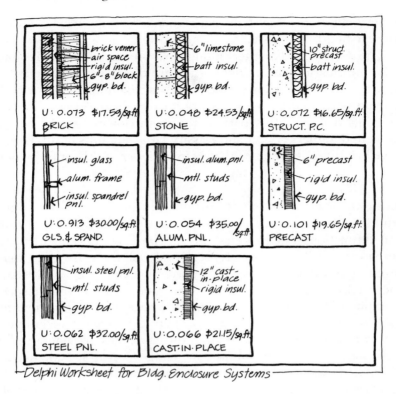

FIGURE 3-6. Delphi session products: exterior closure.

Evaluation

Obviously, all the alternatives developed during the speculative phase do not equally satisfy the project objectives. The evaluation phase critically evaluates those solutions. An important criterion by which to judge during evaluation is the long-term cost implications of various building components. Life-cycle cost analysis measures the effectiveness of a range of building components in terms of costs that will be incurred during the useful life of a building. Each closure system in figure 3-7 carries different implications in terms of construction costs, maintenance costs, energy costs, and replacement and salvage costs. Several of the system options come out much better in life-cycle cost performance.

Post-occupancy evaluation can also be used for evaluation. Again, in terms of closure system evaluation, each solution was examined in existing building designs, and the design team noted insulation qualities, solar-gain and heat-loss capacities, and exterior appearance and aesthetic image.

During the evaluation phase, design team members carefully eyed particular building closure, structural, mechanical, and electrical subsystems within very specific areas of concern, such as life-cycle costing, functional use, and environmental controls. Particular individuals on the team possessed expertise in certain areas. This is the point at which the entire design team has specialized knowledge about discrete pieces of the building but no clear picture as to how all these elements intertwine. The next phase requires that the team begin to make larger decisions about how the specific components constitute the building as a whole.

Synthesis

Perhaps the most delicate task of the decision-making methodology is how the design team combines the separate pieces of a design problem to create a finished program, design, or building. In the process of synthesis, the design team must finally satisfy the original goals of the client and building users. Those goals now become important measures for reassembling and testing the components of the closure, structural, mechanical, and electrical subsystems.

After reviewing the client's design goals, the design team begins to measure the performance of individual components against these goals. The various alternatives are consolidated into design solutions that maximize the project objectives. Figure 3-8 illustrates the team's assessment of how the exterior closure alternatives performed in relation to the original goals regarding cost, comfort, image, building function, and expansion capability, as well as the more specific objectives of durability and environmental protection. This figure applies a decision analysis technique (weighted evaluation) that structures the decision-making process. The technique allows the team to weigh the alternatives and compare them carefully against design goals. The process of synthesis, therefore, is one in which design alternatives—in this case dealing with building exterior closure—are compared to a complex set of objective standards and related to a large-scale view of the building as a whole. The next step is to combine the building exterior closure system with alternative forms of structural framing systems in order to create increasingly larger and more detailed architectural solutions.

Life-Cycle Cost Analysis
Using Present-Worth Costs

Life-Cycle Costing Estimate
General Purpose Work Sheet

Study Title: Exterior Closure
Discount Rate: 10%   Date:
Economic Life: 25 years

			Alternative 1 Describe: Brick & Block		Alternative 2 Describe: Structural Precast		Alternative 3 Describe: Aluminum Panel		Alternative 4 Describe: Steel Panel	
			Estimated Costs	Present Worth	Estimated Costs	Present Worth	Estimated Costs	Present Worth	Estimated Costs	Present Worth
Initial/Collateral Costs										
A. Brick & Block Wall (51,000 usf)			$11.59/usf	$591,100	—	—	—	—	—	—
B. Precast Concrete (51,000 usf)			—	—	$16.65/usf	$849,100	—	—	—	—
C. Aluminum Panel (51,000 usf)			—	—	—	—	$35.00/usf	$1,785,000	—	—
D. Steel Panel (51,000 usf)			—	—	—	—	—	—	$32.00/usf	$1,632,000
E. Windows (13,000 usf)			$25.00/usf	$325,000	$25.00/usf	$325,000	$25.00/usf	$325,000	$25.00/usf	$325,000
F.										
G.										
Total Initial/Collateral Costs				$1,722,100		$1,174,100		$2,110,000		$1,957,000
Replacement/Salvage (Single Expenditure)	Year	PW Factor								
A. minor repair & cleaning	6	0.564	—	—	—	—	30,600	17,300	55,100	31,100
B. sand blast cleaning	12	0.319	—	—	91,800	29,300	—	—	—	—
C. minor repair & cleaning	12	0.319	—	—	—	—	30,600	9,800	55,100	17,600
D. repointing joints	15	0.239	91,800	21,900	—	—	—	—	—	—
E. minor repair & cleaning	18	0.180	—	—	—	—	30,600	5,500	55,100	9,900
F. sand blast cleaning	24	0.102	—	—	91,800	9,400	—	—	—	—
G. minor repair & cleaning	24	0.102	—	—	—	—	30,600	3,100	55,100	5,600
H.										
Salvage	25	0.092		NIC		NIC		NIC		NIC
Total Replacement/Salvage Costs				21,900		38,700		35,700		64,200
Annual Costs	Diff. Escal. Rate	PWA W/Escal.								
A. Energy-Wall (a=0.073)	1%	9.894	20,000	197,900	—	—	—	—	—	—
B. -Wall (a=0.012)	1%	9.894	—	—	—	—	—	—	17,000	168,200
C. -Wall (a=0.054)	1%	9.894	—	—	19,700	194,900	—	—	—	—
D. -Wall (a=0.062)	1%	9.894	—	—	—	—	14,800	146,400	—	—
E. -window (a=0.045)	1%	9.894	38,400	379,900	38,400	379,900	38,400	379,900	38,400	379,900
F. Maint.- Window Washing	0%	9.077	2,300	20,900	2,300	20,900	2,300	20,900	2,300	20,900
G.										
Total Annual Costs				598,700		595,700		547,200		569,000
LCC — Total Present-Worth Life-Cycle Costs				1,842,700		1,808,500		2,692,900		2,542,700
Life-Cycle Present-Worth Dollar Savings				—		34,200		(850,200)		(747,500)

PW — Present Worth   PWA — Present Worth Of Annuity

FIGURE 3-7. Life-cycle cost analysis: exterior closure.

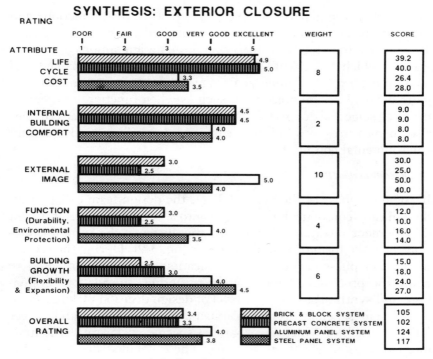

FIGURE 3-8. Synthesis: exterior closure.

As synthesis progresses, the design team begins to exchange information on individual building elements among team members. In synthesis the smaller pieces of a design project are collected and analyzed in a continually expanding evaluative context.

The technique of decision analysis provides a uniform framework for measuring building alternatives against the design objectives established earlier. During the synthesis phase, the Delphi method again becomes a useful tool that allows revised and expanded design ideas to emerge at the same time that the decision analysis framework is being used to weigh and measure the effectiveness of these new solutions. Eventually, all aspects associated with the design of the exterior closure system are analyzed by the design team to form complete building components and design concepts. The technique of decision analysis focused the attention of design team members on alternatives that particularly satisfied the design objectives. A major outcome of the synthesis phase is a rethinking and redefinition of this original list of objectives. Just as cost, function, and image goals helped the design team refine and weigh various design alternatives, the process of analyzing those design options provides a way in which the client's goal statements can be questioned and made more explicit. Some goals may be broken into smaller and more detailed design objectives, such as when function was seen in the later stages of design to consist not only of activity patterns but also to measure how building components perform under certain environmental conditions.

Recommendations

In the final phase of the methodology, the design team collapses all the building component alternatives into a limited number of design development recommendations. In this instance the recommendations take the form of graphic analyses (fig. 3-9). During the recommendation phase, concise communication techniques are used to relate the processes of information gathering, speculation, evaluation, and synthesis to the next level of design decision making. Here two design schemes were recommended—the Tower and Street schemes, each of which incorporated specific enclosure, structural, mechanical, and electrical systems. These detailed design options moved the project from a context of general architectural concepts to one in which specific proposals for building materials, construction details, and unit-price cost data had been analyzed and integrated into complete building assemblies.

Although communication in this phase relied on traditional architectural formats, the design team might have considered new presentation media such as new forms of electronic and photographic techniques. Computer-aided design and electronic animation also effectively transmit ideas from one phase of the facility cycle to the next.

CONCLUSION

Just as in preceding stages of design, the products of conceptual design in this example form the context for the next phase of design development. An expanded set of design objectives is formulated. This revised set of objectives clarifies measurements of life-cycle costs and of image and functional requirements of the proposed building design. Because design development tasks are concerned

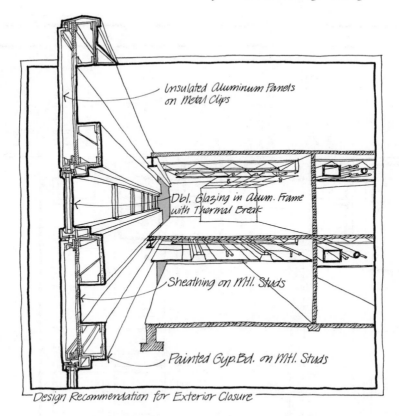

Insulated Aluminum Panels on Metal Clips

Dbl. Glazing in Alum. Frame with Thermal Break

Sheathing on MtI. Studs

Painted Gyp.Bd. on MtI. Studs

Design Recommendation for Exterior Closure

FIGURE 3-9. Design recommendation for exterior closure.

with materials selection and the small-scale arrangement of human activities, the design team has to elaborate the design objectives and address more specifically behavioral and building performance objectives. Additional cost data, for example, are needed to assess the economic consequences of the project at the unit-price level, and the reactions of building occupants are needed to explain behavioral consequences of color selections, room configurations, and comfort levels.

Figure 3-10 outlines the decision-making process as applied within a single phase of the case study. The use of specific techniques illustrates how the five-step methodology structures design-team decisions and facilitates the exchange of information. These techniques will be explained in detail in the next six chapters, and an

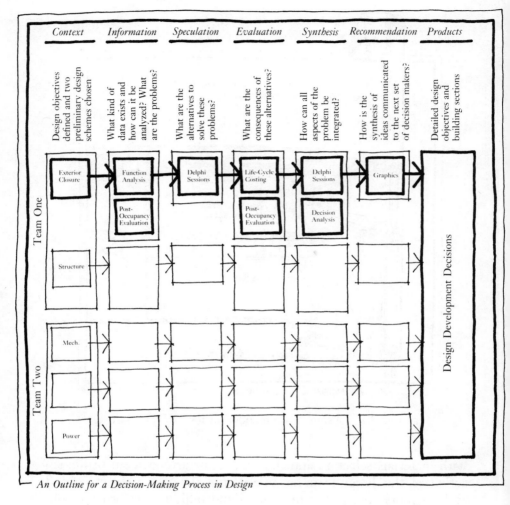

Context Information Speculation Evaluation Synthesis Recommendation Products

Design objectives defined and two preliminary design schemes chosen

What kind of data exists and how can it be analyzed? What are the problems?

What are the alternatives to solve these problems?

What are the consequences of these alternatives?

How can all aspects of the problem be integrated?

How is the synthesis of ideas communicated to the next set of decision makers?

Detailed design objectives and building sections

Team One

Exterior Closure → Function Analysis → Delphi Sessions → Life-Cycle Costing → Delphi Sessions → Graphics

Post-Occupancy Evaluation

Post-Occupancy Evaluation

Decision Analysis

Structure

Team Two

Mech.

Power

Design Development Decisions

An Outline for a Decision-Making Process in Design

FIGURE 3-10. Outline for a decision-making process in design.

expanded design application will illustrate the decision-making methodology in chapter 10.

NOTES

1. Many references outline the scientific method as an approach to problem solving. A good source for an introduction to this approach can be found in Ackoff and Sasieni (1968). For a philosophical understanding of how the scientific method relates to the more creative aspects of problem solving, Bronowski (1955) is an

excellent source. Finally, for those interested in reviewing the history of the scientific method as it is applied to design, reference is to Laseau (1980), Jones (1981), and Cross (1984).

2. William Peña is probably the best-known practicing architect who has made analysis an integral part of the architectural profession. His book, *Problem Seeking: An Architectural Programming Primer* (1977), is the standard by which most of the profession has viewed and applied analytic techniques within the design process.

3. See Spreckelmeyer (1982) for a discussion of why the traditional view of architectural programming should be reconsidered and for ways that the analytic process of decision making can be extended into the creative and synthetic act of design.

4. Recent changes in standard contractual arrangements between architects and clients may enhance this expanded view of the decision process in architecture. The introduction of the *Designated Services* Owner-Architect contract (AIA Form B-161/162) encourages a much broader definition of the design process and enlarges the scopes of architectural services.

5. This example is taken from an architectural project executed by the Tulsa firm of Murray Jones Murray. Stephen Kirk participated in this project and was the consultant for life-cycle cost analyses.

CHAPTER 4

Function Analysis

FUNCTION ANALYSIS allows decision makers to determine *why* a building, system, or component is being designed and *how* a design is to be executed. It describes this purpose in direct terms using verbs and nouns, and it assigns both an actual cost and a minimum cost (worth) to each function in order to measure whether good value for the owner or user will be achieved by the building, system, or component. The relative value of a design element in this context is defined by the ratio:

$$\text{Value Index} = \frac{\text{Cost}}{\text{Worth}},$$

where the best value is achieved when the cost of a building, system, or component approaches the worth, or when the value index approaches 1.0.[1] Refinements of this technique include graphical function analysis and Function Analysis Systems Technique (FAST), both of which are discussed in this chapter.

HISTORY

Function analysis was developed during World War II at the General Electric Company when a shortage of materials and labor compelled the introduction of substitutes (Dell'Isola 1982, 1–3). Company management found that these substitutes often reduced costs and at the same time improved the product. Lawrence Miles was asked to explore why this occurred and how cost reductions could be achieved intentionally. Miles developed a series of techniques that brought about significant quality (value) improvements systemati-

59

cally rather than serendipitously. One technique, function analysis, allowed designers to pinpoint the purpose a substitute material needed to suit in order to qualify for use. Miles formalized this analysis of functions, as well as the follow-on activity of attaching cost and worth to these functions. He also noted that when function analysis was applied consistently during the design of a project, other benefits were achieved as well, such as improved flexibility, maintainability, safety, reliability, and even aesthetics. The collection of techniques that has evolved since function analysis was introduced is known variously today as value analysis, value engineering, and value management.[2] Before the development of FAST, function analysis was performed randomly, analysts never quite knowing if all functions had been identified.

The U.S. Department of Defense adopted value analysis in 1954 when the Navy's Bureau of Ships applied the concept to procurement. Secretary of Defense Robert McNamara in 1964 expanded the cost-reduction program, leading to further use of value analysis principles. During the same period, many federal, state, and local government agencies adopted formal value analysis programs as part of their management improvement efforts.

Al Dell'Isola was the first to apply function analysis to buildings when he introduced value engineering to the Navy's Facilities Engineering Command in 1963.[3] The U.S. General Services Administration (GSA), Public Building Services (PBS), under Don Parker, began formally to apply function analysis shortly thereafter.[4] The National Aeronautics and Space Administration (NASA) utilized value analysis during facilities design starting in 1968. The design and construction branches of other federal agencies initiated programs shortly thereafter. The Environmental Protection Agency (EPA) mandated that value engineering techniques be used during the design of all wastewater treatment facilities over $10 million beginning in 1975.[5]

Interest in improving the value of building designs using value analysis began in the early 1970s in the United States. To promote the concept of value engineering among designers and building owners, the American Institute of Architects and the American Consulting Engineers Council jointly sponsored value engineering seminars beginning in the mid-1970s. Mountain Bell (then part of AT&T) was the initial user of value engineering in communications facilities in 1972. Not long afterward, the corporate facilities office of AT&T

initiated value engineering nationwide. Other large corporations, including United Technologies (applying it to top-down process engineering), Owens Corning Fiberglass, Johns Manville, Ciba-Geigy, and Union Carbide, have institutionalized function analysis as part of their building programs.

Other countries have taken advantage of value and function analysis. Japan has trained over 90,000 persons since value analysis was introduced in 1970 by the Tokyo Institute of Business and Management. In 1978 Bell Telephone of Canada, the British Columbia Building Corporation, and Public Works of Canada began using function analysis. Other countries using these techniques include Italy, Australia, South Korea, Greece, India, South Africa, England, France, Sweden, West Germany, and Saudi Arabia.

Function Analysis Systems Technique (FAST) uses a graphics technique to show the logical relationships linking the various functions of a building, system, or component. Charles B. Bytheway developed FAST at the UNIVAC Division of Sperry Rand Corporation and first introduced it at the 1965 national meeting of the Society of American Value Engineers.[6] Since FAST's origin, a wide variety of applications has evolved for its use.

THEORY

Use functions and aesthetic functions serve owner and user needs. Use functions involve an *action* that owners and users want performed. They want space provided, rain excluded, air cleaned, and the environment heated or cooled within a certain range of tolerance. Aesthetic functions *please* the owners and users of the facility. Owners want a color, shape, aesthetic "look," texture, and view that will please themselves as well as the users of the building.[7]

All facilities and designs for facilities involve both use and aesthetic functions. Some buildings emphasize use, while others emphasize aesthetics. Hospitals, schools, shopping centers, airports, art museums, and warehouses entail both in variable proportions. A warehouse in a remote location might embrace use over aesthetics. An art museum in an urban setting might exhibit primarily aesthetic functions.

An intense study of functions forms the basis of function analysis and advances the value and quality of the facility being designed. Any action that sacrifices performance or utility reduces its value to the owner and user. On the other hand, expenditures that increase the functional capabilities of a facility beyond necessities are also of questionable value to the owner and user.

Function analysis involves:

- Identifying
- Clarifying
- Naming
- Associating cost and worth
- Assessing value

To achieve optimum value, functions must be carefully defined so that their associated costs may be determined and properly assigned.

How owners' needs are expressed often implies their satisfaction, but it is the designer's responsibility to make certain the satisfaction is explicit and tangible. Therefore, the owner's needs are the objectives; the design specifies how the objectives are satisfied. But defining the owner's needs in quantitative terms is a difficult task.

Identifying Use Functions

In function analysis, a function is normally expressed using two words—a verb and its object. The verb specifies the desired action—enclose, support, control, illuminate, heat, cool, protect, convey. The noun identifies what is to be acted on (space, landscape, parking, temperature, light, people, sound). The noun must be specific enough to be quantifiable because later in the function analysis process a specific cost value will be associated with it. For example, the function of a data processing center could be to "provide service." "Service," too broad to be readily measurable, does not enable alternatives to be generated and analyzed. However, if the function is "process data," "data" are measurable, and acceptable processing alternatives can be suggested (GSA 1978, 3–2).

Defining a function in two words, a verb and a noun, allows conciseness, avoids combining functions, and disassociates the actual item from the function(s) it performs. Figure 4-1 provides a partial listing of verbs and nouns typically associated with building use functions.

Identifying Aesthetic Functions

As with use functions, aesthetic functions are expressed using a verb and noun (Miles 1972, 28). Because the functions themselves address

Verbs		*Nouns*	
absorb	heat	air	oxidation
alter	illuminate	compression	parking
amplify	impede	current	people
change	improve	elements	power
circulate	increase	energy	protection
collect	induce	fire	radiation
condition	insulate	flow	sheer
conduct	interrupt	fluids	sound
connect	modulate	force	space
contain	prevent	heat	temperature
control	protect	landscape	tension
convey	provide	light	torque
cool	rectify	load	voltage
detect	reduce	materials	weight
distribute	repel	objects	
emit	resist		
enclose	shield		
exclude	support		
extinguish	transmit		
filter	ventilate		
finish			

FIGURE 4-1. Use functions.

more subjective issues, the naming of aesthetic functions is more difficult. The broadest verb–noun combination that applies to all aesthetic functions is "please owner–user." Specifying *what* will please the owner–user requires the analyst to discover exactly what aesthetic functions the owner–user wants and will pay for. The more precisely aesthetic functions can be named, the more appropriate are solutions that can be promoted. Typical aesthetic function verbs and nouns are listed in figure 4-2 (GSA 1978, 3–4).

Basic and Secondary Functions

Once the use and aesthetic functions have been identified, they are further classified as either basic or secondary. The owner–user is again required to communicate what performance feature (use or aesthetic) must be attained. It reflects the primary reason for the existence of the building, system, or component. A basic function

	Verbs		*Nouns*	
create	improve	appearance	image
enjoy	reflect	balance	prestige
establish	see	beauty	preparation
experience	smell	color	space
feel	taste	convenience	style
finish	think	ego	symmetry
hear		features	texture
		feeling	tone
		form	view

FIGURE 4-2. Aesthetic functions.

satisfies owner–user needs, not desires. Secondary functions are those features the owner–user desires beyond needs. Secondary functions also sometimes arise because of the particular design selected to meet a basic function. Sometimes it is a feature of an item that is not essential to the owner (Dell'Isola 1982, 20).

The point of view from which a function is defined is key in identifying the basic function. What is considered basic will normally differ depending on whether the function analyst is the owner, user, designer, or builder. The basic function can also change over time. A facility may come to be used for something other than its original basic function. A warehouse designed to "protect materials" might be purchased to be used as office space to "house tenants." A window may serve to "view outdoors." The same window in a bank, if the glass is bulletproof, is probably there to "protect teller."

A facility, system, or component may perform more than one basic function. This would be true in the case of an item that satisfies several required use functions or both use and aesthetic functions. An exterior wall that keeps the rain out also acts as a thermo-barrier, thus fulfilling two basic use functions. This same wall might also project an image that serves an aesthetic function.

The basic function is identified in the broadest possible terms to allow the greatest leeway for optimum satisfaction. In this way the greatest freedom in creativity for generating design alternatives should help to overcome preconceived ideas regarding how the function will be accomplished. For example, consider limiting the amount of glass on a building to control heat loss. Rather than "minimize windows," the function would be better articulated as "control heat loss," since minimizing windows is only one way to control heat loss. Insulation could be added, perimeter walls could be reduced, building height could be lowered.

A secondary function is a performance feature aside from those that *must* be accomplished. Secondary functions are also increments of performance in excess of minimum performance levels (GSA 1978, 3–5). The basic function of office partitions may be to "enclose space," with secondary functions of "providing status" or "controlling noise."

COST AND WORTH OF FUNCTIONS

Determining Cost

Function analysis requires the designer to determine the present cost of fulfilling functions. In order to do this, the designer first estimates the present cost of the facility, system, or component being examined. If detailed cost estimates are not available, professional cost analysts should be consulted to prepare reasonable projections of the costs involved. These estimates should include material, labor, equipment, and overhead costs for each functional element (GSA 1978, 3–7).

Since an owner is interested in expending money only for a use or aesthetic function he or she wants, costs must be specified for all previously defined functions. However, the cost for a specific building, system, or component is much more available than are data detailing the costs for specific functions. Where a building, system, or component serves more than one function, the cost of the item often can be prorated among the functions. For example, assume a detailed cost estimate projects $300,000 for the exterior closure system of a bank. Assume also that the exterior closure system serves two functions: it encloses space and it provides image (to the public). Examination of the wall consisting of face brick, insulation, block backup, furring, and gypsum board interior reveals that the face brick provides the "image" function at a cost of $120,000. The balance of $180,000 performs the function of enclosing space. When a building, system, or component serves only one function, its cost equals the cost of the function (GSA 1978, 3–9).

Figure 4-3 illustrates the function analysis of an office complex in

Project: Office Complex   Item: House Office Activities / Process Data / Improve Image   Date

Basic Function

Quantity Unit	$/sf	Component (UNIFORMAT Category)	Function Verb	Noun	Kind *	Explanation	Original Cost $/sq.ft.	Worth $/sq.ft.
46,070	$/sf	01 Foundations	support	loads	U/B	Conc. Spread Ftg.	0.68	0.68
"		02 Substructure	"	"	"	Conc. Basement Walls	6.10	3.00
"		03 Superstructure	"	"	"	Conc. Waffle Slab	10.91	9.00
"		04 Exterior Closure	enclose	space	A/B	Brick, Precast Conc., Glass	5.61	1.00
			improve	(corp.) image	A/B			2.00
			exclude	elements	U/B			2.00
"		05 Roofing	enclose	space	U/B	4 ply – Built up	1.59	0.50
			exclude	elements	"			1.00
"		06 Interior Construction	divide	space	"	Gyp.Bd., Paint, Carpet	5.31	2.00
			finish	space	A/B			3.31
"		07 Elevators	convey	people & objects	U/S	Hydraulic Elevators	1.34	1.30
"		081 Plumbing	convey	fluids	U/B	Piping & Fixtures	1.72	1.08
"		082 HVAC	condition	space	"	Variable Air Volume	8.80	4.00
			circulate	air	A/B			2.45
"		083 Fire Protection	extinguish	fire	U/S	Halon in Computer Room	1.11	0.50
"		091 Service & Distribution	transmit	power	U/B	480/277 volt, 3phase wye	1.22	0.90
"		092 Lighting & Power	illuminate	objects	"	4 tube Fluorescent	2.23	1.50
			distribute	power	"			.60
"		093 Special Elect. Systems	provide	emergency power	U/S	Generator	1.51	0.80
"		10 General Conditions	manage	project	"		10.02	5.68
			provide	profit	"			0.80
"		12 Sitework	improve	(base) image	A/B	Landscaping	2.74	2.24

Total $\dfrac{Cost}{Worth} = \dfrac{60.89}{46.34} = 1.31$

* Function Type: Use or Aesthetic / Basic or Secondary

FIGURE 4-3. Functional analysis worksheet.

the midwestern area of the United States. It distributes cost among each of the facility's functions. Note that both use and aesthetic functions are recorded on the format worksheet. Figure 4-3 also identifies each function as basic (B) or secondary (S). Finally, it assigns "worth" to functions and calculates the cost-to-worth ratio also known as the "value index." In this case, the value index equals 1.31, indicating improvement in value is possible.

Determining Worth

In function analysis, worth is tied only to essential building functions, not to the existing design of the facility or system. Worth, by definition, is the least cost of fulfilling a given function in the most elementary manner using current technology. The worth of a function is usually arrived at by comparing the present design for performing the function with other methods of performing essentially the same function. For example, "conduct electricity" is the function of an electrical cable. Although copper wire might be the present solution, the "worth" might be established by the cost of aluminum wire which also "conducts electricity" (Dell'Isola 1982, 22). Worth can also be established retrospectively by using minimum costs of recently completed designs. Worth is used to indicate value in the performance of a particular function. Complete accuracy in determining this cost is not crucial since it is used merely for comparison.

Some designers allocate worth only to basic functions, assigning the worth of secondary functions as zero. This is done because secondary functions exist only as a result of the design solution that has been chosen to satisfy the basic functions. When an alternate way to accommodate basic functions is discovered, all the previous secondary functions become moot (GSA 1978, 3–10).

Worth can be established during any point of the design process as well as at various levels of detail. At the schematic design stage, historical parameter costs can be used to judge such things as cost per square foot for a courthouse facility, cost per occupant for a church, cost per bed for a hospital, or cost per student for a school. At the design development stage, a designer might judge the least cost of the various functions a roofing system provides. For example, the designer might determine the least cost to "seal roof," "insulate roof," and "allow daylight" (GSA 1978, 3–10).

Building system worth can be established by measuring building parameters. Some examples: building exterior closure using a cost per square foot of wall; air conditioning by cost per ton; electrical systems by cost per connected kilowatt load; structural systems by cost per kip or structural steel pounds per square foot; and plumbing by cost per fixture. These unit costs can be applied to quantities of each desired function. For example, the worth of an air conditioning system to "cool people" might be established by reviewing historical parameter data to determine the lowest cost per ton of air conditioning achieved for that function (GSA 1978, 3–11).

Judging Value

Assigning cost and worth to a function allows assessment of the function's value. Then the value received for a series of functions being performed by a system or component can be compared and ranked. Ranking is arrived at by determining the cost-to-worth ratio, known as the "value index." The value index helps the designer determine whether to proceed with a formal review. A study should proceed only if poor value exists, indicated when the value index is greater than one. Good value is indicated by an index of one. If a review is indicated, the designer pinpoints where the cost-to-worth ratio is the greatest. Generally these areas will have the greatest cost savings potential and are the more profitable parts of the problem to select for study (GSA 1978, 3–11).

In summary, function analysis addresses the functions of buildings, systems, and components. Function means the "purpose" of a building, system, or component and is defined by the owner-user in verb-noun descriptions. Function analysis first determines what functions are required by the owner-user; only afterward is the element itself considered.

GRAPHICAL FUNCTION ANALYSIS

Graphical function analysis permits a visual inspection of the function of a building, system, or item and its relative cost and worth. Normally the cost and worth of a function are expressed as bar graphs descending from highest cost to lowest cost. The worth of each function is shaded to permit a visual register of the relative cost-to-worth ratio of the function. This type of graphic expression of function allows the design team quickly to assess the areas of greatest cost improvement potential. Not only can initial costs of various functions be expressed; so also can the space, energy, or life-cycle cost requirements of a project's elements (Dell'Isola 1982, 22).

Cost-to-Worth Graphical Function Analysis

The most common graphical function analysis uses the initial cost and worth for each function of a building, system, or component. Figure 4-4 applies cost-to-worth graphical function analysis to the office complex mentioned earlier in this chapter. Each major system has been rearranged and displayed in descending order from highest to lowest cost per square foot. It quickly becomes apparent that the superstructure and substructure carry the most cost. Their function, to "support loads," accounts for over $17 per square foot of the building cost. The superstructure consists of a concrete frame and waffle slab system for the two-story building. The substructure is made up of concrete basement walls and foundations. The worths of these systems were established by contemplating how else these functions might be met at the least cost possible. Ideas such as use of a steel frame, concrete flat plate, or prestressed concrete frame for the superstructure, or raising the basement above the water table level for the substructure suggested that there were many ways to reduce cost. The worths of these two systems were then estimated to be $9 per square foot (sq.ft.) for the superstructure and $3 for the substructure, indicated by the shaded areas on the graph.

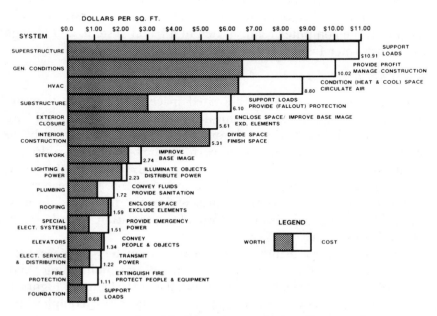

FIGURE 4-4. Graphical function analysis: office complex.

Similarly the HVAC system was examined since it also cost a significant $8.80/sq.ft. Its principal functions were to condition (heat and cool) space and to circulate air. The HVAC system consisted of a variable volume air system with six air handlers, two per floor. The worth was established by thinking of least-cost solutions such as a constant volume system, consolidated air handling units, and a packaged chiller system. The worth was established at $6.45/sq.ft., represented in the shaded area on the graph.

Following this procedure in descending order through the remainder of the systems turns up areas where the most significant impact might be made in further study. Totaling all worth figures and subtracting them from the total cost yields the potential savings if further study is pursued. In this example $58.15/sq.ft. (cost) − $44.10 (worth) = $14.05/sq.ft. (potential savings). Analyses have shown that this scale of savings will normally be identified by the design team if further study is done. Actual recommendations, however, may be quite different from those used to estimate the least cost (worth) of the systems during function analysis. Recommendations from this study included the following: use a steel frame with concrete on a metal deck; raise the basement by two feet; reconfigure the interior exitway to eliminate a stairway; reduce the building height; consolidate the six air handlers to one per floor; use a constant volume system; omit ducted air returns; use dry pipe fire protection in the computer room in lieu of a halon system; and change the transformer from 750 KVA to 500 KVA.

Space, Energy, and LCC Graphical Function Analysis

Architects have traditionally allocated space by listing the function of each type of space. The graphical function analysis discussed here simply extends the traditional approach by adding the "worth" or least amount of space required to perform the basic function. Figure 4-5 illustrates the space graphical function analysis of the office complex. Visual inspection of this design indicates that the greatest potential for space minimization exists within the functions "process data," "provide expansion," "provide circulation," and "store HVAC equipment."

In addition to using space-related parameters—square feet, square meters—other units such as tons of air conditioning, kilowatts of power, or total life-cycle-cost dollars may be used. Figure 4-6 presents an energy function analysis of the office complex dis-

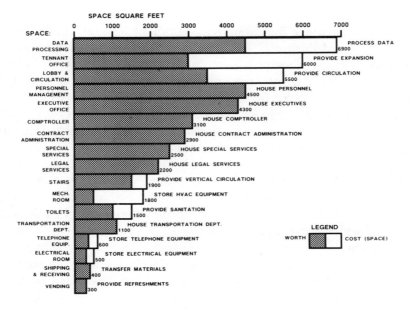

FIGURE 4-5. Space graphical function analysis: office complex.

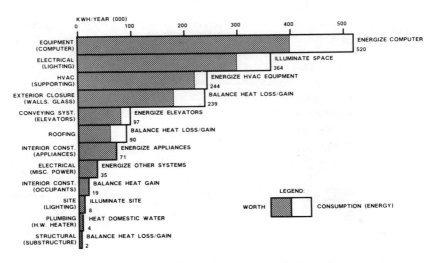

FIGURE 4-6. Energy graphical function analysis: office complex.

cussed earlier. It illustrates that over 30 percent of the load is required to energize the computer equipment. Of the remainder, 31 percent is used to provide illumination. Both the computer and the lighting system generate a large amount of heat in the building, which then must be removed by the air conditioning system (this accounts for over half of the HVAC load). Based on this energy function analysis, designers would examine the computer and lighting systems with a view toward reducing the amount of equipment required and the heat emitted by that equipment.

A major criticism of value analysis has been its focus on reducing initial costs. Function analysis is not limited to first costs. Most of its proponents advocate a total cost (life-cycle cost) approach to value analysis.[8] Figure 4-7 is a graphical function analysis of the life-cycle costs of the office complex.[9] The present worth and cost of each component of the office complex consists of initial cost, operation (energy) cost, maintenance cost, and alterations and replacement costs. This illustration clearly shows that for this office building design, the initial cost is less than half the life-cycle cost for the facility. Designers would do well to balance low first cost and long-term cost efficiency ratios when considering each building system.

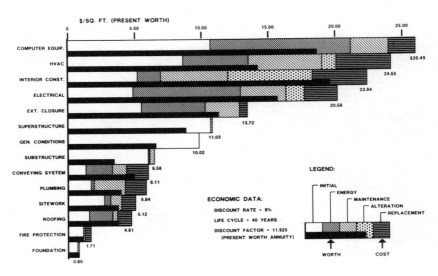

FIGURE 4-7. Life-cycle cost graphical function analysis: office complex.

FUNCTION ANALYSIS SYSTEMS TECHNIQUE (FAST)

The Function Analysis Systems Technique (FAST) is a diagramming procedure that demonstrates the logical relationships among the functions of a building, system, or component.[10] Before FAST diagramming was introduced, functions were identified randomly. The basic function had to be identified by trial and error, and the designer was never quite sure that all functions had been revealed.

Used in conjunction with function analysis, the FAST diagram organizes random listings of functions and places them at the proper level of indenture. A FAST diagram also checks for functions that may have been overlooked in the random function identification process described in function analysis. A properly assembled FAST diagram yields a consensus in defining the problem in terms of function and aids in developing valid yet creative alternatives. Finally, it is particularly helpful in explaining resulting changes to decision makers (GSA 1978, 5–1,2).

The greatest benefit of a FAST diagram is the thinking process that occurs during the diagramming procedure. If the diagram is logical to the diagrammer, it will usually be logical to others who may review it. If it doesn't make sense to others, then it has highlighted a misunderstanding in the statement of the problem.

Diagramming Procedure

Figure 4-8 depicts diagramming conventions used in preparing a FAST diagram. The relative positions of functions as displayed in the diagram are called levels of indenture. The higher-level functions appear on the left side of the FAST diagram, with the lower-level functions successively graphed to the right. The two vertical dashed lines (scope lines), one to the extreme left and one to the extreme right of the diagram, indicate the scope of the problem under study. Every function between these two scope lines composes the problem under study.

In each FAST diagram, at least one critical path of functions moves from left to right across the scope lines. The critical path includes only the basic function(s), the higher-order functions, and sequential supporting functions. All functions on the critical path must be part of the basic function. All other functions on the FAST diagram are subordinate to the critical-path function and are not necessary to the basic functions.

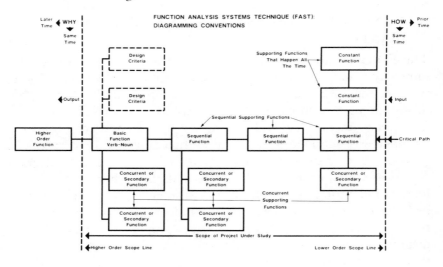

FIGURE 4-8. Function Analysis Systems Technique (FAST): diagramming conventions. (Reprinted, by permission, from Alphonse J. Dell'Isola, *Value Engineering in the Construction Industry* [New York: Van Nostrand Reinhold, 1982] 40)

The higher-order function lies to the immediate left of the scope line. The basic function(s) will always be immediately to the right of the left scope line and the higher-order function. All other functions on the critical path will lie to the right of the basic function. All supporting or secondary functions will lie below the critical path of functions. If the function is performed simultaneously and/or is caused by a function on the critical path, the secondary function is placed below that particular critical-path function.

Constant functions are placed above the critical path to the extreme right of the diagram. Specific design criteria/objectives to keep in mind as the diagram is constructed are usually placed above the basic function and are shown as dashed boxes.

Diagramming Steps

A FAST diagram is typically constructed in this order: (1) list functions, (2) place each function on a separate card, (3) organize functions into a critical path and supporting logic, and (4) locate scope lines (GSA 1978, 5–3,7). The positions of the next higher and lower function cards are determined by answering the following logic questions:

1. Asking the question "How?" of any function should produce an answer to the immediate right. If it does not, the function is either improperly described or in the wrong place.
2. The second question "Why?" works in the opposite direction. The answer should be in the function to the immediate left.

Whether a function belongs on the critical path or immediately beneath a given critical-path block depends on whether it is basic or secondary. Constant functions go immediately above the critical path to the right. Criteria and objectives may also be added at this time above the critical path to the left in dashed boxes.

A FAST diagram is completed by determining where to place the scope lines. Moving the left scope line from left to right lowers the level of indenture of the problem to be studied. The basic function to be studied shifts because it is always to the immediate right of the left scope line. Locating the right scope line determines the assumptions and known information at the start of function analysis. Location of both scope lines is also subject to the owner-user's viewpoint.

FAST Example

An example of FAST diagramming will illustrate the preceding discussion. Figure 4-9 is a simplified diagram for the office complex discussed earlier in this chapter. The higher-order function for this project is "consolidate office space." Three basic functions must be provided:

1. House office activities (use function)
2. Process data (use function)
3. Improve corporate image (aesthetic function)

The functions sequential to these basic functions are to the right of these boxes. Critical paths are indicated by heavier boxes and connecting lines. Subordinate (secondary) functions occurring currently with the functions on the critical path are indicated by lighter lines below the appropriate function. Constant functions, such as "receive supplies" and "receive people," are located above the critical path on the right. Design criteria or, in this case, objectives are listed above the scope line to the left in dashed boxes. These objectives

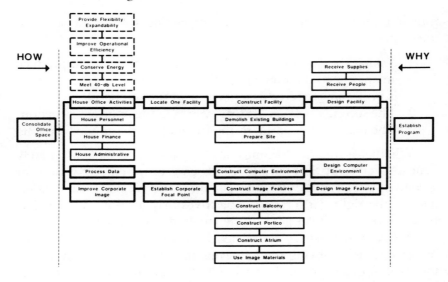

FIGURE 4-9. Function Analysis Systems Technique diagram: office complex.

included providing building flexibility/expandability, improving operational efficiency, conserving energy, and meeting the 40-decibel noise criterion. The scope of study includes those factors between the dashed lines.

CONCLUSION

FAST is a structure diagramming method of function analysis that results in defining the basic function and establishing critical-path and supporting functions. FAST diagrams are always constructed at a level low enough to be useful but high enough to allow a creative search for alternate methods. FAST diagrams communicate an understanding of problems between owner, user, designer, and constructor to define, simplify, and clarify problems.

A FAST diagram, when it is first constructed, may not completely follow the "How" and "Why" logic implied in the finished example shown in figure 4-9. The main benefit of using FAST diagramming and performing extensive function analysis is to produce a clear understanding of the subject. Once function analysis is performed, it becomes apparent that the only reason a lower-level function has to be performed is because a higher-level function brought it into being. Essentially, whenever a functional relationship is presented by a FAST diagram, greater opportunities for creativity emerge.

NOTES

1. Value in the traditional sense is often defined as worth/cost. The reverse is used in this text as the "Value Index." Refer to Miles (1972) for a complete discussion of the theory of value analysis. That text, by the originator of function analysis, is especially good regarding application to the manufacturing industry.

2. Although additional techniques have been added to value analysis over the years, most have been modified from other fields such as creativity, life cycle costs, and group dynamics. The heart of value analysis remains function analysis.

3. See Dell'Isola (1982) for a more complete historical perspective of value analysis in the construction industry. Dell'Isola's book remains the most complete and authoritative text on the subject, containing many examples from the construction industry.

4. The U.S. GSA publication #PBS P9000.1 (1978) was the first text to explain many related techniques of value analysis as applied to both hardware (materials and products) and software (systems, procedures, and paperwork). It is an excellent source of additional information regarding value management.

5. See EPA, *VE Workbook for Construct Projects* (July 1976) for applications in wastewater treatment processes. Any process-related facility can be studied following the steps outlined in this text.

6. See Bytheway (1965) for a more complete discussion of FAST diagramming. The incorporation of FAST into function analysis is considered to be the only significant addition to the body of knowledge since Lawrence Miles began value analysis twenty years earlier.

7. Miles (1972, 25–26) was the first to identify aesthetic functions. Some authors such as Parker (1977) and Dell'Isola (1982) describe aesthetic functions as "esteem" functions.

8. Dell'Isola (1982) makes clear that value analysis should be applied to the total cost of ownership.

9. Dell'Isola and Kirk (1981) were the first to introduce function analysis using the life-cycle cost parameters of initial, energy, maintenance, and replacement costs.

10. The authors have found FAST diagramming to be most useful in defining processes that occur within a facility, such as people or material movements to complete an operation. To date the design profession has made very little use of this more advanced form of function analysis. It can be most useful during architectural programming and early schematic design to understand and define more fully the problem to be solved.

CHAPTER 5

Group
Creativity

G ROUP CREATIVITY involves a collective search for design solutions.[1] Traditional design processes typically concentrate the attention of the architect on the first idea that will work and develop it into a solution. Typically, a designer works as an individual and strives to produce a solution that is unique and original. Group creativity, by contrast, employs the collective thinking of many individuals and identifies as many ideas as possible, then picks the one that best satisfies the needs of the building owner and users. Function analysis identifies the owner-user needs, defines them in verb-noun descriptions, and associates value measures with these functions. Group creativity considers a wide range of ideas that suit the basic functions (use and aesthetic) of the problem. *Quantity* is a focus, because the probability of happening onto an excellent idea is higher in a longer rather than a shorter list of alternatives. No idea is criticized and no idea is dismissed as impractical. Judgmental and negative thinking is detrimental to the group creativity process and stifles the free flow of ideas. Diversity encourages cross-fertilization of ideas and fosters creative solutions.

The use of a multidisciplinary group in design—composed of the owner, user, architect, engineer, and builder—has been shown to yield from 65 to 93 percent more ideas than issue from an individual working alone (Dell'Isola 1982, 47). The team not only generates more ideas but also stimulates the creative potential of each participant. One person's idea nudges the associative processes of other group members. This chain reaction triggers many ideas, and the cycle repeats itself. Thomas Edison, for example, worked during his most productive years not as a solitary inventor, but surrounded by a creative group of technicians, engineers, and scientists. The insights he picked up from his interaction with this team sparked his own imagination.[2]

HISTORY

Much research has concentrated on group creativity processes and techniques since the late 1930s. Probably the earliest group creativity technique was brainstorming, one person's stimulation of another person's mind. Alex F. Osborn first applied this technique to generate ideas as part of a marketing strategy in his advertising firm. The concept of brainstorming was promoted at the Creative Education Foundation in Buffalo, New York, which was founded by Osborn. This technique was also described in his book *Applied Imagination* (1957). Osborn also devised a checklist of verbs to change a person's mental set as he or she contemplates a problem: *magnify*, *minify*, and *rearrange*, for example.

Another early proponent of formalized creativity techniques was William J. J. Gordon, a former Harvard engineering professor who founded his own creativity-training firm in Cambridge, Massachusetts. He called it Synectics, after the name of his technique, which encouraged the use of metaphors and analogies to spawn inventiveness in problem solving. Synectics, from the Greek *synektik*, means joining together different and apparently irrelevant elements to form new and effective ideas and schemes. The purpose of synectics is to multiply ideas by stimulating the imagination through various types of analogies. In *Synectics: The Development of Creative Capacity* (1961), Gordon described four types of analogy: symbolic, direct, personal, and fantasy. Analogies relating to nature have given rise to bionics and biomechanics.

Gordon also modified the brainstorming approach in one respect: no one but the group leader is to know the exact nature of the subject under consideration. This keeps the group from focusing too narrowly. Because the session is open ended, more ideas result (Gordon 1961, 77–78). Design sketches are often similarly characterized by ambiguity, allowing the designer to think flexibly and in general terms. This fluidity and free association allow the designer to shape decisions about the exact location of spaces and boundaries between spaces. Alvar Aalto's sketches (fig. 5-1) are reminiscent of the approach suggested by Gordon's open-ended technique.

FIGURE 5-1. Open-ended sketch by Alvar Aalto. (Reprinted, by permission, from Aarno Ruusuvuori, *Alvar Aalto* [Helsinki: The Museum of Finnish Architecture, 1978] 9)

The Delphi technique, a more structured and analytic form of group dynamics, is used as a means to achieve a consensus in a decision-making process. A Rand Corporation research group developed this technique in the early 1950s as a way to collect ideas and estimates from a multidisciplinary group of comparably qualified individuals. This technique has subsequently become a fundamental tool for technological forecasting in government, industry, and professional organizations.[3] However, Delphi has only recently been applied to complex design problems such as the environment, health, and transportation. The American Institute of Architects first proposed using the Delphi technique in building design through a self-help guide published in 1975.

Larry Miles (1972) also recognized the power of disciplined applications of group creativity to problem solving for General Electric. Since the formulation of value analysis at GE in the mid-1940s, formalized creativity sessions have been part of the value analysis methodology. In fact, creativity was made a separate step in the earliest value analysis job plan. Every value engineering text written since has included in its methodology a separate step for creativity.

THEORY

The mental activity of creativity begins by combining and recombining past experience to form new arrangements that will meet a particular design need (GSA 1978, 6–3). Creativity is perceived by many to be an effortless flash of insight. In fact, however, creativity requires extensive preparation.

Osborn, Gordon, and other creativity experts agree that creative potential exists in everyone. Creative thinking techniques enable people to maximize their creative potential. Certain characteristics distinguish people who exhibit more creative ability than others.[4] Creative people tend to be more open-minded, more tolerant of complexity, less inclined to assume that there is only one best way to solve a problem, and less authoritarian in attitudes than noncreative people (Zimmerman and Hart 1982, 87–88). *Primary creativity* generates completely new ideas and concepts, and *secondary creativity* develops, expands, modifies, and reorders another's ideas. People who display secondary creativity are usually better at carrying ideas through to practical conclusions. Humor is an important fuel for the creative process. Studies have shown a high correlation between creativity and humor.[5] Often a playful jest will lead to a useful idea. Use of art and symbols also is helpful. Picture drawing and guided fantasy, called on when a group is "blocked," can break an unproductive pattern of thinking. In fact, a general principle that has evolved in group creativity techniques is that it really doesn't matter which techniques or how many techniques you use, as long as they take your mind out of one mode of thinking and allow you to explore unconventional ideas.

Creative Process

A study of the creative process will yield a better knowledge of the workings of creativity. To search for a solution to any problem, the mind uses and follows a certain pattern or routine.[6] The steps to this creative process have been defined by some to be these:

1. Identify the problem to be solved.
2. Gather information.
3. Analyze the data.
4. Produce alternative solutions.
5. Evaluate ideas and allow time for additional ideas to occur.
6. Synthesize ideas into a whole.
7. Verify the proposed solution through evaluation.

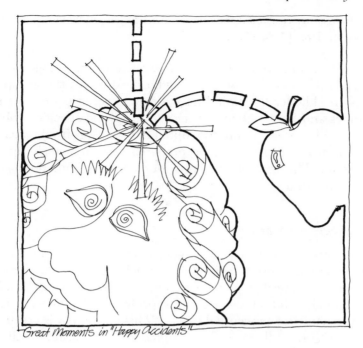

Great Moments in "Happy Accidents"

FIGURE 5-2. Great moments in "happy accidents."

A person's creative ability becomes somewhat diminished with more formalized education and older age. Traditional education and advanced age tend to steer people into narrow, noncreative thought processes. With appropriate training in creative thinking and applied techniques, however, traditional learning patterns and expectations can be channeled into productive thought processes (Australia 1983, 8.3–8.4).

Rapid societal change means that designers must switch more and more from random creativeness to deliberate and focused creativeness. With shorter amounts of time to solve increasingly complex problems, a systematic process is necessary if ideas are to be produced on purpose. Most designers develop attitudes such as the following:

- The first idea that works is used, in lieu of continuing to search for possible better alternatives.
- Decisions that originally seemed sound may now, due to changed circumstances, guarantee excessive cost or lower performance.

- Changes are resisted if they defy old attitudes and beliefs that now are out of date. [Australia 1983, 8.6]

Equally as important as the creative talent of the individual team member is that of the team leader who must direct the group to a conclusion. The leader should have a firm grasp of many creativity techniques and know when to use each to solve a specific problem. In order to encourage an uninterrupted flow of ideas from all participants, the team leader must be prepared to switch techniques as appropriate. The team leader provides order, stimulation, and a sense of direction.

Roadblocks to Creativity

All architects and engineers experience roadblocks in their thinking.[7] A team member alert to this is in a much better position to take positive and practical steps to overcome the blocks. Roadblocks can be perceptual, habitual, emotional, or professional. "Tunnel vision" is another name for perceptual blocks. This restriction is created by the failure to use all the senses—sight, hearing, taste, smell, and touch—to tackle a problem. It has been said that experts tend to "overlook the obvious," also a perceptual block (Australia 1983, 8.6).

Habitual blocks involve the continuance of what has always been done or thought before. They may be generated internally or prescribed by an outside authority. Some individuals conform to existing standards and expectations in order to protect themselves and ensure job security.

Emotional blocks result from fears concerning how one's peers might feel toward one if one were to suggest something different than the way the problem would normally be solved. Blocking stems from fear of making an unpopular decision, unwillingness to let one's guard down, or fear of what others might think. Some individuals play it safe by making adequate, but not creative, decisions.

Professional blocks are caused by the academic, professional, educational, and working environment in which one functions. Some individuals are unable to branch out into concepts proposed by other disciplines. Architects, for example, tend to believe that their profession promulgates the "truth" about design, to the exclusion of disciplines concerned with environmental problems (Australia 1983, 8.7).

Techniques

A number of techniques have been found to improve creativity and to be particularly appropriate for architects and engineers because of the relative ease with which they can be applied in design problems. These techniques are:

- Brainstorming (splitting the judgmental and creative minds)
- Delphi (predicting the future and reaching consensus)
- Manipulation (looking at generalities rather than specifics)
- Pattern (looking at specifics rather than generalities)

Each of the above techniques emphasizes the use of open-ended problem-solving philosophies and the elimination of criticism during the early stages of the decision-making process.

BRAINSTORMING

Brainstorming is based on the stimulation of one person's mind by another's. A typical brainstorming session involves four to six people spontaneously generating ideas to solve a specific problem. Brainstorming, as defined by its originator Osborn (1957), is an organized way to allow the mind to produce ideas without getting bogged down in trying to judge the value of those ideas at the same time (Australia 1983, 8.8).

Group Brainstorming

Prior to brainstorming, a group leader is designated to be responsible for monitoring and guiding the session. Since a rule of this technique is to exclude criticism, the group leader must stop the group when a word, tone, gesture, or anything else indicates rejection of an idea. In fact, the group leader encourages "freewheeling" thinking—the wilder the idea, the better. The greater the quantity of ideas, the more likely a quality solution will result. Because the group is working together, participants can suggest not only ideas of their own, but how others' ideas can be improved or how two or more ideas can be combined into still another idea. Figure 5-3 provides an outline of how a brainstorming session might proceed.

Group members are selected to represent various points of view and diverse backgrounds in brainstorming. Ideally the owner, architects and engineers, user groups, construction managers, and building operators and maintenance managers will participate in brain-

**Why/How Logic Diagram of
Rules for Brainstorming**

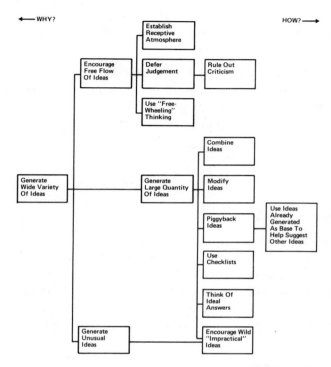

FIGURE 5-3. Brainstorming rules. (Reprinted, by permission, from A. J. Dell'Isola and S. J. Kirk, *Life Cycle Costing for Design Professionals* [New York: McGraw-Hill, 1981] 102)

storming sessions. Group members should represent parallel levels of responsibility (GSA 1978, 6.6). If some team members' superiors are present, the employees might hesitate to suggest ideas for fear of being judged by his or her boss. If such a team must work together, the Delphi technique could be used in lieu of brainstorming.

Criticism during brainstorming can have a stifling and debilitating effect. It may take some practice to shed this mind set, and so a warm-up session can be useful, addressing a simple problem familiar to the whole group. For example, how many ways can a window be designed to allow a view outside without increasing solar gain? This warm-up session does in fact limber up the mind as a runner would limber up his or her muscles prior to a race.

The group leader then opens the regular session by posing a well-defined problem expressed in functional language (see chapter 4). All ideas should be listed on a blackboard or flip sheet, no matter how frivolous or impractical they may seem—sometimes a difficult task because the ideas usually come too fast to be recorded. The final product of the brainstorming session is a host of ideas that with evaluation and refinement may generate a solution to the problem being studied.[8]

Reverse Brainstorming

Reverse brainstorming produces a list of undesirable possibilities. The focus is to identify as many ways as possible that an idea might fail to be implemented. The advantages of this process are that weaknesses are highlighted and can be rectified; all assertions of fact are questioned and, if necessary, validated; negative questions are anticipated and answers prepared. Using this technique permits team members to be more assured that their recommendations are valid and will satisfy the needs in a better way than any other idea (Australia 1983, 8.11).

DELPHI

Delphi is a method of achieving consensus by identifying design options and speculating on their outcome. This involves individual contributions of information, assessment of the group judgment, an opportunity for individuals to debate and revise their views, and a degree of anonymity. Because individual responses in a Delphi session are recorded on paper and submitted anonymously, the technique is especially useful in overcoming the emotional blocks often encountered in brainstorming. A Delphi group would normally include project managers, designers, value engineers, constructors, and client representatives.

A major advantage of Delphi is that it minimizes the bias of personality in achieving a group opinion.[9] This method may be used for:

- Exploring design options
- Identifying the pros and cons of potential design options
- Developing relationships in complex facilities
- Exposing priorities of personal values and design goals

Any group discussion is likely to produce a majority position, but it is often a compromise rather than a true consensus. This compromise may reflect the opinion of the most verbal, most dynamic, or most persistent group members. In early design, where a significant degree of uncertainty prevails, it is imprudent to assume that any one person's opinion is more valid than that of another group member. It is desirable to gain an idea of the range of opinions within the group and the reasons for individual estimates. It is immaterial whether Delphi participants are actually involved in the design under consideration, so long as each person provides a reasonable estimate based on knowledge of various design alternatives. Once assimilated, these estimates provide valuable information in their differences as well as in their similarities.

Design Options

The logic of the Delphi methodology is such that it will gradually converge on a set of design alternatives judged, by consensus, to provide optimum performance for the problem in question. As shown in figure 5-4, the Delphi process goes through a number of individual and group exploration cycles and concludes with a group recommendation. The first Delphi cycle provides an a priori set of inputs (subjective in nature) about a desired system. On the basis of these inputs, the team compiles a set of design alternatives. Estimated cost targets are then reviewed—without revealing their authorship—in order to determine the range of target values. The group can then begin to order the desired system properties into logical and probable design options, each of which is associated with an index of desirability known only to each participant.

The second cycle of the Delphi process allows each participant to digest the group ranking and focus on the most desirable design options. Participants can add or modify design options at this stage, while empirical confirmation of the range of target cost values further reinforces the validity of previous choices. As a part of the search, Delphi may predict the obsolescence of building systems or layout concepts. It is then possible to take corrective action by adding features such as flexible layouts or innovative technology.

Once participants have completed the second, individual cycle of Delphi, the group reassembles. Individual responses are fed into a formal group discussion in order to integrate a priori and a posteriori data. If the design options remain virtually unchanged (with an

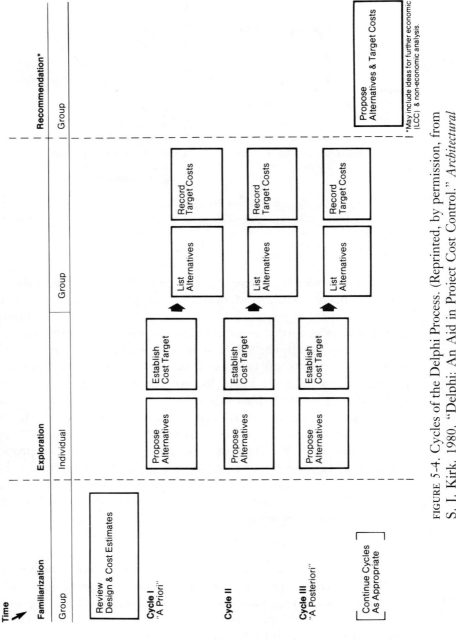

Cost Control Chart for Phases of The Delphi Process

Time

Familiarization	Exploration		Recommendation*
Group	Individual	Group	Group

Review
Design & Cost Estimates

Cycle I
"A Priori"

| Propose Alternatives | Establish Cost Target | → | List Alternatives | Record Target Costs |

Cycle II

| Propose Alternatives | Establish Cost Target | → | List Alternatives | Record Target Costs |

Cycle III
"A Posteriori"

| Propose Alternatives | Establish Cost Target | → | List Alternatives | Record Target Costs |

Continue Cycles
As Appropriate

Propose
Alternatives & Target Costs

*May include ideas for further economic analysis.
(LCC) & non-economic analysis.

FIGURE 5-4. Cycles of the Delphi Process. (Reprinted, by permission, from S. J. Kirk. 1980. "Delphi: An Aid in Project Cost Control." *Architectural Record* 12:51)

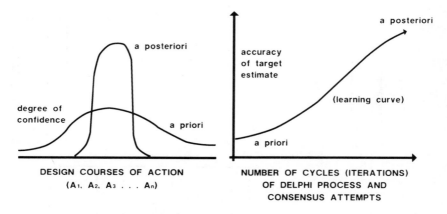

FIGURE 5-5. Reaching group consensus. (Reprinted, by permission, from S. J. Kirk. 1980. "Delphi: An Aid in Project Cost Control." *Architectural Record* 12:53)

indication of which alternatives are more desirable), the group is ready to make recommendations. Usually, however, at least one additional cycle is required before consensus is reached, although target cost values for the system should continue to converge.

The graphs in figure 5-5 illustrate the degree of each participant's confidence in her or his target estimate for various design courses of action. The a priori estimate (before consensus) greatly improves with the number of Delphi cycles. As the cycles converge on a group consensus (a posteriori) so do the design courses of action. In this manner, design cost control is exercised.

The final step of Delphi involves group participation in proposing alternatives and target costs for the system(s) under study. Design options recommended at this stage may still require further economic (life-cycle cost) and noneconomic review as details of specific components are identified.

A Delphi Case Study

A worksheet (fig. 5-6) can be used to aid decision making during each cycle of the Delphi process. The form is organized to document all pertinent information submitted by each individual during every cycle of the Delphi process. The building component or system being studied is described in the block in the upper left. The estimated cost of that element may be entered and a system component

Cost Control
The Delphi Method

Building	Element
Fl. to Fl. height req.'d.	Description
57.50/GSF	Target Cost
$62.39/GSF	Estimated Cost

Project _Health Care Ctr._ Cycle _#1_
Location _Southwest U.S._ Sheet _6_
Bldg. Type _Medical_ Date _____
Const. Type _Steel Frame_ Phase _Concept_

Functions (Verb/Noun)

provide (computer)	environment
provide (personnel)	environment
house (support)	equipment
provide	aesthetics

Alternatives

use trusses to run ducts - all flr.'s
use dual ducts to reduce height
pipe refridgerated water in lieu of air
reduce fl. to ceiling ht. to 8'-0"
eliminate raised flooring
relocate mech. to MESA II
roof top units
floor units

Components

	Cost	savings	
foundations	1.15/GSF	5%	
substructure	2.10/GSF	5%	run ducts under basement floor
superstructure	7.93/GSF	2%	use struct. system as plenum
exterior closure	2.78/GSF	10%	vary basement fl. height for functions
roofing	1.60/GSF	0	step down corridor height to 8'-0"
interior construction	8.07/GSF	5%	integrate lighting w/ struct. & HVAC
conveying system	.84/GSF	1%	use indirect lighting in spaces
HVAC system	8.85/GSF	1%	reduce 48" ⌀ ducts to 36" ⌀
plumbing	.52/GSF	1%	consider rectangular ducts
fire protection	2.55/GSF	1%	use high velocity ducts
spec. mech. & bldg. man.	4.07/GSF	1%	supply air from ducts outside bldg.
electrical	14.35/GSF	1%	expose ducts & HVAC dist. in space
gen. cond., o.h. & profit	7.40/GSF	1%	use 50k steel structural

Rationale / Assumptions

Goals : conserve energy, satify codes, meet (owner) program,
provide reliability
basement floor from 15'-0" to as little as 12'-0" (selected areas)
first floor from 18'-0" to 15'-0"
second floor & third floor 15'-0" to 14'-0"
total height potential = 6'-8'-0" (10% - 15%)

FIGURE 5-6. Delphi worksheet.

breakdown with related costs may be listed on the lines below the block. Functions to be performed by the element may be entered as conventional function analysis (verb-noun) descriptions.

As each participant begins to understand the design through function analysis, alternatives will come to mind. Space is provided on the right side of the sheet to record design options. After adequate consideration of alternative courses of action, each participant estimates a minimum target cost necessary to perform the required functions. The rationale and assumptions underlying the target cost are noted at the bottom of the sheet. Upon completion of the Delphi consensus process, this target figure becomes the cost objective for the element under study.

Applying this format to the design of a health care center and following the Delphi method, a multidisciplinary team consisting of a group leader, a client representative, the architect, a structural engineer, and a mechanical engineer reviews floor-to-floor height requirements for the project. Since this study area overlapped all design disciplines, the entire building was treated as the "element" under study. A list of functions the building is expected to satisfy is provided to the team along with an estimate of costs. After design requirements are reviewed, each participant is asked to list ideas for reducing the floor-to-floor height. Figure 5-6 illustrates how one individual completes the Delphi sheet during the first cycle.

After each participant has completed the worksheet, including a "targeted cost" for reducing the floor-to-floor height, the team is assembled. All ideas are then listed on a flip chart for group discussion. In all, forty-four different ideas are listed in this example. Ideas range from increasing the cross-sectional area of structural steel (to reduce depth) to the use of Vierendeel trusses, creating interstitial space for lights and HVAC distribution. Coffered ceilings are considered as a means of enhancing apparent height while reducing actual clearance from nine to eight feet. Estimated building costs range from $55.00 per gross square foot (GSF) to a high of $62.00/ GSF. As group discussion begins to organize random ideas into packages, certain ideas are judged as having significantly more potential than others. Additional study teams are invited to participate in the discussion.

The second cycle of Delphi begins with individual team members excluding some ideas from further consideration and developing new alternatives. A list of alternatives that meet functional criteria is discussed by team members. The client is also given an opportunity to comment on proposed alternatives.

By the third and final iteration, various team members begin to agree on key points. The structural engineer proposes using open-web trusses in lieu of spandrel beams. The mechanical engineer balances air distribution over the space, taking care to integrate this system into the structure. The architect suggests that a nine-foot flat ceiling be maintained for future flexibility within the health care center.

The team recommends that the floor-to-floor height be reduced from fifteen to fourteen feet on each of the three upper floors and from eighteen to fourteen feet on the ground floor. The basement height is varied to satisfy individual functions. Because of the large floor area involved, this review realizes an estimated saving of approximately $300,000.

The Delphi process is repeated until a satisfactory consensus is reached. However, at times not all participants might agree on a single outcome. Some opinions may be based on significantly different rationales, each of which is so cogent to the individuals proposing them that consensus is impossible. This situation may lead to a more thorough follow-up analysis and revisions of the design problem.[10]

MANIPULATION

Until now, creativity techniques have concentrated on generating ideas around a specific problem. Manipulation obscures the nature of the problem being studied. Creative effort is directed toward seeing commonplace elements in a totally new way. One reason for keeping the specific definition of the problem vague is to avoid a premature or predetermined solution. Ambiguity helps the designer to think more flexibly and generally. An open-ended problem description allows designers to be noncommittal about the exact locations or shapes of spaces. Figure 5-1 illustrated this obscurity in the sketches of Alvar Aalto. Minimal information allows the group process to focus on general issues while establishing the essential character of design solutions (Laseau 1980, 91–94).

Several manipulation techniques allow the group to diverge rather than converge as in the Delphi process. In the Gordon technique, only the group leader knows the exact nature of the problem under consideration. Synectics permits divergence by looking at analogies of the problem, rather than the problem itself. Bionics and biomechanics rely on the analogies of nature.

Gordon Technique

The Gordon technique engenders a free-flowing discussion of ideas regarding a loosely defined problem. No one but the group leader knows the exact nature of the problem. Thus, the most difficult aspect of conducting a session like this is selecting a topic for discussion. While the exact problem cannot be known by the participants, the subject selected should be related as nearly as possible. Normally the subject selected will be related to the actual problem by a physical principle. For example, the actual problem might be to seek solutions to a warehousing problem for a manufacturing company, so the group leader might have the group discuss how to "store things." Another example might be to design individual classrooms for a new school, so the group leader could have the group discuss "enclosures" or "how things are enclosed and given privacy."

The Gordon technique seeks to avoid the pitfall an ordinary brainstorming session is open to, the feeling on the part of participants that they have found the "correct" solution, and therefore there is no need to look for any other solution to a problem. The Gordon session avoids this danger because no best solution can be proposed for an unspecified problem. This technique can frustrate creative people who strive for leadership when none is provided. With only a broad area to discuss, these individuals go in circles, discussing the problem but getting nowhere. The benefit is that they may cover aspects that would never have been touched had they known the specific problem. The technique's strength is that it does not allow people to get bogged down in specifics (GSA 1978, 6.7).

Synectics

In synectics, analogies are the mechanisms for making the familiar strange and the strange familiar. Synectics means "the joining together of different and apparently irrelevant elements" to form new ideas and schemes. Analogies can be seen in everyday architectural inventions: a Bedouin tent in the desert of Saudi Arabia inspires a cable fiberglass structure for the airport in Jiddah; the design of a bird cage leads to the structural steel frame for high-rise buildings.

Gordon describes four types of analogy: personal, direct, symbolic, and fantasy (Gordon 1961, 36–53). Personal analogy injects individual identification into the problem situation in order to experience the effects under study. The individual becomes a part of the thing being designed. Imagine, for instance, trying to improve an entry lobby. Imagine being the receptionist; list various ways the lobby could be redesigned. Designers visualize themselves walking through the building they have just designed. This technique has also been used with great success in technical problems where the designer has thought of himself or herself as an actual part of a machine or system, subject to its motions and forces.

A direct analogy compares similar facets and procedures of dissimilar objects. For example, the cooling system of a dwelling might be designed to act in the same way the human body cools itself (see fig. 5-7). Bionics and biomechanics are creative techniques that look to nature to see whether a solution already exists there (Laseau 1980, 118).

Symbolic analogy uses the actions and structure of one object to create the image of something completely different. It is a way of condensing a complex system or object into a simpler representation. The intricate network of corridors in a hospital is compared to the circulation system of a living organism. Symbolic analogy helps the designer see the underlying structure of something that appears to have no structure. It is a form of conceptual "poetic license" in that it obscures reality in order to simplify the analysis of that reality.

The fourth form of analogy is fantasy, the use of conscious self-deceit by unrestrained imagination to explore a situation. Existing laws and rules are temporarily suspended. Focus is put on functions while fantasy is used to explore options. If the construction of exterior walls is at issue, considering synthetic materials might yield walls made of nylon or bamboo-reinforced concrete. Fantasy helps the decision maker break away from the conventional mind set in order to find a simple solution in unexpected places.

A group creativity session using analogy techniques typically consists of the following steps (Australia 1983, 8.13).

1. *Discussing a general concept:* Only the session leader is aware of the precise problem definition.
2. *Personal analogy:* Having discussed all information about the concept, the group then verbalizes impressions as to what it might feel like to be the various aspects of the concept they have been discussing.

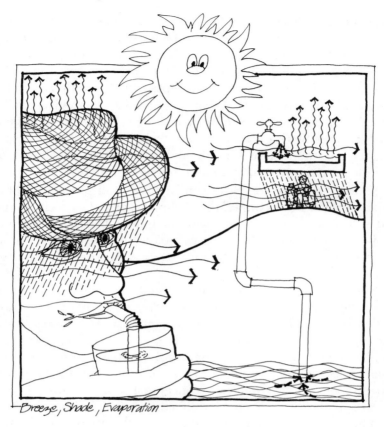

Breeze, Shade, Evaporation

FIGURE 5-7. Direct analogy.

3. *Direct analogy:* The group then makes direct comparisons among the various ideas raised in the previous subsession.
4. *Symbolic analogy:* This type of analogy may be used with direct analogy in the same session.
5. *Fantasy analogy:* Members are encouraged to discuss or compare anything they wish along the lines of the previous analogies, provided it has at least peripheral relevance to the subject.
6. *Free talk:* This session develops into a free discussion once the leader believes that the group has expended all relevant knowledge on the previous phase.
7. *Problem introduced:* At this stage the leader reveals a precise definition of the problem.

8. *Direct problem analysis:* Steps 1 through 5 are repeated, this time addressing the defined problem.
9. *Gestation period:* The team allows all ideas to sink into the subconscious.
10. *Recommendations:* Various ideas are edited (evaluation) and solutions are stated.

Bionics and Biomechanics

Designers throughout history have looked to nature for ideas, which may appear as direct applications or as modifications to the problem under consideration. Avian flight and aerodynamics illustrate this connection. Bionics and biomechanics look at nature to see whether a solution already exists there (Australia 1983, 8.20–8.21).

Example A. How can containers be shifted when normal lifting techniques are not applicable? The weight might be floated on a buoyant medium much the same way driftwood is transported.

Example B. How can tunnels be constructed under rivers? The nineteenth-century British inventor Isambard Brunel watched shipworms tunnel into timber by constructing protective tubes for themselves as they went; Brunel developed a similar tunneling process.

Engineering and design problems usually can be solved from ideas stemming from nature. For example, high-rise building design is structurally analogous to a tree and its roots. Mechanical engineers take advantage of the heat storage capacity of water to collect the sun's rays and reradiate this heat at night. Architects have long recognized the aesthetic value of natural objects and patterns in buildings, and routinely use them as ways of expressing function and direction. Flowers in nature occur in unpredictable combinations of color and are innately pleasing. Letting tenants paint their own apartments various colors or hanging their own window blinds might provide a similar effect in an otherwise homogenous and sterile apartment block (Laseau 1980, 120).

Because designers work primarily in a visual medium, other senses may be ignored and the designer cut off from a large number of possible design solutions. For example, if a house designer were to consider the tactile qualities of nature, a building might begin to respond to the way that surfaces "feel" as well as the way they appear (Laseau 1980, 122).

PATTERN

The opposite of the purposeful creation of vagueness is the establishment of an orderly way of going about identifying and creating ideas. Several techniques encompass this systematic approach: checklists, which provide suggestions or leads to yield more ideas; morphological analysis, a structured way to list combinations of characteristics to yield new alternatives; listing all attributes of an item, then changing or modifying them; pattern language, combining prototypes of smaller types to form a building concept.

Checklisting

The checklist, one of the most common designer aids in the search for new ideas, can unearth a number of clues to be compared against the problem definition to identify new possibilities and design options. Checklists range from specialized to generalized. An example of a generalized checklist is as follows:

Adapt	What else is like this? Copy nature.
Modify	Change the meaning, size, color, direction.
Magnify	Make stronger, heavier, more costly.
Minify	Miniaturize, omit, lighter, lower.
Substitute	What could be used instead? Parts, materials, power, process.
Rearrange	Is there an alternative design?
Reverse	Can it be transposed, used in reverse upside down?
Combine	Blend ideas; perform multiple functions. [Australia 1983, 8.16–8.17]

Suppose, for example, a designer is interested in enhancing cooperation among departments in a university. If the design team applies the word "magnify," it might come up with the following ideas: "Invite more outsiders, such as local business associates"; "Increase the number of classes offered in the week." Relating to "minify" might be the idea, "Provide smaller informal gathering areas outside classrooms," or "Do away with the faculty club and institute small cafés in the corridors." Or, "reverse" the normal daily activities by having a meeting before classes begin.

A number of specialized checklists also exist to deal with specific issues. The U.S. General Services Administration has published two books of guidelines for conserving energy. Checklists are broken down by systems: site, building, lighting, power, HVAC, domestic water, vertical transportation, solid waste, and operation and maintenance. Edwin Feldman in *Building Design for Maintainability* (1975) presents a checklist of designer ideas to improve a building's maintenance.

Another type of checklist is known as the "bug" or "problem" list.[11] Examples of "bugs" in buildings are these: dirty windows, leaky roof, noisy mechanical system, uneven floors, lack of privacy, computer screen glare, unswept floors, lack of office location signs, broken sidewalks, and clogged drains.

Checklists can be both helpful and obstructive. A list that is not open-ended can restrict thinking. Checklists are aimed at solving a specific problem. At the very least they assure the designer that successful approaches used in the past have been considered for the present situation.

Morphological Analysis

Morphological analysis lists and examines all possible combinations that might be useful in solving a problem. The first step is to define the problem clearly. Brainstorming can be very useful here. A visual model helps in cross-relating or seeing combinations of characteristics. For example, the following matrix of lighting systems might be useful:

	Lens Type			
Lighting Type	*Prismatic*	*Polarized*	*Parabolic*	*Indirect*
Incandescent	X			X
Fluorescent	X	X	X	
Mercury vapor			X	

This matrix becomes a cube when the size, shape, appearance, or wattage characteristics are listed. With more than three characteristics, a model can be made by listing the parameters in columns.

The number of combinations quickly runs into the hundreds as illustrated in this example for work stations:

Characteristic (parameter)	No. of Types	Total Alternatives
1. Type—single, shared, closed, open, computer, reception	6	6
2. Shape—rectangular, square, circular	3	18 (6 × 3)
3. Material—wood, steel, plastic	3	54 (18 × 3)
4. Finish—painted, natural, fabric	3	162 (54 × 3)
5. Features—task lighting, file storage, drawing, interviewing	4	648 (162 × 4)

The best time to apply morphological analysis is during the concept stage of design. The greatest benefit of this approach is its clear patterning in uncovering new ideas (GSA 1978, 6.10).

Attribute Listing

This technique involves listing all attributes that characterize an item under study. The group then tries to modify the attributes to yield new alternatives. By means of this technique, it is possible to raise new combinations of attributes that improve on the existing solution.

For example, consider the standard venetian blind developed a number of years ago (GSA 1978, 6.10–6.11). Its attributes are a number of horizontal slats, pivoted at each end for opening and closing; vertical pulls on a cord for opening and closing; and vertical raising for storing when not in use. Each attribute can be changed by:

1. Changing horizontal slats to vertical slats
2. Changing horizontal pivoting to vertical pivoting
3. Changing pulley cord to twisting on a fiberglass rod
4. Changing overhead storage through vertical raising to side storage by horizontal sliding

Pattern Language

Pattern language permits buildings to be dissected into component parts, then reassembled into new designs. It was developed by Christopher Alexander at the University of California at Berkeley.[12] Identification of prototypical elements allows designers to assemble environments from small-scale individual rooms to large-scale urban settings. The approach is best used by a team of design professionals at the conceptual stages of a project. Three steps are usually involved.

A set of prototypes for a particular building is identified and the best selected for the review team. Simple sketches and a few words illustrate each prototype. The sketches or diagrams are grouped into patterns that represent the building elements and layout. The last step is manipulation of patterns to meet the owner-user requirements, climatic conditions, and urban context.

The prototypes that are the cornerstones of this process are collected by designers from architectural images and concepts, previous projects, and post-occupancy evaluations. The base information can include:

- A statement of need (function) and context
- A verbal and graphic statement of a prototypical response to the need or function
- A detailed description of the prototype (including cost and other performance data)

The conceptual patterns for a project are normally the product of a team effort. Groupings of possible combinations of patterns are proposed and discussed by the team. The most appropriate pattern is selected for further refinement (Laseau 1980, 130–31). Chapter 10, figure 10-2 is an example of the use of pattern language in exploring building expansion alternatives. When the matrix of "building height" levels versus "direction of expansion" was analyzed, nine alternatives became apparent.

The office of CRS-Sirrine in Houston uses pattern language to identify and record concepts during the programming stage of the design process. Texts such as Clark and Pause, *Precedents in Architecture* (1985) have been written to help identify the patterns of current and historic architectural styles. Pattern language draws on solutions of the past to create new solutions for the future.

CONCLUSION

The purpose of group creativity techniques is the expansion of options and ideas through the collective insight of a decision-making team. Together with the techniques outlined in chapter 4, these methods provide ways to open the creative impulses of the group and broaden the search for design solutions. They are characterized by unrestricted concepts, free association, and lowering of inhibitions. The decision-making techniques which will be discussed in subsequent chapters assume a different approach to problem solving and require a more focused view of design problems. Whereas function analysis and group creativity techniques guided the design team into areas that dealt with "possibilities" in design, the techniques formed in chapters 6 through 9 will deal with "feasibilities."

NOTES

1. See Judson (1980) for a review of the creative process of group problem-solving techniques in scientific settings.

2. Refer to William J. J. Gordon's book *Synectics* (1961, 8–19) for a number of specific examples involving group creativity techniques.

3. See Linstone and Turoof (1975) for a thorough discussion of the Delphi technique.

4. Edwards (1979) is cited as a source for information concerning the creative versus analytic skills required by designers.

5. Refer to Koestler (1967, 27–80) for a thorough discussion of the relationship between creativity and humor.

6. These steps are fairly standard in most group creativity texts, although they vary slightly from one author to the next. See GSA (1978) for a discussion of the steps outlined in this book.

7. Adams (1979) provides an excellent summary of mental blocks encountered during the creative process of problem solving.

8. Refer to Clark (1958) for a complete discussion of the history and theory of brainstorming techniques.

9. The following discussion of Delphi techniques is reprinted by permission from S. J. Kirk. 1980. "Delphi: An Aid in Project Cost Control." *Architectural Record* 12:51–55.

11. See Adams (1979) for a detailed discussion of this type of checklist.

12. See Alexander et al. (1977) for a detailed analysis of pattern language techniques.

CHAPTER 6

Life-Cycle Costs

THE EFFECTIVE USE of natural and synthetic resources is a matter of concern to all segments of the construction industry. Large numbers of these resources are committed by the architect through decisions made during facilities design. Today, more than ever, these design decisions are examined closely by both government and private building owners seeking to conserve resources while maintaining or improving the value and quality of facilities. Life-cycle costing (LCC) measures the economic value of decisions of a design project. Figure 6-1 illustrates the life-cycle costs for a manufacturing facility in Texas.

Life-cycle costing can be defined as "an economic assessment of competing design alternatives, considering all significant costs over the economic life of each alternative, expressed in equivalent dollars."[1] P. A. Stone, a British economist, has coined the terminology "cost-in-use" and suggested that the technique is concerned with "the choice of means to a given end and with the problem of obtaining the best value for money for the resources spent."[2] The U.S. Department of Health, Education, and Welfare has defined life-cycle cost analysis as the systematic consideration of cost, time, and quality.[3]

HISTORY

Both government and private-sector clients have established LCC guidelines for the design and maintenance of facilities. The General Services Administration has developed elaborate procedures for pre-

Life-Cycle Costs

Economic assumptions: $i = 15\%$, $n = 25$ yrs

	Present Worth (1986)
Initial Costs	
Facility	$19,700,000
Equipment	38,300,000
Operation (Energy) Costs	
16,000,000 kwh × $0.04/kwh = $640,000/yr PWA (6.464)	4,137,000
Maintenance	1,642,000
Alteration Costs	
$2.30/GSF × 127,000 GSF = $292,100/yr × PWA (6.464)	1,888,000
Major Replacements	
yr. 5: $500,000 × PW_5 (0.49)	245,000
yr. 10: 500,000 × PW_{10} (0.25)	125,000
yr. 15: 500,000 × PW_{15} (0.13)	65,000
yr. 20: 500,000 × PW_{20} (0.09)	45,000
	480,000
Functional Use (Staffing) Costs	
Professional (technical) $2,500,000/yr × PW (6.464)	16,160,000
Nonprofessional 2,500,000/yr × PW (6.464)	16,160,000
	32,320,000
Associated Costs	
Water (ultra pure and sewer) $500,000/yr × PW (6.464)	3,232,000
Process gases and chemicals 1,150,000/yr × PW (6.464)	7,434,000
Waste handling, trash, laundry 140,000/yr × PW (6.464)	905,000
Telephone/communication 200,000/yr × PW (6.464)	1,293,000
Misc. other 250,000/yr × PW (6.464)	1,616,000
	14,480,000
TOTAL LIFE-CYCLE COST	$112,947,000

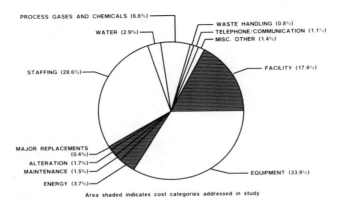

PROCESS GASES AND CHEMICALS (6.6%)
WASTE HANDLING (0.8%)
TELEPHONE/COMMUNICATION (1.1%)
MISC. OTHER (1.4%)
WATER (2.9%)
STAFFING (28.6%)
FACILITY (17.4%)
MAJOR REPLACEMENTS (0.4%)
ALTERATION (1.7%)
MAINTENANCE (1.5%)
ENERGY (3.7%)
EQUIPMENT (33.9%)

Area shaded indicates cost categories addressed in study

FIGURE 6-1. Life-cycle costs—microchip manufacturing facility.

dicting a facility's total cost.[4] Large corporations such as United Technologies and AT&T routinely require designers to prepare LCC studies as part of the design process.

The classic reference on life-cycle cost theories, *Principles of Engineering Economy*, was written by E. L. Grant in 1930.[5] The United States government began using LCC principles in supplies and equipment acquisition in the 1930s and relied heavily on LCC during the World War II defense build-up. During the decade following the war, when material and labor shortages spawned searches for alternative construction and manufacturing methods, Larry D. Miles originated the concept of value analysis, known also as value engineering (VE).[6] This theory was conceived as a much broader analysis of building costs. Incorporating subjective measures of economic value, it was geared toward measuring the "total cost" of a building or manufacturing process. In 1972, Alphonse J. Dell'Isola promoted value engineering theories in the construction industry when he published a design guide that demonstrated the relationships between design theories and long-term building costs.[7]

From 1960 to the mid-1970s, the use of LCC in the design profession declined, primarily because of reduced interest rates and low energy costs, two major determinants of life-cycle costs in buildings. In 1972, however, the comptroller general of the United States issued a major report on the long-term costs of hospitals because of enormous investments that were being made at that time in such facilities. The report concluded that the costs of operating and maintaining hospital facilities can exceed the initial, or capital, costs as soon as one to three years after construction.[8] This was the first dramatization of the impact that life-cycle cost decisions can have on design, and it lent credibility to findings by the National Bureau of Standards which suggested that capital costs typically accounted for only 2 percent of the long-term economic impact of buildings.

The most influential event in the development of LCC techniques in the construction industry was the 1973 oil embargo and the rapid increase in inflation with higher energy costs. Designers and builders could no longer escape the reality that operating costs, not construction costs, were the most critical economic variables in building design. Since 1975, the United States federal government and more than two-thirds of the states have enacted legislation that mandates analyses of long-term costs of building designs based on energy standards produced by the American Society of Heating, Refrigeration, and Air Conditioning. In 1977, the American Institute of Architects issued guidelines providing designers with methods for computing long-term economic impacts of design decisions and using UNIFORMAT to organize cost data.[9] In 1978, the National Energy Conservation Policy Act required all new federal buildings to be designed to be life-cycle cost effective.[10] In 1983, the American Society for Testing and Materials (ASTM) issued a standard practice for measuring life-cycle costs of buildings and building systems.[11] Design and construction professions in Britain have also employed LCC techniques since the 1970s, using the term "terotechnology" to describe those practices of engineering and management directed at minimizing life-cycle costs of buildings.[12]

THEORY

A simple example illustrates the application of life-cycle cost principles.[13] A hospital corporation is considering two alternatives for a nursing-care addition to an existing building. One requires a greater initial investment because it relies on the use of automated patient-monitoring and recording systems. The second is less expensive in terms of initial costs because it relies on conventional data-collection technology. The question arises: "Do the long-term savings in operating expenses (nurses' salaries) associated with the first solution justify the initial capital investment over the life of the building?"

In order to answer this question, the decision maker would use LCC principles first to remove from consideration any factors that might have the same impact in any given design solution. This reduces the complexity of the analysis since it focuses the decision maker's attention only on design variables that represent significant fluctuations in long-term costs. Second, the most critical costs associated with each alternative are isolated and computed. The automated nursing system would have higher capital, operation, and maintenance costs than a conventional design but would result in lower functional-use costs in terms of staff salaries. The costs for each alternative are grouped by year over the expected life of the building, and anticipated replacement, alteration, and salvage costs are estimated. Third, all costs are converted to a common economic point of reference by using an appropriate discount factor.[14] This discounting is done because a cost incurred at any given point in the

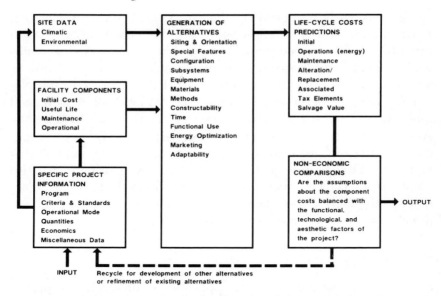

FIGURE 6-2. Life-cycle costing logic. (Reprinted, by permission, from A. J. Dell'Isola and S. J. Kirk, *Life Cycle Costing for Design Professionals* [New York: McGraw-Hill, 1981] 12)

future of a building's life cycle does not have the same impact—because of interest rates, inflation, or other economic variables—it might have if it were incurred today. Finally, discounted costs for each alternative are summed up and solutions ranked in terms of LCC impact. It may be necessary at this point to perform a number of separate analyses in order to test the validity of this ranking. Although the final selection of an alternative will probably be based on economic variables, the effects of noneconomic factors—such as a design's functional and technological feasibility—must be considered as well.

Figure 6-2 summarizes this process. Initially, input data are based on programmatic and client-defined information in addition to economic constraints associated with local cost factors, interest rates, and tax credits. Next, input data for specific components of the facility such as construction costs, equipment costs, site and climate factors, functional or use costs, operation and maintenance costs, and energy factors, are enumerated for each alternative. These costs are then computed and predicted using discounting methods, and careful considerations of noneconomic design variables are made to temper the ranking of the alternative solutions.

Figure 6-3 shows that LCC may be applied at any time during the facility cycle—in pre-design, design, and post-design activities. The greatest potential for effecting life-cycle savings in buildings exists in the early stages of design. The costs of making changes in planning documents are much less than those associated with the revision of construction documents or completed buildings. As a design project moves from conceptual design into construction, LCC analyses provide design information for future design efforts. The most important impacts of LCC techniques should be felt during the feasibility and design phases of the cycle.[15] Study areas for LCC technique in design might include the following:

- Facility construction versus other economic investment
- New facility versus retrofit existing structure
- High-rise versus low-rise construction
- Active/passive solar energy versus conventional HVAC
- Design layouts versus staffing efficiencies
- Spatial flexibility versus interior partitioning
- Natural versus artificial lighting
- Native versus irrigated landscaping
- Fire sprinkler systems versus insurance premiums
- Fixed versus demountable partitions

ECONOMIC PRINCIPLES

Life-cycle costing is based on several major economic principles: time value of money, equivalence approaches, and the type of economic decision to be made. The concept of time value of money is based on the notion that money has earning power that accrues to its investor over time. On the other hand, for the borrower a continuing or periodic cost offsets this earning power. Because of the earning power or cost of money, dollars spent in the future do not equal dollars spent today. For purposes of comparing these dollars, the concept of equivalence allows monies spent over time to be brought to a common basis.

Interest formulas (or tables) are used to calculate the equivalent values of expenditures that occur over time. The annualized method of LCC converts all present and future expenditures to an

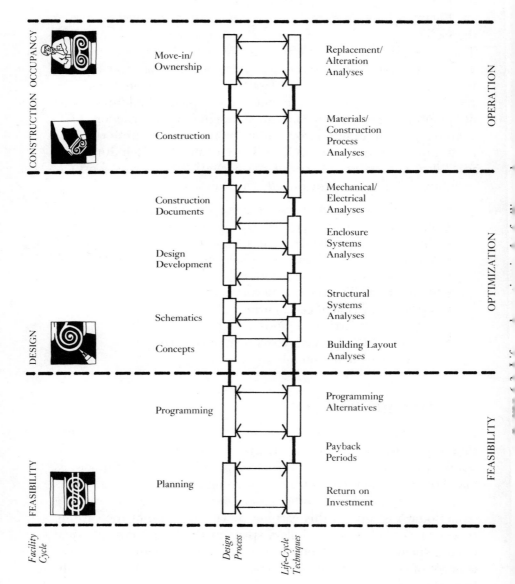

CONSTRUCTION OCCUPANCY

Move-in/
Ownership

Replacement/
Alteration
Analyses

OPERATION

Construction

Materials/
Construction
Process
Analyses

Construction
Documents

Mechanical/
Electrical
Analyses

Design
Development

Enclosure
Systems
Analyses

OPTIMIZATION

Structural
Systems
Analyses

Schematics

Concepts

Building Layout
Analyses

DESIGN

Programming

Programming
Alternatives

FEASIBILITY

Payback
Periods

Planning

Return on
Investment

FEASIBILITY

Facility
Cycle

Design
Process

Life-Cycle
Techniques

equivalent uniform annual cost. The present-worth method is used to convert present and future costs to an equivalent one-time expenditure today (present worth). Each method accounts for the time value of money and, therefore, is a valid measure of life-cycle cost. Economic analyses are generally classified as investment or design analyses. Generally, *investment* analysis determines what overall course of action to take, and *design* analysis continues to optimize the selected course of action as the design is refined. The technique of life-cycle costing is used in both types of economic analysis.

Time Value of Money

The value of money is time-dependent because money can be invested over time to yield a return. This is true also for the borrower. For this reason, a dollar amount today will be worth more than that same dollar amount in a year's time. For example, if $100 were deposited in a savings account paying 7 percent annual interest compounded annually, it would grow to $100 \times \$1.07 = \$107.00$ by the end of the first year, to $100 \times (\$1.07)^2 = \$114.49$ at the end of the second year, and to $100 \times (\$1.07)^3 = \$122.50$ at the end of the third year. Figure 6-4 illustrates the effects of time on an investment of $100 over 25 years at a 7 percent interest rate.

Two methods of calculating the effects of time or money can be

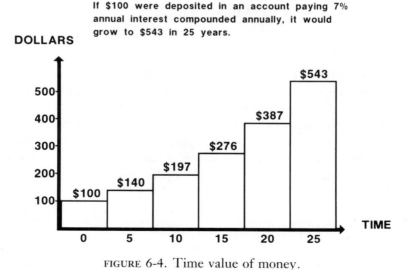

FIGURE 6-4. Time value of money.

used in LCC analysis. The first is the present-worth method, which converts all present and future costs to a common reference point, namely, the value of money today. Because initial building costs are expressed in today's dollars, this method is used to convert long-term or recurring costs that will come up during the life of a building to a single present-worth value. Although a number of assumptions must be made in this analysis concerning the rate of inflation, interest rates, and payback periods, the example in table 6-1 shows the worth of a monetary value now and over the years. All costs associated with design, construction, and operation are converted to a single lump-sum payment. The second method, the annualized method, transforms a project's initial costs into a series of annual payments. An example of the worth of a dollar using the annualized method is illustrated in table 6-2. Table 6-3 shows the effect of a uniform series of payments (present-worth annuity) converted to a single equivalent amount. Table 6-4 is similar to table 6-3 except that it also reflects the effects of inflation rates over time.[16]

Given certain fundamentals, it is possible to define LCC terminology and key elements of an LCC analysis. First, the analysis approach is selected, that is, the annualized or present-worth method, which uses dollars as the measuring stick. The effects of inflation have historically continued to change the dollar yardstick; thus inflation has become a key element in an LCC analysis. Other key elements include the discount rate, the analysis period (life cycle), and when the present time begins.

Discount Rate

The discount rate (or interest rate) is the time value of money. It is commonly established as the nominal rate of increase in the value of money over time, or as the actual rate of increase in the value of money; that is, that rate over and above the general economy's inflation rate. The discount rate for a given study might range from 7 percent to 15 percent. Much has been written on discount rates and how to determine them, but no universally accepted method or rate results.[17]

Inflation and Cost Growth

Inflation is the general increase in the price of goods and services over the economy as a whole without a corresponding increase in value. Cost growth, on the other hand, is the price increase of an item without a corresponding increase in value. An inflating economy as a whole usually does not favor one alternative over others. The same is not true with respect to cost growth. For example, the cost of labor to replace light fixtures will probably not tip the balance toward one lighting alternative over another. However, the cost growth of energy may indicate that an alternative consuming the least amount of energy is the better choice. Two methods have been established to deal with the effects of inflation and cost growth: current dollars and constant dollars.

The current-dollars approach deals with dollars that are current in the year they are spent. When future costs are stated in current dollars, the figures given are the actual amounts that will be paid, including any amount due to projected inflation or cost growth. The constant-dollars approach deals with dollars that have constant purchasing power. Constant dollars are always associated with a base year. An advantage of the current-dollars approach is that it presents the actual dollar figures that will be spent in any given year. The constant-dollars approach provides comparison dollar figures (for a specified year) and does not represent the dollar figures that actually will be spent. The difficulty with the current-dollars approach is in predicting actual inflation rates over the life cycle. The constant-dollars approach eliminates this guesswork by stating all figures in terms of dollar values as of a particular date. Because the primary purpose of a life-cycle cost analysis in most cases is to compare alternatives, the constant-dollars approach is most commonly used. When the constant-dollars approach is used in a life-cycle cost analysis, it is necessary only to reflect the cost growth of individual items that may rise above the general economy's inflation rate. This cost growth of individual items is the "differential escalation rate."[18]

Analysis Period or Life Cycle

The analysis period, or life cycle, is also a key element in an LCC analysis. It is that time frame selected to compare alternatives in order to determine which is more economical for a particular application. Normally an LCC analysis is based on a life-cycle period of between twenty-five and forty years. Whether a short or long time frame is selected, the same LCC approach is utilized. The selection of the analysis period will depend to a large extent on the owner's objectives and perspectives or on established organizational policy.

TABLE 6-1. Present worth: compound interest factors—what $1 due in the future is worth today (present worth), single payment.

Yrs.	6 Percent Present Worth	7 Percent Present Worth	8 Percent Present Worth	9 Percent Present Worth	10 Percent Present Worth	12 Percent Present Worth	14 Percent Present Worth	16 Percent Present Worth	18 Percent Present Worth	20 Percent Present Worth	Yrs.
1	0.943396	0.934579	0.925926	0.917431	0.909091	0.892857	0.877193	0.862069	0.847458	0.833333	1
2	0.889996	0.873439	0.857339	0.841680	0.826446	0.797194	0.769468	0.743163	0.718184	0.694444	2
3	0.839169	0.816298	0.793832	0.772183	0.751315	0.711780	0.674972	0.640658	0.608631	0.578704	3
4	0.792094	0.762895	0.735030	0.708425	0.683013	0.635518	0.592080	0.552291	0.515789	0.482253	4
5	0.747258	0.712986	0.680583	0.649931	0.620921	0.567427	0.519369	0.476113	0.437109	0.401878	5
6	0.704961	0.666342	0.630170	0.596267	0.564474	0.506631	0.455587	0.410442	0.370432	0.334898	6
7	0.665057	0.622750	0.583490	0.547034	0.513158	0.452349	0.399637	0.353830	0.313925	0.279082	7
8	0.627412	0.582009	0.540269	0.501866	0.466507	0.403883	0.350559	0.305025	0.266038	0.232568	8
9	0.591898	0.543934	0.500249	0.460428	0.424098	0.360610	0.307508	0.262953	0.225456	0.193807	9
10	0.558395	0.508349	0.463193	0.422411	0.385543	0.321973	0.269744	0.226684	0.191064	0.161506	10
11	0.526788	0.475093	0.428883	0.387533	0.350494	0.287476	0.236617	0.195417	0.161919	0.134588	11
12	0.496969	0.444012	0.397114	0.355535	0.318631	0.256675	0.207559	0.168463	0.137220	0.112157	12
13	0.468839	0.414964	0.367698	0.326170	0.289664	0.229174	0.182069	0.145227	0.116288	0.093464	13
14	0.442301	0.387817	0.340461	0.299246	0.263331	0.204620	0.159710	0.125195	0.098549	0.077887	14
15	0.417265	0.362446	0.315242	0.274538	0.239392	0.182696	0.140096	0.107927	0.083516	0.064905	15
16	0.393646	0.338735	0.291890	0.251870	0.217629	0.163122	0.122892				16
17	0.371364	0.316574	0.270269	0.231073	0.197845	0.145644	0.107800				17
18	0.350344	0.295864	0.250249	0.211994	0.179859	0.130040	0.094561				18
19	0.330513	0.276508	0.231712	0.194490	0.163508	0.116107	0.082948				19
20	0.311805	0.258419	0.214548	0.178431	0.148641	0.103667	0.072762	0.051385	0.036506	0.026084	20
21	0.294155	0.241513	0.198656	0.163698	0.135131	0.092560	0.063826				21
22	0.277505	0.225713	0.183941	0.150182	0.122846	0.082643	0.055988				22
23	0.261797	0.210947	0.170315	0.137781	0.111678	0.073788	0.049112				23
24	0.246979	0.197147	0.157699	0.126405	0.101526	0.065882	0.043081				24
25	0.232999	0.184249	0.146018	0.115968	0.092296	0.058823	0.037790	0.024465	0.015957	0.010482	25

26	0.210810	0.172195	0.135202	0.106393	0.083905	0.052521	0.033149				26
27	0.207368	0.160930	0.125187	0.097608	0.076278	0.046894	0.029078				27
28	0.195630	0.150102	0.115914	0.089548	0.069343	0.041869	0.025507				28
29	0.184557	0.140563	0.107328	0.082155	0.063039	0.037383	0.022375				29
30	0.174110	0.131367	0.099377	0.075371	0.057309	0.033378	0.019627	0.011648	0.006975	0.004212	30
31	0.164255	0.122773	0.092016	0.069148	0.052090	0.029802	0.017217				31
32	0.154957	0.114741	0.085200	0.063438	0.047362	0.026609	0.015102				32
33	0.146186	0.107235	0.078889	0.058200	0.043057	0.023758	0.013248				33
34	0.137912	0.100219	0.073045	0.053395	0.039143	0.021212	0.011621				34
35	0.130105	0.093663	0.067635	0.048986	0.035584	0.018940	0.010194	0.005546	0.0030488	0.001693	35
36	0.122741	0.087535	0.062625	0.044941	0.032349	0.016910	0.008942				36
37	0.115793	0.081809	0.057986	0.041231	0.029408	0.015098	0.007844				37
38	0.109239	0.076457	0.053690	0.037826	0.026735	0.013481	0.006880				38
39	0.103056	0.071455	0.049713	0.034703	0.024304	0.012036	0.006035				39
40	0.097222	0.066780	0.046031	0.031838	0.022095	0.010747	0.005294	0.002640	0.001333	0.000680	40

Source: Dell'Isola 1982, 138.

TABLE 6-2. Periodic payment: compound interest factors—periodic payment necessary to pay off a loan of $1 (capital recovery), annuities (uniform series payments).

Yrs.	6 Percent Capital recovery	7 Percent Capital recovery	8 Percent Capital recovery	9 Percent Capital recovery	10 Percent Capital recovery	12 Percent Capital recovery	14 Percent Capital recovery	16 Percent Capital recovery	18 Percent Capital recovery	20 Percent Capital recovery	Yrs.
1	1.060000	1.070000	1.080000	1.090000	1.100000	1.120000	1.14000000	1.16000000	1.18000000	1.20000000	1
2	0.545437	0.553092	0.560769	0.568469	0.576190	0.591698	0.60728972	0.62296296	0.63871560	0.65454545	2
3	0.374110	0.381052	0.388034	0.395055	0.402115	0.416349	0.43073148	0.44525787	0.45992386	0.47472527	3
4	0.288591	0.295228	0.301921	0.308669	0.315471	0.329234	0.34320478	0.35737507	0.37173867	0.38628912	4
5	0.237396	0.243891	0.250156	0.257092	0.263797	0.277410	0.29128355	0.30540938	0.31977784	0.33437970	5
6	0.203363	0.209796	0.216315	0.222920	0.229607	0.243226	0.25715750	0.27138987	0.28591013	0.30070575	6
7	0.179135	0.185553	0.192072	0.198691	0.205405	0.219118	0.23319238	0.24761268	0.26236200	0.27742393	7
8	0.161036	0.167468	0.174015	0.180674	0.187444	0.201303	0.21557002	0.23022426	0.24524436	0.26060942	8
9	0.147022	0.153486	0.160080	0.166799	0.173641	0.187679	0.20216838	0.21708249	0.23239482	0.24807946	9
10	0.135868	0.142378	0.149029	0.155820	0.162745	0.176984	0.19171354	0.20690108	0.22251464	0.23852276	10
11	0.126793	0.133357	0.140076	0.146947	0.153963	0.168415	0.18339427	0.19886075	0.21477639	0.23110379	11
12	0.119277	0.125902	0.132695	0.139651	0.146763	0.161437	0.17666933	0.19241473	0.20862781	0.22526496	12
13	0.112960	0.119651	0.126522	0.133567	0.140779	0.155677	0.17116366	0.18718411	0.20368621	0.22062000	13
14	0.107585	0.114345	0.211297	0.128433	0.135746	0.150871	0.16660914	0.18289797	0.19967806	0.21689306	14
15	0.102963	0.109795	0.116830	0.124059	0.131474	0.146824	0.16280896	0.17935752	0.19640278	0.21388212	15
16	0.098952	0.105858	0.112977	0.120300	0.127817	0.143390	0.15961540				16
17	0.095445	0.102425	0.109629	0.117046	0.124664	0.140457	0.15691544				17
18	0.092357	0.099413	0.106702	0.114212	0.121930	0.137937	0.15462115				18
19	0.089621	0.096753	0.104128	0.111730	0.119547	0.135763	0.15266316				19
20	0.087185	0.094393	0.101852	0.109546	0.117460	0.133879	0.15098600	0.168667	0.186820	0.205356	20
21	0.085005	0.092289	0.099832	0.107617	0.115624	0.132240	0.14954486				21
22	0.083016	0.090106	0.098032	0.105905	0.114005	0.130811	0.14830317				22
23	0.081278	0.088714	0.096422	0.104382	0.112572	0.129560	0.14723081				23
24	0.079679	0.087189	0.094978	0.103023	0.111300	0.128463	0.14630284				24
25	0.078227	0.085811	0.093679	0.101806	0.110168	0.127500	0.14549841	0.164012	0.182919	0.202119	25

26	0.076904	0.081561	0.092507	0.100715	0.109159	0.126652	0.14480001				26
27	0.075697	0.083426	0.091448	0.099735	0.108258	0.125904	0.14419288				27
28	0.074593	0.082392	0.090489	0.098852	0.107451	0.125244	0.14366449				28
29	0.073580	0.081449	0.089619	0.098056	0.106728	0.124660	0.14320417				29
30	0.072649	0.089586	0.088827	0.097336	0.106079	0.124144	0.14280279	0.161886	0.181264	0.200846	30
31	0.071792	0.079797	0.088107	0.096686	0.105496	0.123686	0.14245256				31
32	0.071002	0.079073	0.087451	0.096096	0.104972	0.123280	0.14214675				32
33	0.070273	0.078408	0.086852	0.095562	0.101499	0.122920	0.14187958				33
34	0.069598	0.077797	0.086304	0.095077	0.104074	0.122601	0.14164604				34
35	0.068974	0.077234	0.085803	0.094636	0.103690	0.122317	0.14144181	0.160892	0.180550	0.200339	35
36	0.068395	0.076715	0.085345	0.094235	0.103343	0.122064	0.14126315				36
37	0.067857	0.076237	0.084924	0.093870	0.103030	0.121840	0.14110680				37
38	0.067358	0.075795	0.084539	0.093538	0.102747	0.121640	0.14096993				38
39	0.066894	0.075387	0.084185	0.093236	0.102491	0.121462	0.14085010				39
40	0.066462	0.075009	0.083860	0.092960	0.102259	0.121304	0.14074514	0.160423	0.180240	0.200136	40

Source: Dell'Isola 1982, 139.

TABLE 6-3. Present worth of annuity: compound interest factors—what $1 payable periodically is worth today (present worth of annuity).

Yrs.	6 Percent Present worth	7 Percent Present worth	8 Percent Present worth	9 Percent Present worth	10 Percent Present worth	12 Percent Present worth	14 Percent Present worth	16 Percent Present worth	18 Percent Present worth	20 Percent Present worth	Yrs
1	0.943396	0.934570	0.925926	0.917431	0.909001	0.89286	0.877193	0.862089	0.847458	0.833333	1
2	1.833393	1.808018	1.783265	1.759111	1.735537	1.69005	1.646661	1.605232	1.565642	1.527778	2
3	2.673012	2.624316	2.577097	2.531295	2.486852	2.40183	2.321632	2.245890	2.174273	2.106481	3
4	3.465106	3.387211	3.312127	3.329720	3.169865	3.03735	2.913712	2.798181	2.690062	2.588735	4
5	4.212364	4.100197	3.992710	3.889651	3.790787	3.60477	3.433081	3.274294	3.127171	2.990612	5
6	4.917324	4.766540	4.622880	4.485919	4.355261	4.11140	3.888668	3.684736	3.497603	3.325510	6
7	5.582381	5.389289	5.206370	5.032953	4.868419	4.56375	4.288305	4.038565	3.811528	3.604592	7
8	6.209794	5.971299	5.746639	5.534819	5.334926	4.96764	4.638864	4.343591	4.077566	3.837160	8
9	6.801602	6.515232	6.246888	5.995247	5.759024	5.32825	4.946372	4.606544	4.303022	4.030967	9
10	7.360087	7.023582	6.710081	6.417658	6.144567	5.65023	5.21116	4.833227	4.494086	4.192472	10
11	7.886875	7.498674	7.138964	6.805191	6.495061	5.93771	5.452733	5.028644	4.656005	4.327060	11
12	8.383844	7.942686	7.536078	7.160725	6.813692	6.19437	5.660292	5.197107	4.793225	4.439217	12
13	8.852683	8.357651	7.903776	7.486904	7.103356	6.42356	5.842362	5.342334	4.909513	4.532681	13
14	9.294984	8.745468	8.244237	7.786150	7.366687	6.62818	6.002072	5.467529	5.008062	4.610567	14
15	10.712249	9.107914	8.559479	8.060688	7.606080	6.81088	6.142168	5.575456	5.091578	4.675473	15
16	10.105895	9.446649	8.851369	8.312558	7.823709	6.97399	6.265060				16
17	10.477260	9.763223	9.121638	8.543631	8.021553	7.11962	6.372859				17
18	10.827603	10.059087	9.371887	8.755625	8.201412	7.24969	6.467420				18
19	11.158116	10.335595	9.603599	8.950115	8.364920	7.36578	6.550369				19
20	11.409921	10.594014	9.818147	9.128546	8.513564	7.46943	6.623131	5.928844	5.352744	4.869580	20
21	11.764077	10.835527	10.016803	9.292244	8.648694	7.56201	6.686957				21
22	12.041582	11.061240	10.200744	9.442425	8.771540	7.64462	6.742944				22
23	12.303379	11.272187	10.371059	9.580207	8.883218	7.71843	6.792056				23
24	12.550358	11.469334	10.528758	9.706612	8.984744	7.78434	6.835137				24
25	12.783356	11.653583	10.674776	9.822580	9.077040	7.84314	6.872927	6.097094	5.466905	4.947590	25

26	13.003186	11.825779	10.809978	9.928972	9.160945	7.89565	6.906077				26
27	13.210536	11.986709	10.935165	10.026580	9.237223	7.94256	6.935155				27
28	13.406166	12.137111	11.051078	10.116128	9.306567	7.98441	6.960662				28
29	13.590721	12.277674	11.158406	10.198283	9.369606	8.02182	6.983037				29
30	13.764831	12.409041	11.257783	10.273654	9.426914	8.05516	7.002664	6.177200	5.516805	4.978940	30
31	13.929086	12.531814	11.349799	10.342802	9.479013	8.08499	7.019881				31
32	14.084013	12.646555	11.434999	10.406240	9.526376	8.11162	7.034983				32
33	14.230230	12.753790	11.513888	10.464441	9.569432	8.13537	7.048231				33
34	14.368141	12.854009	11.586934	10.517835	9.608575	8.15654	7.059852				34
35	14.498246	12.947672	11.654568	10.566821	9.644159	8.17548	7.070045	6.215337	5.538618	4.991535	35
36	14.620987	13.035208	11.717193	10.611763	9.676508	8.19242	7.078987				36
37	14.736780	13.117017	11.775179	10.652993	9.705917	8.20749	7.086831				37
38	14.846019	13.193473	11.828869	10.690820	9.732651	8.22098	7.093711				38
39	14.949073	13.264928	11.878582	10.722523	9.756956	8.23303	7.099747				39
40	15.046297	13.331700	11.924613	10.757360	9.779051	8.24375	7.105041	6.233500	5.548150	4.996600	40

Source: Dell'Isola 1982, 140.

TABLE 6-4. Present worth of an escalating annual amount, 10 percent discount rate.

Year	Escalation Rate (percent)															Year
	0	1	2	3	4	5	6	7	8	9	10	11	12	13	14	
1	0.909	0.918	0.927	0.936	0.945	0.955	0.964	0.973	0.982	0.991	1.000	1.009	1.018	1.027	1.036	1
2	1.736	1.761	1.787	1.813	1.839	1.866	1.892	1.919	1.946	1.973	2.000	2.027	2.055	2.083	2.110	2
3	2.487	2.535	2.584	2.634	2.684	2.735	2.787	2.839	2.892	2.946	3.000	3.055	3.110	3.167	3.224	3
4	3.170	3.246	3.324	3.403	3.483	3.566	3.649	3.735	3.821	3.910	4.000	4.092	4.185	4.280	4.377	4
5	3.791	3.899	4.009	4.123	4.239	4.358	4.480	4.605	4.734	4.865	5.000	5.138	5.279	5.424	5.573	5
6	4.355	4.498	4.645	4.797	4.953	5.115	5.281	5.453	5.630	5.812	6.000	6.194	6.394	6.599	6.812	6
7	4.868	5.048	5.234	5.428	5.628	5.837	6.053	6.277	6.509	6.750	7.000	7.259	7.528	7.807	8.096	7
8	5.335	5.553	5.781	6.019	6.267	6.526	6.796	7.078	7.372	7.680	8.000	8.334	8.683	9.047	9.426	8
9	5.759	6.017	6.288	6.572	6.871	7.184	7.513	7.858	8.220	8.601	9.000	9.419	9.859	10.321	10.806	9
10	6.145	6.443	6.758	7.090	7.441	7.812	8.203	8.616	9.053	9.513	10.000	10.514	11.057	11.630	12.235	10
11	6.495	6.834	7.194	7.575	7.981	8.411	8.868	9.354	9.870	10.418	11.000	11.619	12.276	12.974	13.716	11
12	6.814	7.193	7.598	8.030	8.491	8.983	9.510	10.072	10.672	11.314	12.000	12.733	13.517	14.355	15.251	12
13	7.103	7.523	7.972	8.455	8.973	9.530	10.127	10.770	11.460	12.202	13.000	13.858	14.781	15.774	16.842	13
14	7.367	7.825	8.320	8.853	9.429	10.051	10.723	11.449	12.233	13.082	14.000	14.993	16.068	17.231	18.491	14
15	7.606	8.103	8.642	9.226	9.860	10.549	11.296	12.109	12.993	13.954	15.000	16.139	17.378	18.729	20.200	15
16	7.824	8.358	8.941	9.576	10.268	11.024	11.849	12.752	13.738	14.818	16.000	17.294	18.713	20.267	21.971	16
17	8.022	8.593	9.218	9.903	10.653	11.477	12.382	13.377	14.470	15.674	17.000	18.461	20.071	21.847	23.806	17
18	8.201	8.808	9.475	10.209	11.018	11.910	12.895	13.985	15.189	16.523	18.000	19.638	21.454	23.470	25.708	18
19	8.365	9.005	9.713	10.496	11.362	12.323	13.390	14.576	15.895	17.363	19.000	20.825	22.862	25.137	27.679	19
20	8.514	9.187	9.934	10.764	11.688	12.718	13.867	15.151	16.588	18.196	20.000	22.024	24.296	26.850	29.722	20
21	8.649	9.353	10.139	11.015	11.996	13.094	14.326	15.711	17.268	19.022	21.000	23.233	25.756	28.610	31.839	21
22	8.772	9.506	10.329	11.251	12.287	13.454	14.769	16.255	17.936	19.840	22.000	24.453	27.243	30.417	34.033	22
23	8.883	9.647	10.505	11.471	12.562	13.797	15.196	16.784	18.591	20.650	23.000	25.685	28.756	32.274	36.307	23
24	8.985	9.776	10.668	11.678	12.822	14.124	15.607	17.299	19.235	21.454	24.000	26.927	30.297	34.181	38.664	24
25	9.077	9.894	10.819	11.871	13.069	14.437	16.003	17.800	19.867	22.250	25.000	28.181	31.866	36.141	41.106	25

26	9.161	10.003	10.960	12.052	13.301	14.735	16.384	18.287	20.488	23.038	26.000	29.446	33.464	38.154	43.638	26
27	9.237	10.102	11.090	12.221	13.521	15.020	16.752	18.761	21.097	23.820	27.000	30.723	35.090	40.222	46.261	27
28	9.307	10.194	11.211	12.380	13.729	15.291	17.107	19.222	21.695	24.594	28.000	32.012	36.746	42.346	48.979	28
29	9.370	10.278	11.323	12.528	13.926	15.551	17.448	19.671	22.283	25.361	29.000	33.312	38.433	44.528	51.797	29
30	9.427	10.355	11.426	12.667	14.112	15.799	17.777	20.107	22.859	26.122	30.000	34.624	40.150	46.770	54.717	30
31	9.479	10.426	11.523	12.798	14.287	16.035	18.095	20.532	23.426	26.875	31.000	35.947	41.898	49.073	57.743	31
32	9.526	10.491	11.612	12.920	14.453	16.261	18.400	20.944	23.982	27.622	32.000	37.283	43.678	51.438	60.879	32
33	9.569	10.551	11.695	13.034	14.610	16.476	18.695	21.346	24.527	28.362	33.000	38.631	45.490	53.868	64.129	33
34	9.609	10.606	11.771	13.141	14.759	16.682	18.979	21.736	25.063	29.095	34.000	39.992	47.335	56.365	67.497	34
35	9.644	10.657	11.843	13.241	14.899	16.878	19.252	22.116	25.589	29.821	35.000	41.364	49.214	58.929	70.988	35
36	9.677	10.703	11.909	13.335	15.032	17.065	19.516	22.486	26.106	30.541	36.000	42.749	51.127	61.564	74.606	36
37	9.706	10.745	11.970	13.423	15.158	17.244	19.770	22.845	26.613	31.254	37.000	44.147	53.075	64.270	78.355	37
38	9.733	10.784	12.027	13.505	15.276	17.415	20.014	23.195	27.111	31.961	38.000	45.558	55.058	67.050	82.241	38
39	9.757	10.820	12.079	13.582	15.389	17.578	20.250	23.535	27.600	32.661	39.000	46.981	57.077	69.906	86.268	39
40	9.779	10.853	12.128	13.654	15.495	17.733	20.478	23.866	28.080	33.355	40.000	48.417	59.133	72.840	90.441	40

Source: Dell'Isola 1982, 143.

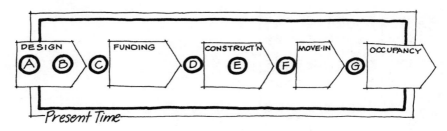

FIGURE 6-5. Present time diagram.

Present Time

The present time in a life-cycle cost analysis marks the beginning point of a series of expenditures. For present-worth analysis, it also represents the point at which all life-cycle costs are combined (by discounting), compared, and analyzed. The present time in an LCC analysis is typically selected from those points identified in figure 6-5.

The points usually selected for present time are Point B (during design) and Point E (midpoint construction). Selection of Point B normally results in the most realistic baseline values for various cost items, developed from contractor quotes or designer cost sources. Projections made from these costs can be more readily evaluated for uncertainty. All points subsequent to Point B provide a less realistic baseline value, with greater uncertainty pervading all cost figures. Nonetheless, Point E is often selected because project budgets are based on the construction midpoint and initial costs become the costs expected to be paid to a contractor.

Costs

The designer needs to consider various costs and cost relationships, the proper understanding of which is essential to the completion of an effective LCC analysis. These costs and cost relationships can be classified as types of costs, common costs, collateral costs, and sunk costs.

All costs attributable to an alternative are considered in any LCC analysis. These include construction, construction-related, and pro-curement costs at the beginning of the analysis period; disposal, demolition, and other salvage costs at the end; and costs incurred between those times. Whether any particular type of cost should be included depends primarily on two factors: (1) whether that type of cost is relevant for the particular facility under design and for the specific design feature under consideration; and (2) whether the projected magnitude of that type of cost is significant in comparison to other relevant costs for the LCC analysis. For convenience, these costs have been divided into the following categories:

- Initial investment costs
- Energy costs
- Maintenance, repair, and custodial costs
- Replacement and alteration costs
- Salvage (terminal) costs
- Other types of costs, such as staffing, insurance, tax, elements, and other utilities (water, sewer, and so forth)

Monetary benefits, which are normally considered as negative costs in the life-cycle cost analysis, include all benefits that can be readily quantified in terms of dollars, such as salvage values and other forms of income, cost reduction, and marketable by-products. The decision as to whether any particular monetary benefit should be included in an analysis is usually based on relevance and significance.

Because the usual purpose of an LCC analysis is to select the best alternative from among a number of alternatives, it is not necessary to estimate *all* costs. Costs that characterize all alternatives, with no differences in magnitude, can be excluded without affecting the relative economic ranking of the alternatives. Consider, for example, two hot water heater systems, both having the same impact on, say, the size of the maintenance staff; it is not necessary even to consider maintenance staff costs (no matter how high or how low they may be) in the life-cycle cost analysis. Care is taken, however, to include differential costs. If the two systems place a different load on a building's electrical system, these costs are included in order to develop an accurate comparison.

It is sometimes necessary to include costs not directly attributable to the system. For example, in evaluating various lighting systems, some alternatives may have differing ceiling and HVAC interface costs. Because these costs impinge on the selection of the most cost-effective system, they are included in the analysis. Such costs are referred to as collateral costs. At times, these costs are so small they may be excluded from the analysis because only the differential or incremental costs are important to the results of the analysis. However, the assumption that such costs can be neglected in any given situation may not be valid and probably should not be made without some evidence and careful analysis of the consequences of these costs.

Sunk costs are those that have been incurred before a study is begun. Only costs expected to be incurred during the life cycle of the analysis (beyond the present) are included in the cost estimates of alternatives. Therefore, sunk costs have no direct bearing on the results of the analysis because the asset or benefit already purchased is available regardless of the alternative selected.

ANNUALIZED AND PRESENT-WORTH METHODS

To illustrate the principles of LCC, two examples will outline the similarities and differences between annualized and present-worth methods of analysis. The annualized method expresses all life-cycle costs as annual expenditures. Recurring costs are expressed as annual costs and require no time adjustment, while initial costs require equivalent-cost conversions. Say an owner is preparing a feasibility study to determine whether he should lease or build a dental clinic he will need for fifteen years. Were he to build, his financing rate of interest would be 12 percent. Leasing would cost $16.00/sq.ft./year over the next fifteen years, a cost that includes utilities, maintenance, and replacement costs. The following data summarize the costs for the build option:

	Build Option
Initial construction cost (including land)	$65.00/sq.ft.
Energy cost (per year)	1.50/sq.ft.
Maintenance cost (per year)	2.75/sq.ft.
Carpet replacement cost (year 8)	2.00/sq.ft.
Resale/salvage (year 15)	35.00/sq.ft.

The LCC analysis would begin by converting initial costs to an annualized cost using the periodic payment schedule in table 6-2.

Initial costs for the build option would be converted to an annualized figure by the following calculations:

Initial cost (annualized) = $65.00 × (0.1468) = $9.54/sq.ft.

No conversion is necessary for energy and maintenance costs since they are already expressed as annualized figures. Replacement costs would then be converted first to present-worth values using the information in table 6-1 and then expressed as annualized costs, using the periodic-payment schedules as in the above initial cost calculations. The replacement cost calculation would proceed as follows:

Carpet replacement, year 8 (PW) = $2.00/sq.ft. × (0.4039) = $0.81/sq.ft.

Carpet replacement (annualized) = $0.81/sq.ft. × (0.1468) = $0.12/sq.ft.

The resale/salvage value (treated as a negative cost) would also be converted to an annualized cost:

Resale/salvage, year 15 (PW) = ($35.00/sq.ft.) × (0.1827) = $6.39/sq.ft.

Resale/salvage (annualized) = ($6.39/sq.ft.) × (0.1468) = 0.94/sq.ft.

Here is a summary of the life-cycle costs expressed as annualized figures:

	Build Option *(annualized LCC)*
Initial construction cost	$9.54/sq.ft.
Energy cost	1.50/sq.ft.
Maintenance cost	2.75/sq.ft.
Carpet replacement (year 8)	0.12/sq.ft.
Resale/salvage (year 15)	0.94/sq.ft.
Total life-cycle costs	12.97/sq.ft.

Based on these figures, the owner sees that he should build ($12.97/sq.ft. per year) rather than lease ($16.00/sq.ft. per year).

The present-worth method allows all costs incurred over a specified life cycle to be converted to equivalent costs at one point in time.

Consider the selection between two air-handling units. A 10 percent discount rate, a twenty-four-year life cycle, and a differential energy rate escalation of 2 percent per year are assumed. Other relevant data are:

Type of Cost	Alternative One	Alternative Two
Initial cost	$15,000	$10,000
Energy (annual)	1,800	2,200
Maintenance (annual)	500	800
Useful life	12 years	8 years

The solution begins by converting all annual or recurring costs to the present time. Using the present-worth annuity factor (table 6-3), the recurring costs of maintenance would be:

Alternative One: maintenance (present worth) = $500 × (8.985) = $4,492

Alternative Two: maintenance (present worth) = $800 × (8.985) = $7,188

According to table 6-4, the present worth of the energy costs for each alternative would be:

Alternative One: energy (escal = 2%) = $1800 × (10.668) = $19,202

Alternative Two: energy (escal = 2%) = $2200 × (10.668) = $23,470

Replacement or nonrecurring costs are considered next. When one or more alternatives has a shorter or longer life than the life cycle specified, an adjustment for the unequal life is necessary. If the life of an alternative is shorter than the project's life cycle, the item continues to be replaced until the life cycle is reached. On the other hand, if the item life is longer than the specified life cycle, then a terminal or salvage value for the item is recognized at the end of the life cycle. This treatment, using the present-worth factors in table 6-1, is illustrated as follows:

Alternative Two: replacement (n = 8) = $10,000 × (0.4665) = $4,665

Alternative One: replacement (n = 12) = $15,000 × (0.3186) = $4,779

Alternative Two: replacement (n = 16) = $10,000 × (0.2176) = $2,176

The salvage value for both systems equals zero since they both complete replacement cycles at the end of the twenty-four-year life cycle. A summary of present-worth life-cycle costs follows:

Type of Costs	Alternative One	Alternative Two
Initial cost	$15,000	$10,000
Maintenance (recurring) cost	4,492	7,188
Energy (recurring) cost	19,202	23,470
Replacement (nonrecurring), year 8	0	4,665
Replacement (nonrecurring), year 12	4,779	0
Replacement (nonrecurring), year 16	0	2,176
Salvage, year 24	0	0
Total present-worth life-cycle costs	$43,473	$47,499

The first alternative should be selected on the basis of this life-cycle cost analysis. To simplify the above example, a uniform worksheet (using the present-worth method) is presented in figure 6-6. Each cost element for the second example is entered on the present-worth format worksheet. This worksheet is divided into three major categories. The upper third is devoted to initial costs. In this example, the purchase cost is listed for each air-handler alternative. Note that the estimated cost and the present-worth cost are the same for the initial cost category. The total initial cost for each alternative is then determined and recorded in the appropriate place on the form.

The middle third of the worksheet is used for recording replacement and salvage values. In this example, replacement costs occur at years eight and sixteen for the economy air handler and year twelve for the performance air handler. These values are listed under the estimated-cost column of the worksheet. To calculate the present worth of replacement costs, the present worth (single amount) factor must be obtained for years eight, twelve, and sixteen from table 6-1 under the column headed "10 Percent," which is the discount rate of this example. Once these factors are obtained, the estimated cost of repair is simply multiplied by the appropriate factor to arrive at the present-worth equivalent cost. For example, $10,000 \times 0.4665 = 4,665$ is the present worth for the year eight replacement cost for the

Life-Cycle Cost Analysis
Using Present-Worth Costs

Life-Cycle Costing Estimate
General Purpose Work Sheet
Study Title: Rooftop Air Handler System   Date: _____
Discount Rate: 10%   Economic Life: 24 years

				Alternative 1 Describe: performance air handler		Alternative 2 Describe: economy air handler		Alternative 3 Describe:		Alternative 4 Describe:	
				Estimated Costs	Present Worth	Estimated Costs	Present Worth	Estimated Costs	Present Worth	Estimated Costs	Present Worth
Initial/Collateral Costs	Initial/Collateral Costs										
	A. Air Handler System			15,000	15,000	10,000	10,000				
	B.										
	C.										
	D.										
	E.										
	F.										
	G.										
	Total Initial/Collateral Costs				15,000		10,000				
Replacement/Salvage Costs	Replacement/Salvage (Single Expenditure)	Year	PW Factor								
	A. replace economy AH	8	0.4665			10,000	4,665				
	B. replace performance AH	12	0.3186	15,000	4,779						
	C. replace economy AH	16	0.2176			10,000	2,176				
	D.										
	E.										
	F.										
	G.										
	H.										
	Salvage air handlers	24	0.1015	0	0	0	0				
	Total Replacement/Salvage Costs				4,779		6,841				
Annual Costs	Annual Costs	Diff. Escal. Rate	PWA W/Escal.								
	A. maintenance	0%	8.985	500	4,492	800	7,188				
	B. energy	7%	10.668	1,800	19,202	2,200	23,470				
	C.										
	D.										
	E.										
	F.										
	G.										
	Total Annual Costs				23,694		30,658				
LCC	Total Present-Worth Life-Cycle Costs				43,473		47,499				
	Life-Cycle Present-Worth Dollar Savings				4,026		—				

PW — Present Worth   PWA — Present Worth Of Annuity

FIGURE 6-6. Life-cycle cost worksheet.

economy air handler. The total replacement and salvage present-worth cost is then determined and recorded in the appropriate place on the worksheet.

The final third of the worksheet records annual costs such as maintenance and energy costs. In this example, maintenance and energy costs are listed for each alternative. To convert these estimated annual costs to an equivalent present-worth cost, the present-worth annuity factor must be obtained from table 6-3. For electrical energy costs, the fuel is anticipated to escalate by 2 percent per year. Therefore, referring to table 6-4, under the "2 Percent" column heading for a 10 percent discount rate and a twenty-four-year life cycle, the factor is 10.668. Multiplying this factor by the estimated annual energy cost for each alternative yields the equivalent present-worth cost. For example, the performance air handler = 1,800 × 10.668 = $19,202. Other annual costs are calculated similarly. The total annual present-worth cost is then determined and recorded in the appropriate place on the form.

The total present-worth life-cycle cost for each air handler is established by totaling the initial, replacement/salvage, and annual operating costs. As a result of life-cycle costing, one can see that although the performance air handler was the most expensive initially, it costs much less to operate. These calculations show that, over its life, the performance air handler will save $4,026 over the economy air handler.

INVESTMENT ANALYSIS

Economic approaches best suited to investment analyses may be useful during design in performing an analysis in response to an owner directive or a special situation that requires detailed economic consideration.

Return on Investment

This approach is often used to evaluate private-sector investment alternatives; it is also used by government agencies. The expected annual savings due to an investment (return on an investment) are expected as a discounted percentage of the investment. This discounted percentage may be viewed as analogous to an interest rate. The present-worth annuity (PWA) factor is used to discount the equal periodic savings. For example, suppose an investment of

$1,000,000 in a new metal halide lighting system is expected to net an annual energy-cost reduction of $150,000 over ten years. To compute the rate of return on investment, the PWA is found using the formula:

$$\text{PWA} = \frac{\text{Investment}}{\text{Savings}} = \frac{1,000,000}{150,000} = 6.667$$

The figure of 6.667 is somewhere between the PWA for 8 percent and ten years (6.710 in table 6-3) and the PWA for 9 percent and ten years (6.418 in table 6-3). Interpolation between 8 percent and 9 percent yields a rate of return of approximately 8.4 percent.

Savings-to-Investment Ratio

The savings-to-investment ratio (SIR) is used to measure investment effectiveness. The SIR is calculated by dividing the present worth of the annual cost savings by the initial cost. If the SIR is higher than 1, the investment can be considered cost effective; the higher the ratio, the greater the dollar savings per dollar spent. By comparing SIRs of various alternatives, the most effective course of action can be determined. The SIR is similar to the ratio of benefits and costs used to compare alternatives for U.S. Army Corps of Engineers civil works projects. Suppose the installation of loading dock shelters is proposed to reduce heat loss at a northern facility. The estimated cost of a shelter is $15,000, and the estimated annual savings, over eight years, are $4,000. The discount rate is 10 percent. For eight years and 10 percent, the PWA (from table 6-3) is 5.335. The SIR would be:

$$\text{SIR} = \frac{\text{Annual Savings}}{\text{Investment}} \times \text{PWA}$$

$$= \frac{4,000}{15,000} \times 5.335$$

$$= 1.423$$

An SIR in excess of 1 indicates an economically viable investment. However, this alternative should be analyzed with at least one additional design solution with a different set of investment and annual savings figures to judge how well this SIR compares.

Payback-Period Method

The payback-period method of LCC is particularly useful in making investment decisions regarding energy-saving measures for existing facilities. It would be appropriate when considering such design decisions as switching from existing fluorescent fixtures to metal halide fixtures, installing electronic ignition systems on existing water heaters, adding insulation, replacing outdated street lamps, or installing energy management systems.

To use this procedure, the capital improvement under consideration is analyzed to determine:

- The initial dollar cost of the energy-saving feature
- The expected annual energy savings in dollars that will result from the purchase
- The expected useful life of the energy-saving improvement

With this information, the decision maker can determine when the invested capital can be recovered—the number of years to payback. This method assumes that (1) available money that is invested has the potential to earn interest and should be worth more in the future, and (2) the costs of energy will increase in the future, making expected annual savings for energy-conscious design grow as well. By assuming constant energy prices and establishing a discount rate, designers may reject an investment in which the payback period exceeds the useful life of the improvement. But by assuming that energy prices will increase and by using the same discount rate, the designer can see that the investment will yield a shorter payback period.

To perform this analysis in a project that evaluates the impact of energy prices on a proposed capital investment, it is necessary to know the initial cost of investment, the estimated annual energy and associated cost savings, and the useful life of the improvement. Two variations of the payback-period approach are *simple payback period* and *discounted payback period*. The simple payback-period method uses the formula:

$$\frac{\text{initial cost}}{\text{annual savings}}$$

Consider the case where additional insulation around an existing hot water boiler costs \$2,000 to install but is estimated to save \$500 per year in energy consumption. The simple payback period would be calculated:

$$\text{Simple payback period} = \frac{\$2,000}{\$500} = 4 \text{ years}$$

In this example, the simple payback period is estimated to be four years. The time value of money, life expectancy, and future costs are ignored in the simple payback approach.

The discounted payback period is arrived at by first converting each year's savings to present-worth savings. The discounted payback period is achieved when the present worth of cumulative savings equals the initial expenditure. Table 6-5 summarizes payback periods assuming a discount rate of 10 percent. Using the same example, it can be seen that if no price escalation is assumed, the payback period would actually be 5.36 years. On the other hand, if energy prices are estimated to rise 6 percent per year, that period would be reduced to 4.42 years. This method produces a more realistic picture of investments made, especially when operating costs are expected to increase with time.

SOURCES OF COST DATA

Cost data for a specific LCC analysis are developed from the best information available and at a level of accuracy commensurate with a level of effort appropriate to the importance of the decision being made. Initial costs normally present the least challenge to the designer. But reliable post-occupancy costs may be difficult to obtain. As a result, the best information available often may be no better than a best guess. The appropriate sources for any particular application are determined case by case.

Construction costs are developed from standard sources: the cost estimator, designers, construction manager, or a cost consultant, who may use *Building Construction Cost Data*, published annually by Robert Snow Means Company, and the *Dodge Manual for Building Construction*, published annually by McGraw-Hill Information Systems.

Energy costs are derived from simulation models that take into account climatic data, insulation and orientation factors, and building occupancy. Various energy analysis models are discussed in publications of the American Society of Heating, Refrigeration and

TABLE 6-5. Years to payback at 10 percent discount rate (DPP).

Ratio of Initial Cost to First Year Savings	Price Escalation Rate (percent)					
	0	2	4	6	8	10
1	1.11	1.08	1.06	1.04	1.02	1.00
2	2.34	2.26	2.19	2.12	2.06	2.00
3	3.74	3.55	3.39	3.24	3.12	3.00
4	5.36	4.99	4.68	4.42	4.19	4.00
5	7.27	6.59	6.07	5.64	5.30	5.00
6	9.61	8.42	7.58	6.93	6.42	6.00
7	12.63	10.55	9.22	8.28	7.57	7.00
8	16.89	13.08	11.04	9.70	8.74	8.00
9	24.16	16.21	13.06	11.20	9.94	9.00
10	never	20.31	15.34	12.79	11.16	10.00
11	never	26.30	17.95	14.48	12.41	11.00
12	never	37.52	21.01	16.28	13.70	12.00
13	never	never	24.72	18.21	15.01	13.00
14	never	never	29.39	20.29	16.36	14.00
15	never	never	35.75	22.54	17.74	15.00
16	never	never	45.73	24.99	19.15	16.00
17	never	never	70.45	27.69	20.60	17.00
18	never	never	never	30.70	22.10	18.00
19	never	never	never	34.08	23.63	19.00
20	never	never	never	37.94	25.21	20.00

Air Conditioning Engineers (ASHRAE). Energy models in such programs as BLAST and DOE-2 have been developed by the U.S. Corps of Engineers and Department of Energy to provide precise estimates of energy consumption.

Maintenance and repair cost data may be obtained from the facilities engineering and maintenance staffs with direct experience in the operation of those projects. Trade representatives and journals also provide general information, and historic maintenance cost data can be found in Dell'Isola and Kirk, *Life Cycle Cost Data*.[19] Care should be taken to ensure that the data developed through these sources represent similar levels of operating, maintenance, repair, and custodial activity.

Replacement, alteration, and salvage cost sources normally include staff cost estimators, facilities engineers, and designers with experience in the frequency and cost of replacements. Replacement information may also be obtained from manufacturers' representatives, industry associations, and, again, *Life Cycle Cost Data*. Planned alteration time frames can be obtained from the facility owner. Once these time frames and degree of change are established, the cost sources for making the alterations are the same as for initial costs.

UNCERTAINTY ASSESSMENT

Even after calculations are completed and preliminary results obtained, the LCC analysis cannot be considered complete until the effects of uncertainties are taken into account. Because uncertainties dominate decision making in the real world, an important step in an LCC analysis is to examine the uncertainties that affect the design project. Failure to do so can produce distorted or incorrect decisions. Life-cycle cost analyses by their very nature involve substantial uncertainty about the future and about the past, upon which future cost estimates are based. All of this makes LCC more an art than a science, producing not absolute results but credible estimates of the economic consequences of alternative solutions. Uncertainties are inherent in forecasts, estimates, and human judgments. An alternative that is lowest in LCC under one set of reasonable assumptions may be the highest given another set.

Sensitivity analysis best accounts for the effects of uncertainties and assists in decision making. In sensitivity analysis, a decision variable of uncertain value is assigned a range of different values—an upper bound, a lower bound, and the parameter value judged to represent the best estimate. A separate life-cycle cost analysis is conducted for each value. Figure 6-7 illustrates how the economic viability of a proposed solar heating system will vary as changes are made in the discount rate, fuel price escalation rate, and the analysis period. This present value of savings is based on fuel savings estimated initially at $1,000 per year. The analysis period covers zero to twenty-five years. The discount rate is varied in increments of 0, 5, 10, and 15 percent. It can be seen that cumulative savings increase over time but increase less with higher discount rates or lower escalation rates. The dramatic increase in savings is evident when fuel price escalation is large: compare the top line of the graph with the

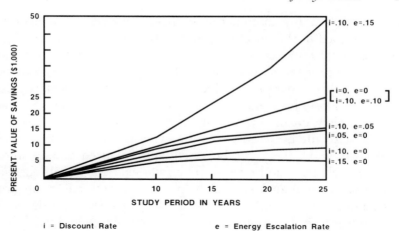

i = Discount Rate   e = Energy Escalation Rate

FIGURE 6-7. Sensitivity of fuel savings to analysis period, discount rate, and energy escalation rate. (Reprinted, by permission, from American Society for Testing and Materials (ASTM), "Measuring Life-Cycle Costs of Buildings and Building Systems" [ASTM E917-83, 1983] 897)

line next to the bottom of the graph. The present value of savings for a fuel escalation of 15 percent is approximately $49,000 at the end of twenty-five years and only $9,000 for a 0 percent escalation. The amount of energy saved is the same, but the present-worth savings vary widely, depending on the fuel price escalation rate used. Figure 6-7 illustrates the impact of alternative assumptions.

Chapter 10, figure 10-10 presents a sensitivity analysis of a lighting system. This analysis tests the sensitivity of the variable employee productivity versus the type of lighting system. It also tests the sensitivity of energy escalation rates to the life-cycle cost of the various lighting systems. The worksheet assists in recording the data.

ALTERNATIVE SELECTION

Economics is the major factor in decision making for many projects. Other than documentation and final report preparation, the last major step in the conduct of an LCC is to select an alternative. The alternative with the highest ranking, all things considered, is judged to be the most economical choice. The designer must determine whether initial cost alone can be used or whether life-cycle costs, energy, solar, or any combination of these, balanced or unbalanced, should be used in the selection process. Based on an owner's objectives, each selection criterion is intended to translate into action through the process of economic analysis. This is where an owner can exercise his or her prerogative to establish the means of carrying out these philosophies. As a consequence, the selection criteria may be based solely on life-cycle costs or give added weight to energy together with life-cycle costs; or the criteria may comprise solely initial costs and energy, or be essentially balanced among initial cost, life-cycle cost, and energy. The following chapter discusses a method of decision analysis that helps the decision maker integrate the economic criteria of initial and long-term costs with the more subjective goals of function, image, user satisfaction, and flexibility.

NOTES

1. See Dell'Isola and Kirk (1981, 1) for detailed discussion of the methodology of life-cycle costing contained in this book. This text also contains numerous examples applied to various buildings and building systems.

2. P. A. Stone's book (1975) addresses life-cycle costing (LCC) from the quantity-surveyor point of view.

3. Refer to the HEW publication *Life Cycle Budgeting as an Aid to Decision Making* (1973) for a complete description of life-cycle cost terminology.

4. GSA developed a computerized planning and budgeting LCC model in the late 1970s which it uses in its Capitalized Income Approach to Project Budgeting (CIAPB) (1977).

5. Grant et al. (1976) provides an excellent discussion regarding the theory of engineering economics.

6. See Miles (1972) for a complete discussion of value analysis as applied in manufacturing.

7. The text by Dell'Isola (1982) discusses value engineering as it relates to the construction industry. The interrelationship of LCC to VE is also addressed in this text.

8. See U.S. Comptroller General (1972) for a complete report of findings.

9. See the American Institute of Architect's document *Life Cycle Cost Analysis, A Guide for Architects* (1977) for a general overview of LCC in the design professions.

10. This law, more than anything else, has focused the attention of architects and engineers on life-cycle cost analyses in the construction industry.

11. Refer to ASTM E 917-83 for the complete standard on LCC. The method measures in present value or annual value dollars the total of all relevant costs associated with an investment in buildings and building systems. It results in an economic evaluation that encompasses designing, purchasing, leasing, constructing/installing, maintaining, operating, repairing, replacing, and disposing of buildings

or building systems. The significance, use, and step-by-step procedures for using LCC are described. In support of applying the standards, this ASTM standard lists a computer program for performing LCC calculations.

12. Refer to *Terotechnology: An Introduction to the Management of Physical Resources* (1976).

13. This methodology was developed by Dell'Isola and Kirk (1981).

14. Ten percent is used by some federal agencies, but many private owners use a higher rate.

15. See Kirk (1979–80) for a more complete list of potential LCC study areas. Much of the remaining material found in this chapter is abstracted from work conducted by Stephen Kirk for the U.S. Army Corps of Engineers.

16. See Grant et al. (1976) for the derivations of the economics formulas used in this discussion.

17. See Grant et al. (1976) for various methods of establishing the discount rate.

18. See Dell'Isola and Kirk (1981) for a discussion of how to deal with inflation when performing life-cycle cost studies.

19. Refer to Dell'Isola and Kirk (1983) for a complete listing of data on building systems.

CHAPTER 7

Decision Analysis

DECISION ANALYSIS is a mathematical theory of choice behavior. It assumes that rational decision makers, given clear options that have well-defined consequences, will choose the course of action that maximizes their satisfaction based on values defined as critical to the solution of a problem. The theory assumes that those consequences and levels of satisfaction can be measured by a single or compatible group of values.[1]

HISTORY

Decision analysis in the design professions has traditionally been applied in problem areas concerned with mechanical or economic issues that required only a single measure of effectiveness. Selection of building components or materials based on long-term or initial construction costs is typical of problems that have been resolved by decision analysis.[2] When such methods were used in problems that were environmental rather than mechanical, a discrepancy between theory and application became apparent. Measures of subjective decision values were often reduced to economic variables that tended to homogenize a complex set of problem attributes into a contrived format. The issues of building image and environmental comfort, for example, were often reduced to cost/benefit measures. A central argument against such decision methodologies in design has been that architects who deal with problems that have a rich mixture of environmental consequences have been forced to discard that richness and base their decisions on a common objective denominator.

The emergence of the design methods movement in the 1960s

focused the designer's attention on the need to weigh and evaluate the consequences of design decisions objectively. A number of techniques from operations research and systems engineering were borrowed by environmental designers to structure the decision-making processes in architecture and industrial design. Christopher Jones (1981) outlined a range of decision-analysis methodologies for the design professions that were modifications of industrial and engineering techniques. The models for these techniques, however, were often viewed by architects as too mechanical or restrictive for the creative and open-ended process of design.[3]

Multi-objective decision analysis evolved from the traditional theory of choice behavior as a response to this weakness. It assumes that the overall structure of the original theory can be maintained while allowing decision makers to use a range of values, rather than a single measurement scale, to weigh the consequences of their actions. This theory, which was developed during the 1970s, has been used in such problems as site selection for large transportation and power facilities as well as in program evaluations of social and environmental activities.[4] The use of this methodology in such complex and diverse problems indicates that designers might take advantage of this technique in architectural settings. William Peña of the Houston firm of CRS-Sirrine, for example, has used a form of this technique to aid the decision process during architectural programming and post-occupancy evaluations.

THEORY

The discussion of decision-analysis techniques here will focus on a simplified version of multi-objective decision methods. A *strict* application of multi-objective decision techniques is difficult to accomplish in design problems, primarily because of the large amount of time required to collect data and the questionable accuracy of the data collected. Most designers are not concerned with precision in environmental data, nor is the time element in most design projects conducive to exhaustive data collection. Decision analysis in this chapter, therefore, combines the theory of multi-objective decision analysis with a simplified format of data collection and mathematics. The reason for this simplification is twofold. First, in order to make the technique useful to architects and designers, the mechanics of its use must be tailored to the demands of the typical design process.

This process is characterized by imprecise and subjective data, short periods of time devoted to decision making, and a design process involving many decision makers. The technique must respond to these pressures. Second, decision-analysis techiques are used in design not to *prescribe* precise answers to complex questions, but rather to *illuminate* for the design team the consequences of a range of design solutions. The critical element of decision analysis, therefore, is the ability to define the criteria of a design problem and to allow a number of decision makers the opportunity to test a range of solutions against those criteria.[5]

The first component of this decision-analysis technique is the definition of independent design criteria. Keeney and Raiffa (1976) have shown that the criteria must cumulatively produce a combined measure or index of overall problem definition. These criteria, referred to as *objectives*, must be selected in a manner that decomposes a problem statement into independent measurement scales. Objectives define the goals and desires of the people who will construct and occupy an environment and the relative degrees of importance of these objectives.

The second component of decision analysis is the generation of a list of feasible alternatives that address design objectives. Examples of design alternatives are space and function diagrams, patterns of people and material flow, and activity analyses which have been discovered during the early phase of the design process. Decision alternatives may also consist of site-plan arrangements of major functional spaces, floor plans, and concept diagrams that describe unique ways in which a set of design criteria might be satisfied. Any alternative must be able, in itself, to satisfy all the criteria established by the decision makers. This is where the term *feasible* alternative becomes important.

The purpose of decision analysis is to establish a structure that allows the design team to weigh the effectiveness of each alternative against the design criteria. The balance of the requirements implied by the design objectives and the potential of each alternative to fulfill these objectives constitutes the decision model outlined in figure 7-1, a simplified view of this process.

Assumptions basic to this technique are:

1. One decision maker or a group of decision makers defines objectives and evaluates alternatives.

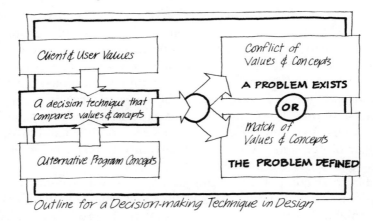

FIGURE 7-1. Decision analysis process chart. (Reprinted, by permission, from R. Bechtel, R. Marans, and W. Michelson, eds., *Method in Environmental and Behavioral Research* [New York: Van Nostrand Reinhold, 1986] 255)

2. The objectives are assumed to be independent of one another and understood by all decision makers.
3. Judgments of the relative importance of the various objectives can be made by the decision makers.
4. Probabilities can be assigned to describe the likelihood of each alternative achieving specific levels of the stated objectives.

Decision analysis is a normative model of decision making and is limited to a finite set of design objectives and alternatives. It helps the decision maker objectively define a design problem and systematically sort through the consequences of distinct design solutions.

Those concerned with design decisions—the owners and users of the environment, the programmer, cost analysts, and designers—must organize the information that has been collected during the design process and provide direction for the project. At critical decision points in the design process, alternatives have been generated, the objectives of the problem have been defined, and the members of the design team are assembled to evaluate the project. This assembly is an opportunity for the decision makers to express their various opinions and pool their experiences to arrive at a collective understanding of the problem. At the completion of these decision meetings, agreements should be reached that outline the direction of the chosen solutions.

DEFINING DESIGN OBJECTIVES

The definition of design objectives is usually the first step in any decision-analysis technique, regardless of which phase of the design process concerns the decision makers. In the earliest phases of programming, for example, these objectives will probably be referred to as program goals and will be general in nature. As the project moves through the schematic design phase, the objectives will take on more specificity. Early program goals dealing with economic feasibility may begin with gross estimates of cost based on *dollars per square foot*. What is important in the selection of design objectives is that the decision makers agree on how each objective will be measured and the relative independence of each objective against the others.

Most design objectives can be put into a limited number of general categories. Peña, for example, groups the major design goals that programmers should concern themselves with under the categories of form, function, time, cost, and energy.[6] Other studies have shown that three kinds of design objectives prevail in design programs: economic factors, visual or image-related factors, and functional factors.[7] Although a unique set of criteria will characterize each decision problem, it is likely that a uniform and repetitive set of concerns will be present, in one form or another, in all design problems. Generally, economic objectives concern either initial construction budgets or life-cycle costs. Image-related objectives are typically associated with symbolic meaning and issues of scale and proportion. They also define the degree to which environments enhance and reinforce the human components of design and touch on the issues of color, texture, comfort, and psychological response to buildings. Functional attributes of environments deal with the physical nature of designed spaces: activity sizes and arrangements, proximity of one activity to another, and degrees of expandability and changeability in environments. Figure 7-2 lists some common design objectives.

Scaling Design Objectives

Once the design objectives have been selected by the design team, a consensus must emerge regarding how each objective will be measured. It can be seen from the range of objectives in figure 7-2 that most are highly subjective and variable. Except for those concerned with economics, they do not have natural measurement scales. It

Design Objective	*Definition*
Image	The visual concept of the building and the way in which the building attracts attention to itself. The form of the building and the degree to which it acts as a symbol for the company
Community	How the building and its site project a "good neighbor" identity in terms of safety, security, and privacy
Functional efficiency	The degree to which the building is able to respond to the work process and flow of people, equipment, and materials
Security	The degree to which the building can segregate sensitive functions from one another and prevent the entry of people to restricted areas
Expansion	The ability of the building to grow to meet projected changes in the work process without disturbing existing building functions
Flexibility	The degree to which the building plan can be rearranged to conform to revised work processes and personnel changes
Technical performance	How the building operates in terms of mechanical systems, electrical systems, and industrial processes
Human performance	How the building provides a physically and psychologically comfortable place for people to work and live
Energy conservation	The degree to which the building is able to conserve energy resources through construction, site orientation, and solar design
Life-cycle costs	The economic consequences of the building in terms of initial capital investment and long-term operating costs
Others	To be defined for specified project requirements

FIGURE 7-2. Typical design objectives.

would be very difficult, for example, to conceive of a system that could effectively measure "Building Image." A method must define in general terms the basic meaning and intent of each objective and establish uniform rating scales for each objective.

One method that has been used to construct objective and relatively accurate measurement scales for environmental design objec-

Decision Analysis
Scaling Objectives

Project___*Corporate Headquarters*___   Date___3/23/81___

Objective Name___*Circulation*___   Objective No.___1___

Objective Descriptions

Low Value	1 Extended amount of employee walking for communication. Circulation system that satisfies simple, clear, and direct movement with safety. Mixed circulation for people, vehicles, and service. Controlled access to buildings.
	2 Tolerable amount of employee walking for communication. Circulation system that satisfies simple, clear, and direct movement with safety. Separate circulation for people, vehicles, and service. Controlled access to buildings
	3 Moderate amount of employee walking for communication. Circulation system that satisfies job function, personal needs, and safety. Separate circulation for people, vehicles, and service Controlled access to buildings.
	4 Minor amount of employee walking for communication and safety purposes. Circulation system that improves job function and personal needs. Separate circulation for people, vehicles, and service. Restricted access to buildings & parking with separate visitor entry pt.
High Value	5 Minimal amount of employee walking for communication and safety purposes. Circulation system that greatly improves job function and personal needs. Separate circulation for people, vehicles, and service. Restricted access to buildings and parking with controlled entry points for employees and visitors.

FIGURE 7-3. Design objective scaling worksheet. (Reprinted, by permission, from R. Bechtel, R. Marans, and W. Michelson, eds., *Methods in Environmental and Behavioral Research* [New York: Van Nostrand Reinhold, 1987] 258)

tives is outlined in figure 7-3. Given a particular design objective, design team members are asked to assess the range of extremes that might be acceptable and desirable in a given problem. Questions are posed to the decision makers to stimulate discussion about the nature of the objective being considered. A question such as "What is the least you would expect in a potential design solution for how people circulate through this facility?" might prompt the design team to define the issue of "Circulation." The question is repeated for the most desirable value, which allows the decision group to establish the upper and lower bounds of a measurement scale (that is, the 5 and 1 values of fig. 7-3). This process is continued for the intermediate points on the scale and then the intervals between the points are tested for accuracy. If the perceived intervals between the first and third, and the third and fifth scalar pairs are judged to be equal, then at least the overall structure of this particular scale can be considered valid. After all comparisons among the various scalar intervals are completed, the circulation design objective scale can be set aside and another objective definition tested.[8]

Scaling the objectives of a problem in this manner not only helps the design team arrive at uniform measurement scales but is also a way to define the general nature and context of that problem. The process of defining and constructing these measurement scales involves the collective participation of the entire team and allows each team member to express his or her own values and expertise to the group as a whole. The establishment of the five scalar points in figure 7-3 represents not only a convenient measuring device for a decision-analysis exercise, but also presents a visible and public statement of the feelings about a specific design criterion that are shared by the design team. If, at a later stage of design, someone disagrees with the circulation scale or new information shows that the scale is incorrect, a mechanism has been created to allow the team to adjust this definition and to reach a new consensus.

Weighing Design Objectives

After each design-objective scale has been constructed, the team turns its attention to the relative degrees of importance—or value priorities—of the objective definitions. In order to verify the relative degrees of importance of the objectives, a trade-off exercise is performed. The exercise begins with the assumption that decision makers believe one particular design objective is more important to the success of the project than all other objectives. Assume, for example, that the team has defined and constructed measurement scales for five independent objectives (fig. 7-4) and has determined, in this particular problem, that functional efficiency should take priority. A trade-off diagram similar to the one found in figure 7-5 is constructed for each of the four trade-off comparisons between the

Decision Analysis
Definitions of Objectives

Project Corporate Headquarters　　Date 3/81

Location Southwest U.S.　　Phase Early Schematic

Objectives

No.	Name	Description/Definition	Rank or Weight
1	Circulation	movement of workers and materials in a well-defined and efficient manner	4
2	Functional Efficiency	organization and arrangement of activities to allow for maximum work productivity	1
3	Expansion	the ability to grow and change within the building and on the site	5
4	Image	comfort of the user in physical and psychological terms positive corporate image	2
5	Life-Cycle Costs	minimization of capital, operating, maintenance, salvage, and tax costs	3
6			
7			
8			
9			
10			

FIGURE 7-4. Initial client and user objectives. (Reprinted, by permission, from R. Bechtel, R. Marans, and W. Michelson, eds., *Methods in Environmental and Behavioral Research* [New York: Van Nostrand Reinhold, 1987] 257)

Decision Analysis
Trade-Off Assessment

Project _____Corporate Headquarters_____ Date __3/81__

Objective "X" Name _____Functional Efficiency_____ Objective "X" No. __2__

Objective "Y" Name _____Circulation_____ Objective "Y" No. __1__

High "X" Objective _____Grouping of functions match organizational needs (in all dept.'s)_____

Low "X" Objective _____Clusters of activity areas are compatible in only two dept.'s_____

High "Y" Objective _____Minimal employee walking distances. Seperate circ. systems_____

Low "Y" Objective _____Extended amount of walking. Clear circ. system. Controlled access_____

Assessing Scaling Constants

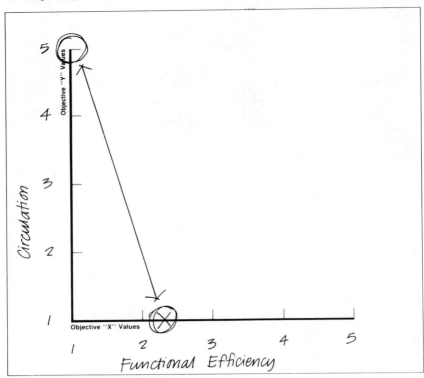

FIGURE 7-5. Trade-off assessment. (Reprinted, by permission, from R. Bechtel, R. Marans, and W. Michelson, eds., *Methods in Environmental and Behavioral Research* [New York: Van Nostrand Reinhold, 1987] 259)

functional efficiency objective and the other, less important criteria. A question is posed to the team: "If circulation and function could be compared one to the other, and if the former were to be increased to its highest scalar value (that is, 5), how much of the preferred function objective could be traded off in order to achieve this level of circulation?" In essence, the group is asked to consider how much of one objective's value can be sacrificed in order to get value from a less important design goal. The distinction of importance between function and circulation is fairly great in this example (fig. 7-5), primarily because the decision makers in this instance apparently consider the way the building is arranged to be much more important from a functional point of view.[9]

The mechanics for rank ordering design objectives are shown in figure 7-6. The completion of this exercise is likely to produce a different rank ordering from that originally expressed by the design team. This is a common outcome of decision analysis and one that should be considered a useful consequence, indicating that a discussion and analysis of the objectives of the problem has produced a deeper understanding of the design project. It is important to remember that the primary goal of decision analysis is not to provide definitive answers to complex questions, but to enhance the ability of *all* decision makers to comprehend the problem at hand.

GENERATION OF ALTERNATIVE DESIGNS

The second component of decision analysis is to generate feasible solutions. During the course of any project, project programmers and designers will suggest hypothetical answers to the problem. Some solutions may be focused on a narrow range of design objectives, while others may be very comprehensive. But to be considered a valid design alternative, each solution must satisfy every design objective *at least* at the lowest acceptable level in the scalar value system. If an alternative does not fulfill the established objectives and if the alternative is viewed as a desirable solution, the objectives not met should be revised to accommodate the alternative or eliminated from consideration.

As a design project progresses from feasibility and programming to schematic and design development, the nature of feasible solutions will change as well. As the process of defining the design

Functional efficiency: This objective was judged to be the most
important. Set the weight at *1.00*   = 1.00

Circulation: A trade-off value at the 2.3 point on the *Function*
scale was established (see fig. 7-5). Since this point is approximately a third of the distance up the scale, use a weight of
importance of *.33.*   = .33

Life-cycle cost: A trade-off value of 3.75 on the *Function* scale
was chosen by the team. Since this value is somewhat less than
three-quarters of the distance up this scale use a weight of importance of *.69.*   = .69

Expansion: A trade-off value at the 3.5 point on the *Function*
scale was chosen. This value is just slightly less than assigned
to the *Life-cycle cost* goal. Assign a weight of importance of *.65.*   = .65

Image: A trade-off value of 2.3 was chosen. Assign the same
weight as *Circulation* at *.33.*   = .33

GRAND TOTAL = 3.00

The new normalized weights of
importance of the value statements
(in descending order) are:

Function = 1.00/3.00   =   .33
Life-cycle cost = .69/3.00   =   .23
Expansion = .65/3.00   =   .22
Circulation = .33/3.00   =   .11
Image = .33/3.00   =   .11

Total =   *1.00*

FIGURE 7-6. Weights of importance and rankings of objectives.

objectives moves from the measurement of abstract goals to precise
design criteria, so too will the alternatives progress from general
functional and conceptual diagrams to specific and dimensionally
accurate spatial arrangements. It is most productive to generate alternatives representing a wide variety of design philosophies that
will test the extremes of the design-objective definitions.

Six alternatives to a hypothetical problem are sketched in figure

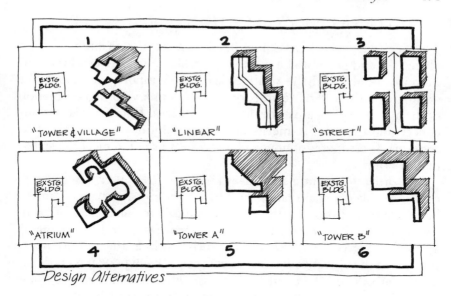

FIGURE 7-7. Design alternatives. (Reprinted, by permission, from R. Bechtel, R. Marans, and W. Michelson, eds., *Methods in Environmental and Behavioral Research* [New York: Van Nostrand Reinhold, 1987] 260)

7-7. The initial task of the decision-making team is to brainstorm informally about the strengths and weaknesses of each scheme.[10] Free association of ideas is encouraged here; no suggestion is considered too unusual for inclusion in the discussion. When a number of ideas have been recorded, the team is asked to respond to each one against the previously constructed design objectives. Each idea is scored as advantageous or disadvantageous to each objective. This exercise begins to highlight the need to clarify and reinforce the rankings that were originally established in the previous definition and scaling exercises.

When widely divergent opinions are investigated in this way, new approaches to a problem are often uncovered. By openly discussing the ideas generated by these discussions, the design team is often able to view the alternatives in a creative, as well as a critical, manner. These discussions are systematically recorded, and modifications to the alternatives should be suggested to the project designer or programmer.

ALTERNATIVE EVALUATION

The decision makers have now detailed a set of measurable design objectives and generated a number of design alternatives. Trade-off exercises established the relative degrees of importance among the design objectives. The team is ready to begin a vigorous evaluation of the alternatives against the design objectives. Informal discussions concerning the relative merits of various solutions have established some crude estimates of how well they meet or fail to meet the stated design criteria.

In order to begin a formal evaluation of the alternatives, each decision maker is again familiarized with the value statements in the objective definitions and the five-point measurement scales of each. Team members are now asked to make very specific value judgments as to the degree to which each solution fulfills the requirements implied in the objective measurement scales. Each person records his or her ratings and the combined assessments are collected and compared. Figure 7-8 illustrates an evaluation session in which a specific design alternative (the "Village and Tower" scheme) has been rated by a ten-person team with respect to the five design objectives discussed above.

After all the alternatives have been assessed, the decision group meets again to discuss the ranges of value assessments that team members have assigned to the various schemes. On the first scheme, for example, it would probably become evident that some decision makers perceive the problem differently than others. It might be asked why Member 1 viewed this alternative so poorly with respect to expansion capabilities while Member 5 so positively assessed this solution in terms of this design criterion. The assessment and questioning generated by this method bring the collective expertise of the group to bear on the problem and highlight design areas that might be too loosely defined or in need of special attention later in the project. By the completion of this discussion, several group members will perhaps have changed their assessments in light of the opinions of their colleagues. At this point a simple arithmetic average of the ten ratings is calculated for each alternative assessment.

The arithmetic average score for each design objective is only a crude approximation of how the collective mind of the team has analyzed the effectiveness of a particular alternative. In order to analyze the overall rankings of the alternative schemes using these average design objective scores, a series of simple equations can be

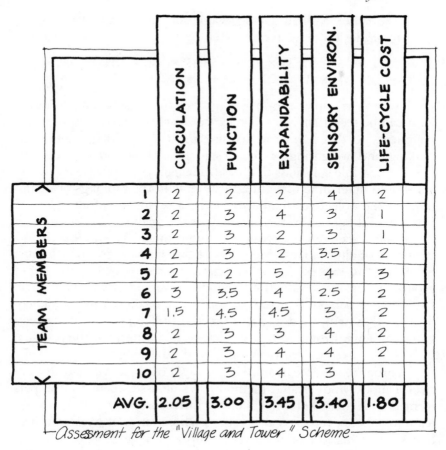

TEAM MEMBERS	CIRCULATION	FUNCTION	EXPANDABILITY	SENSORY ENVIRON.	LIFE-CYCLE COST
1	2	2	2	4	2
2	2	3	4	3	1
3	2	3	2	3	1
4	2	3	2	3.5	2
5	2	2	5	4	3
6	3	3.5	4	2.5	2
7	1.5	4.5	4.5	3	2
8	2	3	3	4	2
9	2	3	4	4	2
10	2	3	4	3	1
AVG.	2.05	3.00	3.45	3.40	1.80

Assessment for the "Village and Tower" Scheme

FIGURE 7-8. Assessments for the "Village and Tower" scheme. (Reprinted, by permission, from R. Bechtel, R. Marans, and W. Michelson, eds., *Methods in Environmental and Behavioral Research* [New York: Van Nostrand Reinhold, 1987] 263)

used.[11] These calculations use the weights of importance from figure 7-6 to determine how well each alternative satisfies—on the average—the full range of design criteria. The "weighted average" value for the first scheme, with respect to the circulation objective, was determined by the equation:

(Weight of Importance for Circulation) × (Average Circulation Score)

or

$$(.11) \times (2.05) = .23,$$

while the *total* weighted average value for this alternative with respect to *all* design objectives is given by the following summation:

$$[(.11 \times 2.05) + (.33 \times 3.00) + (3.45 \times .22) + (.11 \times 3.40) + (.23 \times 1.80)] = [(.23 + .99 + .76 + .37 + .41)] = 2.76.$$

Using the sample set of five objectives and six alternatives (fig. 7-9), it can be seen that two schemes are clearly preferred by the team members. At this point the decision makers should reevaluate the ranking and weighting of the design objectives and consider the range of feasible solutions that has been analyzed. Sensitivity analyses should determine if slight adjustments in the rankings or definitions of the objectives might affect the assessments of alternatives. What would happen to the outcome of the analysis, for example, if the image objective were reduced in importance? Would this change the order of alternatives? Members of the decision group also must be allowed to express individual views in isolation from the larger group. A separate evaluation, therefore, should be undertaken in which each person is asked to analyze the alternatives independently. This will yield a picture of the preferences of individuals who may have strong opinions about certain aspects of the problem or who may possess relevant specialized knowledge.

In order to validate the rankings of a set of objectives and alternatives a more sophisticated method of value assessment can be performed with the aid of a calculator or microcomputer.[12] In this way, team members can assess alternatives with a range of *potential* objective scores. Instead of using the simple average scores shown in figure 7-9, the group can establish a probability distribution for the range of values thought to be likely in each scheme. Although the basic theory of this decision technique is similar to the weighted-average method, the use of a computer program is required to input and calculate the assessments because of the larger number of probability calculations.[13] The team is thus able to take into account the full range of opinions and assessments that surfaced earlier in decision making.

The completion of a decision-analysis session should have specific outcomes. First, a consensus—or at least a friendly understanding—should be reached within the decision group in terms of preferred design solutions. The preferred solutions should be the basis of future design choices and generation of alternatives. Second, the perceived strengths and weaknesses of each alternative should be

Early Schematics
Analytical Phase
Building Layout
Basic Function

List the best ideas from ranking and comparison techniques. Determine which one stacks up the best against the desired criteria.

Desired Criteria: circulation, functional efficiency, expansion, image, life-cycle costs

Alternate Scores (sum of weighted avg values)

Design Alternatives	a circulation .11	b functional efficiency .33	c expansion .22	d image .11	e life-cycle costs .23	f	g	Total
1. Village Tower	.23 / 2.05	.99 / 3.00	.76 / 3.45	.37 / 3.40	.41 / 1.80			2.76
2. Linear	.26 / 2.35	1.01 / 3.05	.59 / 2.70	.30 / 2.75	.56 / 2.45			2.72
3. Street	.40 / 3.65	1.22 / 3.70	.74 / 3.35	.45 / 4.10	.98 / 4.25			3.79
4. Atrium	.41 / 3.70	1.16 / 3.50	.89 / 4.05	.50 / 4.50	.79 / 3.45			3.75
5. Tower A	.32 / 2.95	.83 / 2.50	.51 / 2.30	.31 / 2.80	.30 / 1.30			2.27
6. Tower B	.32 / 2.93	.97 / 2.95	.67 / 3.03	.34 / 3.10	.78 / 3.40			3.08
7.								
8.								
9.								
10.								

Weight of Importance (re: 7-6)

Excellent - 5   Very Good - 4   Good - 3   Fair - 2   Poor - 1

Key:
— Weighted average value (average alternative score × weight of importance)
— average alternate score (see fig. 7-8)

FIGURE 7-9. Weighted average decision analysis. (Reprinted, by permission, from R. Bechtel, R. Marans, and W. Michelson, eds., *Methods in Environmental and Behavioral Research* [New York: Van Nostrand Reinhold, 1987] 264)

further analyzed by the designer to refine the set of potential feasible solutions. A particular scheme may have a low *overall* rating, but it may contain a specific aspect or satisfy a particular objective that should be incorporated into the fabric of the solution. Finally, decision makers should once again focus on defining and ranking design objectives. The most positive outcome of a decision-analysis exercise should be a critical reappraisal of the direction in which a design problem is moving. Again, it should be remembered that the most important benefit of performing group decision exercises is not to select a single, "correct" solution, but systematically to explore the range of alternatives and values within the collective mind of the design team.

USE OF DECISION TECHNIQUES IN DESIGN

Decision analysis is intended to provide a framework for establishing design objectives and evaluating design alternatives. The technique is presented as a general model of decision making, not a prescriptive model of choice behavior. No attempt was made to incorporate information from a large number of users of the proposed facility. Post-occupancy evaluation techniques, however, apply to this model and could be used to enrich decisions made during decision analysis. This model of decision making might come into play during any of the building-cycle phases, although it is probably most useful during early stages of design, when decisions to be made are general in nature and opportunities for suggesting changes are greatest. The level of detail that will form the basis for specificity of alternatives and design objectives depends on the degree to which information entering into the decision process is appreciated and understood by the design team. Information considered early in a project is necessarily general in nature; over time the specificity of the data will become more concrete and less amenable to change.

   The use of decision-analysis techniques in design projects suggests a number of important factors that should be considered by decision makers when these techniques are incorporated in the design process.[14] Architects and programmers generally assume that the definition of client and user goals and objectives should be the initial step in the design process. Furthermore, they assume that these definitions should be limited to general statements of environmental needs and should avoid physical design solutions in the early stages of problem definition. The use of these techniques in practice, however, indicates that decision makers prefer to construct definitions of design objectives on tangible information sources. Cost objectives, for example, are often associated with *known* levels of construction quality. As the design team sets about to construct design objective scales, alternative design solutions are generated to flesh out the feasible range of scalar values for the various design criteria. In general, the most productive format for using decision techniques in design is one which is cyclical and iterative in nature. The structure outlined above should not be viewed as a linear process that begins with criteria definitions and ends with a design solution. Rather, it should be viewed as a uniform format that allows conflicting personalities to argue about and formulate the direction and philosophy of a design problem.

This view of decision making is supported not only by the experience of decision makers using the technique in design projects, but also by principles of human behavior and psychology. In settings that deal with complex human behavior, the distinction between that behavior and the physical environment can be seen only in the context of the other. Many social scientists, for example, have argued that an approach that defines human response in relation to physical objects is a necessary assumption in problem solving:

> We take the view that behaviors and objects are inextricably intertwined. The behavior helps define the object and the object helps define the behavior; interaction between human and object is a joint process.[15]

Therefore, the earliest attempts at resolving design objectives should recognize the relationship between the visual and abstract nature of environmental settings. It is probably counterproductive to think strictly in terms of clients' values without considering what those values might mean in very real and physical contexts.

A client will not necessarily be willing to share with the entire design team enough of his or her values to describe a problem accurately, especially in the case of problems that might be considered controversial, politically or socially sensitive, or unfamiliar.[16] One reason that environmental problems are typically defined in such physical, economic, and spatial terms is that these are the least threatening ways for clients to make their values apparent to designers. A desire for a neoclassical bank façade may say as much about the client's need for security and illusions of stability than could ever be determined in an analytic exercise that abstractly isolates and defines these values.

Finally, environmental problems do not exist as isolated and discrete entities. The idea of packages or portfolios of problem attributes has been used to enrich the examination of human values in, for example, psychology.[17] The fact that problem definitions will not remain constant or in fact ever be fully stated should not be considered detrimental to the use of such techniques. The technique should be seen as a device to help define environmental problems without completely defining a client's system of values.

CONCLUSION

The decision-making model presented in this chapter is a simple framework that structures the process of complex team designs. It implies that process can be described within three distinct parts: a system of well-defined design objectives, a set of at least two feasible design solutions, and a mechanism for comparing those solutions to the design objectives. The discussion of these elements has presented a simplified outline of how the design team collects the values and goals of the users, owners, and designers of the problem together in uniform measurement scales and uses those scales systematically to evaluate a range of design alternatives. On the surface, it may appear that this model of decision making is too sparse to handle the complexity and diversity that is present in almost any but the most simple and direct of design problems. What must be remembered about the model is the term *framework:* all the other techniques outlined in the book must work *within* this framework and help to enrich the processes of establishing the measurement scales, generating alternatives, and evaluating design solutions.

The techniques described in the chapter on function analysis, for example, can now be seen as methods to help the design team construct and evaluate a set of feasible design alternatives. The life-cycle techniques found in chapter 6 now become useful ways to evaluate *precisely* the consequences of long-term economic objectives. The techniques that will be discussed in the following chapter dealing with post-occupancy evaluation will be useful in establishing the complex measurement scales of image and human performance. The group creativity techniques found in chapter 5—especially the

Delphi technique—are valuable aids to the design team in assessing the relative merits of the various design alternatives. In short, the structure that has been described for decision making in this chapter should be viewed as the focus for bringing all the other techniques together during design. It is a way of ordering the decision-making responsibilities of the team and providing a mechanism for monitoring the progress of the problem solution.

NOTES

1. An excellent reference that describes the elementary components of classical decision-analysis theory is found in Raiffa (1970, 1–38). The examples in this chapter are taken from Bechtel, Marans, and Michelson (1987, 247–69).

2. See Mattar et al. (1978) for a decision technique that has been used in selecting materials and assemblies for building enclosures.

3. Seaton (1978) and Thompson (1977) outline technical and philosophical problems associated with the use of decision-analysis techniques in design.

4. Keeney and Raiffa (1976) are the best source for understanding the theoretical foundations and historical uses of multi-objective decision methods.

5. See Behn and Vaupee (1982) for a discussion of how decision techniques can be applied in problems with severe time constraints and social pressures.

6. Peña's *Problem-Seeking* (1977) outlines a systematic approach to problem definition and decision processes in architectural programming.

7. Six decision-making case studies in architectural programming are reviewed in detail in Spreckelmeyer (1981), and a discussion of design objectives is found on pages 88–94.

8. For a complete discussion of this scaling technique, see Coombs (1976), chapters 5 and 6.

9. It should be noted that for the purposes of simplifying this discussion of decision methods, all five measurement scales are assumed to be linear. If it is determined that certain design objects are not linear—meaning that the decision maker assumes a "risk-adverse" or "risk-seeking" attitude—a more complex set of assessment procedures must be used. See Keeney (1977) for the components of this assessment process.

10. A modified form of the traditional Delphi method was used in this project and is outlined in Kirk (1980). See a detailed discussion of Delphi and brainstorming techniques in chapter 5.

11. See Dell'Isola and Kirk (1981, 103–4) for a detailed description of this type of decision analysis.

12. This form of decision analysis, commonly referred to as expected utility theory, is outlined in Keeney and Raiffa (1976), which also details programming uses of this method.

13. See Spetzler and Holstein (1975) for a discussion of this probability assessment technique.

14. See Spreckelmeyer (1982) for a detailed review of these factors and a discussion of six decision-analysis case studies.

15. This quote is taken from Runkel and McGrath (1972, 21–22) and indicates the attitude that behavioral scientists hold concerning this principle of human behavior.

16. See Starr (1969) for a discussion of this problem in the context of defining design objectives concerned with such volatile issues as safety factors and cost-benefit projections.

17. See Coombs and Bowen (1971) for a review of this concept.

CHAPTER 8

Post-Occupancy
Evaluation

ARCHITECTS and environmental designers use post-occupancy evaluation to determine how environments are being used by their occupants and to assess the degree to which that use satisfies specific design objectives.[1] This technique has been used recently in environmental design to establish programmatic criteria for new designs based on the performance of occupied buildings. Post-occupancy evaluation aims to:

- Use existing environments to model future environmental needs and programmatic requirements
- Test the performance of original program and design goals
- Update and modify existing environments based on how they are being used by their occupants

HISTORY

The concept of post-occupancy evaluation is not new to design. Architects and designers have always used existing buildings as models for designing new environments, but post-occupancy evaluation as a formal technique has been used by architects and designers only during the last twenty years.[2] The introduction of social science techniques into architecture has provided models for incorporating post-occupancy evaluation into the design process. The social sciences have provided architects with a formal way to investigate occupied environments by establishing hypotheses of human behavior in physical settings and techniques that are useful to test these hypotheses.[3]

The founding of the Environmental Design Research Association (EDRA) in the late 1960s was designers' and environmental researchers' first formal attempt to establish a method of analyzing existing environments and to conceptualize how post-occupancy evaluation could be incorporated into architectural design.[4] In 1973 the American Institute of Architects (AIA) sponsored the Coolfont Conference in an effort to combine the benefits of formal research methods in design.[5] The rise of programming as a pre-design service in architecture has also led to the conclusion that a post-design service is a logical continuation of the design process. In post-design services, the architect is compensated for examining how a building or building process has met or failed to meet a client's original program requirements. During the 1970s, the AIA established new contractual relationships between clients and architects to allow architects to tender not only traditional design services but also programming, post-occupancy evaluation, and other analytic services.[6]

Post-occupancy evaluations have typically been conducted by academic researchers or governmental bodies interested in establishing specific criteria for complex building types. During the 1970s, for example, the U.S. General Services Administration established such a program for federal buildings, while the governments of New Zealand and Australia formulated similar programs.[7] One of the better-known post-occupancy evaluations of this period was conducted by Clare Cooper-Marcus in Easter Hill Village. In this particular study, Cooper-Marcus tried to determine how public housing met the user need and to establish new criteria for future housing projects.[8]

In Great Britain during the 1960s, Peter Manning established procedures by which office buildings could be evaluated in order to establish office planning guidelines. Manning's work proposed to establish environmental standards for offices and to give a voice to users who normally would not be involved in the design.[9]

Another example of post-occupancy evaluation in an office setting is Robert Marans and Kent Spreckelmeyer's study of the Ann Arbor (Michigan) Federal Building. This was a response to the National Bureau of Standard's desire to develop a model of building evaluation and to test the model in a typical federal office building.[10] Florida A&M University has also conducted an extensive post-occupancy evaluation of the School of Architecture building on its Tallahassee campus in order to establish a procedure by which the Florida

Board of Regents can develop criteria and design standards for new campus buildings.[11]

The future of post-occupancy evaluation seems to be in formalizing it as a professional service in the design process. Just as the pre-design services of site analysis and programming have come to be accepted parts of architectural design, so too should post-occupancy evaluation become the designer's responsibility. The philosophy of post-occupancy evaluation, however, poses the following problems:

- If the project architect is also the evaluator, who assumes the legal responsibility for the project and what degree of objectivity is possible?
- How can the time lag between building design and occupancy be accounted for in the traditional design process? The use of post-occupancy techniques would mean that the traditional process would be lengthened by at least a year to three years.
- What new forms of contractual arrangements and billing procedures will be necessary to account for this longer time lag in the design process?
- What building types lend themselves to post-occupancy evaluation techniques? Hospitals, large office complexes, and multi-family housing are more natural candidates for post-occupancy evaluation than are houses, religious buildings, or other buildings that have unique design criteria and use patterns.

THEORY

Because post-occupancy evaluation techniques have arisen from the social sciences, the model that will be used here assumes a social science bias. The philosophy of this model is a variation of the scientific process and can be summarized by these steps:

1. Observing reality and forming hypotheses about the behavior of an environment's occupants. Why are the occupants reacting to a given environment in a particular way?
2. Designing research methods that allow data to be systematically collected. How can data concerning behavior be gathered to study the hypotheses?
3. Analyzing that data and comparing them to the original hypotheses. What relationships exist between the environment and its occupants?

4. Drawing conclusions about the validity of the original hypotheses. Can general conclusions guide designers in future projects?

The model of post-occupancy evaluation used here is taken from Robert Marans and Kent Spreckelmeyer's *Evaluating Built Environments: A Behavioral Approach* (1981). The scientific approach is followed closely to establish methods by which evaluators and designers can systematically collect information about occupied environments. The evaluation process consists of four independent, yet overlapping, steps (fig. 8-1). In the reconnaissance and information-gathering stage, the evaluator makes preliminary observations of an existing environment. If an office building were being evaluated, the first step would involve informal site visits, interviews with management and supervisory personnel, and establishment of early hypotheses about how certain environments are used by their occupants to accomplish specific tasks.

The research design phase is concerned with how information gathered in reconnaissance is collated and supplemented by systematic data collection procedures. The initial hypotheses are translated into specific, testable issues. One such issue might be how many square feet per work station a worker needs to perform a specific job task. The research hypothesis might be that a minimum floor area of eighty-five square feet is needed. The evaluator would need to design a research procedure to collect data to address this hypothesis.

During the data collection stage, research instruments such as questionnaires, interviews, systematic observations, light and noise

Reconnaissance/Information

Research Design

Data Collection

Documentation/Data Analysis

FIGURE 8-1. A model for post-occupancy evaluation. (Reprinted, by permission, from R. W. Marans and K. F. Spreckelmeyer, *Evaluating Built Environments: A Behavioral Approach* [Ann Arbor: Institute for Social Research, 1981] 11)

meters, and video or time-lapse photography are employed to collect information around issues outlined in research design. Questionnaires dealing with comfort, work-related behavioral criteria, and worker attitudes toward the environment might be administered to clerical workers.

The final step, documentation and data analysis, involves a formal comparison of newly collected data against the original research hypotheses. The information either verifies or modifies the hypotheses and can also be used to establish design criteria for specific environmental attributes. By systematically observing an existing office setting, formulating hypotheses, and collecting information concerning square-footage requirements, an objective standard can be formulated for future square-footage requirements in office environments.

Underlying this model of evaluation is an assumption that people's behavior in buildings can be predicted by measuring specific environmental attributes. A direct and measurable link exists between the environment and how people use that environment. The measurement of these attributes (fig. 8-2) informs the designer of the ways people perceive their environments. Some issues dealt with in the evaluation process are:

- Cost, especially life-cycle costs of buildings
- Functional requirements and circulation

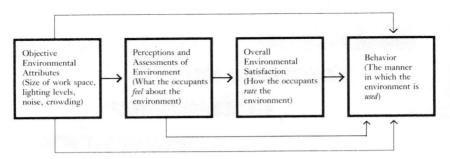

FIGURE 8-2. Conceptual model of environmental behavior. (Reprinted, by permission, from R. W. Marans and K. F. Spreckelmeyer, *Evaluating Built Environments: A Behavioral Approach* [Ann Arbor: Institute for Social Research, 1981] 22)

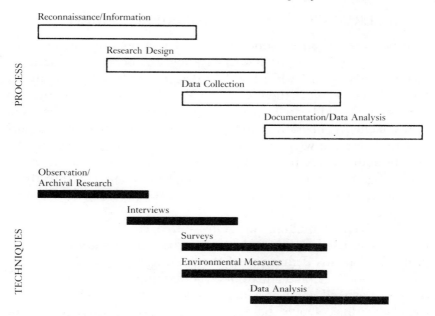

FIGURE 8-3. Sequence of technique usage in evaluation process.

- System performance, especially of heating, ventilating, air conditioning, and passive solar systems
- Human behavior and the response of people to specific environmental conditions
- Ergonomic factors and criteria dealing with the physical requirements of architectural space
- Safety requirements, especially those dealing with fire codes

Evaluation techniques focusing on economic issues were reviewed in chapter 6, while chapter 4 outlined methods for evaluating functional and systems-performance issues. Post-occupancy evaluation techniques are concerned with the behavioral and ergonomic dimensions of design. Five evaluation techniques will be related to the four-step evaluation model just described. These five techniques are used sequentially; each has a particular utility for the evaluator. This sequence, shown in figure 8-3, implies that the evaluator begins the investigation of environmental settings with loosely structured and subjective evaluation methods and moves the investigation into more analytic and narrowly defined techniques.

OBSERVATION AND ARCHIVAL RESEARCH

The purposes of observation are to review a building project's original goals and to assess informally how the occupied building is meeting these goals.[12] If a building design was based primarily on life-cycle economics, then a principal concern of post-occupancy evaluation should be to determine how well the building performs in terms of energy, operating, and maintenance costs. Also, it is important to determine which of the programming goals can most profitably be addressed in post-occupancy evaluations. Goals stated at the beginning of a process do not necessarily lend themselves directly to post-occupancy evaluation; in such cases, the goals may need to be rephrased.

The original building program—often consisting of budgets, functional activities, user inputs, and space-planning guidelines— probably contains definitions of the building's proposed functions, budget guidelines, and square footage requirements. This building program, as well as records describing how the building has been used over time, should be acquired. The records may consist of energy audits, payroll documents, measurements of work areas, and activity logs.

Occupant Response to Present Use

The first action that most evaluation teams take is to observe how the building functions on a daily basis: how people and materials flow through an occupied building, entry sequences, and the use of public spaces within the facility. The evaluator needs to become familiar with the daily rhythms of a building's activities. These unstructured observations will let the evaluation team make mental comparisons of what the building owner wanted and what the building actually allows. These observations should be recorded so that each evaluation team member can make specific judgments of how well the building is meeting the original program goals.

After the initial set of informal observations is completed, the evaluation team should gather to compare notes. At this point detailed descriptions of work areas, density of people in work areas, functional zoning, and furniture arrangements should be prepared. These detailed descriptions will give the team a starting point in determining specific evaluation questions to be addressed during later data collection exercises. Also, general measurements of overall environmental conditions should be conducted, including lighting

Issues to Be Analyzed	*Sources of Information and Analysis Techniques*	
Space requirements	Programming documents On-site measurements Photography of existing conditions (crowding, furniture arrangements)	
Functional efficiency	Programming documents Work logs or production data Time-lapse photography/video taping Observation of people/material flow	
Life-cycle costs	Programming documents Energy bills Construction costs Maintenance logs	
User response to environment	Production data Unobtrusive observation Personnel data (worker turnover, absenteeism)	
Systems performance	Programming Maintenance logs Building "wear and tear" Code checks	

FIGURE 8-4. Observation and archival research checklist.

levels in work areas, task light levels at work stations, heating and cooling levels, noise levels, material wear, and occupant crowding. These measurements in the early stages of evaluation give the team an idea of how the building is responding to use.

Establishment of Evaluation Issues

The team then prepares a list of specific evaluation issues, the most obvious being the original programming goals; other issues will emerge from observations made by the evaluation team, evident through building use during occupancy. Research issues can be segregated into two distinct categories: quantitative and qualitative attributes of an environment. Quantitative attributes consist of issues dealing with the size of activity areas, density of people within the areas, distances between activities, and environmental comfort levels. Quantitative issues can be measured explicitly.

Qualitative attributes deal with human behavior and the human factors of building performance: the movement of people through the building, activity zones, use areas, and attitudes and perceptions about the building. These issues will begin to determine the type of research needed to investigate particular building aspects. Not all issues can be investigated with neatly packaged measurement instruments. It may be necessary to design data-collection techniques that deal with the subjective and specialized aspects of building usage.

Establishment of Research Hypotheses

Specific research hypotheses should emerge from the observation and information-gathering stages, hypotheses that will be tested during the remainder of the evaluation. The purpose here is to investigate the degree to which stated or implicit programming goals are being satisfied by an occupied building. Hypotheses should cover each programming goal uncovered during observation and information gathering.

Specific problem areas and positive aspects of the environment should be recorded with photography and sketches. Such records will be useful during data collection to compare early subjective evaluations with more detailed descriptions of how specific areas within the building are functioning. The statement of hypotheses assumes that the evaluation team has made some initial assessment of the success or failure of the building in meeting specific program goals. For example, a hypothesis might state that certain work areas had been undersized during the programming process and, consequently, work tasks are being frustrated. This assessment is the result of a subjective evaluation and will be tested further on in the process.

INTERVIEWS

One of the most critical periods of the evaluation process outlined in figure 8-3 is the time that elapses between information gathering and the completion of research design. This is when the evaluator will define research issues and construct measurement techniques to test specific research hypotheses, setting the direction of the evaluation effort. Interviewing of the occupants, owners, and designers of an environment is useful for validating or modifying research hypotheses and further expanding the evaluator's subjective assessments.[13]

An interview can be conducted between a questioner and a person being questioned or it might consist of a group discussion between the evaluation team and an audience of building occupants—anything from a private conversation to a press conference. The interview is an opportunity to uncover new information and allow the interviewee(s) to expand the research issues compiled by the evaluation team during observation and information gathering.

For example, if the team feels that the lack of programmed work areas in an office building impedes the performance of office workers, a small and informed sample of building occupants should be asked general questions about this. An area supervisor might be queried about the ability of his or her employees to perform certain tasks. Office occupants should be asked about crowding, comfort, privacy, and productivity. Finally, a number of occupants should be asked very subjective questions: "Are you satisfied with your work space?" "What do you like (or dislike) most about your work area?" If the results indicate that (1) the supervisor feels the work load cannot be met in the building, (2) office workers have perceptions of crowding and little privacy, or (3) the occupants uniformly dislike their environment, the evaluation team can assume that the initial hypothesis regarding a lack of programmed work space in the building is valid and worthy of objective evaluation efforts.

Simply *looking* at a building and how people use it often provides insufficient or inadequate information. What may appear to the evaluator as "crowded," "poorly lit," or "small" may in fact be "roomy," "bright," and "spacious" to the people in the environment. Interviews bridge gaps between those who are *affected* by environments—the occupants and clients—and those who must *measure* the effects of environments.[14]

People to Interview

A general rule in determining the number and kind of people to be interviewed is that only those people who have a general and broad view of a building's performance should be interviewed. This is because the main purpose of conducting interviews is to validate and expand research issues, processes that require interviewees to be familiar with a wide variety of environmental concerns. Decision makers—the architect who designed the building, the client who commissioned it, and the manager who operates it—are obvious candidates. The building owner may be able to provide insight into why the total area of office work space was decreased. People who are not directly concerned with the management of a building project should be questioned also during the interview process. This means that a small, representative sample of building occupants should be included in the process. The purpose of interviewing is not to test exhaustively all research hypotheses or to limit the investigation of issues to narrow building constituencies. If the entire population affected by a building were to be interviewed, definitive answers to an infinite number of questions would be provided. It is unfeasible in even a moderately sized project to expect the evaluator to have time to contact everyone who lives in, works in, or is otherwise connected with the building. Representatives of the occupants, therefore, should be selected either by a process of equity (the occupants choose a spokesperson) or randomly (for example, every thirty-fifth person on the building roster). This should ensure that a broad constituency of occupants has input into the early evaluative process.

Content of Interviews

Interviews should be designed to elicit a wide range of opinions. The interviews should probe into the evaluation issues. Open-ended questions will *invite* the response of the person being interviewed. The person being questioned should not be limited to simple "yes/ no" or "satisfied/dissatisfied" responses but should rather be presented with an issue and asked to enlighten the interviewer with his or her opinion. Since interviews are almost always performed face to face, the interviewer must guide the conversation in a direction that is meaningful to the respondent. For example, the interviewer may begin with, "What is your opinion concerning the amount of floor area in office X?" and be led by the response of the person being interviewed into a discussion of the merits of giving each worker in office X a private cubicle. The interviewer should view this process as an exploration of issues and should not discourage the introduction of new ideas and concepts.

Issues should be presented to the respondent in a neutral and

People to Interview	Information	
Designers/ programmers	Design concepts Program/design objectives Function and space requirements Systems selection Budgets	
Clients/ owners	Organizational goals Budgets Operating costs Efficiency of environment Return on investment	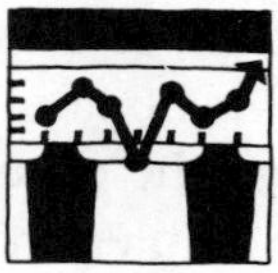
Building users	Environmental comfort Efficiency of environment Building aesthetics Work productivity	
Contractors	Ease of construction Completeness of detailing Change orders Profitability of job	
Building maintenance staff	Systems performance Maintainability Building operations Energy costs	

FIGURE 8-5. Interview checklist.

unbiased manner. Although the evaluation team may have established definitive assessments of the various aspects of a building, the purpose of the interview is to independently verify or reject these initial judgments. If the above question had been posed as "Don't you think the floor area in office X is too small?" the interviewer is trying to elicit a certain answer and, depending on how timid or combative the interviewee is, may predetermine a reactive response. Questions should simply introduce a general topic and allow the respondent to expand on that topic in a variety of ways. The questions should be arranged in categories that address broad evaluative issues. Discussions should begin with general issues and be reinforced with questions that help the respondent focus on more specific environmental issues. Finally, the interview should contain questions that encourage the respondent to introduce new topics and expand the list of evaluation hypotheses. An interview should end with a question like, "Is there anything that has not been discussed that you feel is an important factor in this building?" This will help the evaluator complete the range of concerns that may not have become apparent through an analysis of the stated program goals or during the observation phase.

Completion of the interviewing process leads the evaluation team into the tasks of research design. Having validated and expanded the list of research hypotheses through interviewing, the team is now ready to construct specific data collection tools to test and measure how a building is being used. An analysis of interview responses will provide a refined set of evaluative issues and will suggest specific methods that might objectively measure the validity of the hypotheses. These data collection methods will deal with the human and the physical aspects of building performance. The first method measures the perceptions and attitudes of the people who use a building, while the second measures the physical conditions within a building. The purpose of the data collection phase (fig. 8-6) is to compare the physical conditions with the response of people who are affected by these conditions.

SURVEYS

Surveys (also referred to in this discussion as questionnaires) are data collection instruments that address the human dimension of building performance. They help the evaluator establish norms and objective standards of human behavior and performance in buildings. Unlike interviews, they are designed to narrow the range of responses to a research hypothesis in describing the perceptions of building occupants. They are also distinct from interviews in that they collect data from the entire building population and ensure that all responses can be analyzed and measured using a single standard of comparison. Questionnaires, therefore, should be viewed by evaluators as precise statements of the research hypotheses that ask building occupants to respond to narrow and discrete evaluative issues. The power of the

Data about people's
perceptions of an
environment

Data about the
physical conditions
of an environment

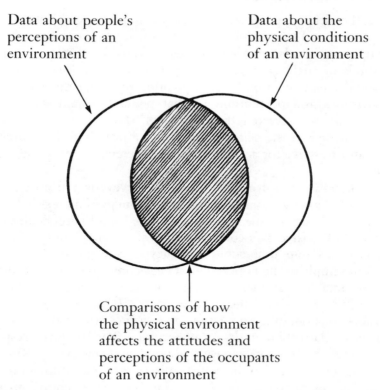

Comparisons of how
the physical environment
affects the attitudes and
perceptions of the occupants
of an environment

FIGURE 8-6. Comparisons of behavioral and physical data. (Reprinted, by permission, from R. W. Marans and K. F. Spreckelmeyer, *Evaluating Built Environments: A Behavioral Approach* [Ann Arbor: Institute for Social Research, 1981] 21)

data collected from surveys depends on the accuracy with which research questions are posed to occupants and the uniformity and number of responses available for analysis.[15]

Whom to Survey

Each person affected either directly or indirectly by a building environment should have the opportunity to express an opinion in a survey. This includes those who work or live in an environment (occupants), those who interact occasionally with the building (visitors to a museum or patrons of a post office), and those who merely experience the building as a visual or functional component of their larger environmental surroundings (the community at large). Because the ultimate purpose of a survey is to measure objectively how people respond to a particular environment, it is necessary to elicit the opinions of a large group of those affected by that environment. Methods of analysis employed in survey research assume that the data collected from a building population represent the entire range of attitudes and perceptions of that population and that general trends can be extracted from the data. This form of analysis is closely linked to the scientific research approach and requires the evaluator to strive for accuracy and completeness during the survey process.

Generally, it is feasible to collect survey data from all those affected by an environment if the population does not exceed 250 to 300 people. Any number greater than this would necessitate a complex and expensive data collection system and may not yield results any more accurate than could be achieved using a carefully selected random sample of the population. The accuracy and repeatability of survey data do not increase proportionately with the size of the survey (fig. 8-7). This means that once 250 to 300 representative members of a building population are surveyed, the evaluator should achieve a relatively high degree of accuracy. For any given response to a survey of 300 representative respondents, chances are 95 out of 100 that the answer will be statistically significant within a range of plus or minus 5 percent. The key to the above statement is *representative*: if only a sample of a large population is surveyed, it is imperative that the people be selected scientifically to ensure that no *bias* is shown (for example, only men surveyed) and that a *proportionate number* representing each major activity or social group is included. These selection criteria are captured in the terms "random" and "stratified" population samples, "random" meaning that a system of statistical chance be employed to eliminate bias and "stratified" meaning that a percentage of every major building occupant or user group be represented in the sample.

The concept of random sampling is especially important when opinions are sought from not only the building occupants but also the people who are affected indirectly by an environment. In the case of an office building, it may be useful to determine the responses of people who visit the building to conduct business and even the people who walk past the building. This community response depends on a large survey population and probably can only be tapped through carefully selected procedures. In the case of visi-

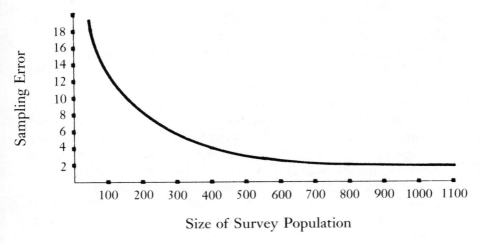

FIGURE 8-7. Sampling error.

tors, a specific number of people entering the building may be surveyed at the site. How these people are selected would depend on the number of surveys the evaluator determines is necessary to give an accurate view of the building and on the random selection techniques used. This is also the case in regard to populations that may be anonymous to the evaluator. A building client may want to know how a large portion of the community views this environment; opinions might be elicited by using directories of residents such as telephone books and visitor lists. A random sample of respondents could be drawn from these lists, and survey forms mailed or phone surveys conducted to gather data.

Survey Contents

Because surveys aim to gather data in response to specific research questions, the questions should address focused topics. The responses are generally closed ended in that a predetermined range of answers is offered to a respondent in order to be able to standardize the data. For example, the issue of work station size may surface during the interviewing process and a hypothesis established that implies that the amount of space in a work area is too small for the tasks being performed. Questions in the survey should attempt to measure users' levels of satisfaction with their work stations and to determine how these occupants perceive their work area size. The interview is designed to *uncover* an issue; the survey is designed to *measure* and *test* the hypothesis associated with that issue.

Because questionnaires are generally returned anonymously to the evaluator for analysis, the format must be clear and unambiguous. Each question should address only *one* issue, and the range of responses for each question should cover all possible answers to this issue. Possible responses to questions can be found in standardized formats that have been used in similar survey instruments. Marans and Spreckelmeyer's survey of the Ann Arbor Federal Building modeled its questions after those found in Lou Harris's 1978 national study of office workers. The Ann Arbor questionnaire was modified for use in a number of succeeding office studies and will be used in future studies as well. (For samples of this instrument, see fig. 10-14).

The benefits of standardizing and revising survey questions are many. First, since the questions have been used in a number of previous studies, the response categories have been tested with a large number of building occupants. Second, the data collected in the current study can be compared to research results from the previous studies. Third, research issues in one building type tend to be of concern in similar buildings, providing a basis for evaluation comparisons. Finally, standardized response categories help the evaluator frame questions that address specific research issues. Using pretested survey questions and building on data collected previously are important features of the evaluation process.

Responses from people who use and occupy buildings will generally fall under the heading of qualitative data. The data are qualitative in the sense that, although the questions are answered with limited and standardized responses, the answers in fact measure only the subjective feelings and opinions of these people. There is no quantitative measure of a person's satisfaction with an environment, although a closed-ended survey question may produce a single, discrete response in one of the four categories *very satisfied, satisfied, dissatisfied,* or *very dissatisfied.* The fact that a respondent answers *satisfied* does not mean that this response indicates a uniform level of satisfaction. For this reason, a number of different survey questions should attempt to elicit responses from building users concerning a particular issue. To measure a person's satisfaction with the amount of working space in an office, several questions should address this subject. The following sequence of questions might be posed:

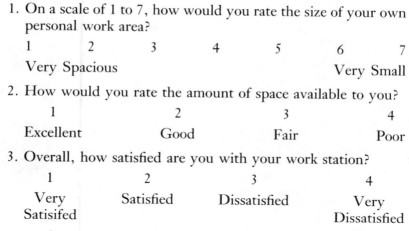

1. On a scale of 1 to 7, how would you rate the size of your own personal work area?

1	2	3	4	5	6	7
Very Spacious						Very Small

2. How would you rate the amount of space available to you?

1	2	3	4
Excellent	Good	Fair	Poor

3. Overall, how satisfied are you with your work station?

1	2	3	4
Very Satisifed	Satisfied	Dissatisfied	Very Dissatisfied

It can be seen that although all the above survey questions deal with work station size, each allows the respondent to think of size in a slightly different way. The first question addresses spatial scale. The second prompts the user to think of the work area in terms of relative value, implying that the area itself may have some intrinsic "goodness" or may in fact be unacceptable. The third question asks the respondent to examine his or her own set of expectations and make a judgment about the degree of satisfaction he or she experiences. If a respondent were to answer "small," "poor," and "very dissatisfied" on the above questions, the evaluator can assume that the amount of space in that particular work area is inadequate.

Survey Administration

Surveys can be administered to building users in a variety of ways: self-administered printed forms to fill out and return to a central collection point, face to face, telephone surveys, or short forms to fill out as people enter a building. In selecting a method the evaluator must consider (1) accuracy of data, (2) response rate, and (3) anonymity.

Accuracy should be a major concern of the evaluator during the research design phase of the evaluation process and is primarily concerned with pretesting the survey instrument. A small sample of the survey population or a sample of a similar set of building users should answer the questions in the same manner that the larger survey will be administered. Such a pretest will highlight ambiguous questions and reveal incongruities in response categories. It will also

Survey Issues	General Guidelines	
Whom to survey	Each group affected by environment Feasible to survey 250 to 300 building occupants Insure representative sample	
Survey contents	Focused and specific topics Standardized response categories Surveys from similar building types (comparison data) Limited number of open-ended questions	
Survey administration	Pretest survey instrument Type of survey (self-administered, face to face, telephone) Accuracy of response data Response rates Confidentiality of respondents	
Topics to address	Population characteristics (age, sex, length of time in building, job setting) Opinions of immediate work area (desk, chair, work surface, office size) Satisfaction with specific attributes (privacy, comfort, lighting) Overall opinions of building (aesthetics, size, access, function) Occupant activities	

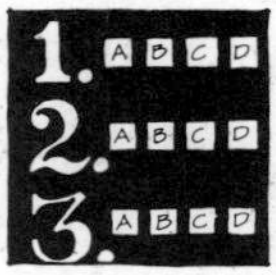

FIGURE 8-8. Survey checklist.

give the evaluation team a sense of the possible range of answers that might be expected from the larger survey population. If one question is answered in exactly the same way by all respondents, it may be an unnecessary or redundant question that will provide little useful information in the larger survey.

The response rate is the percentage of questionnaires that are completed and returned by the building users. Ideally, the evaluator would like to see a 100 percent response rate, but will probably have to settle for between 70 and 90 percent. The return rate can be maximized if the respondents have an incentive to complete the survey and the format is easy to understand. Incentive can be fostered by explaining the survey process to the building users ahead of time. A cover letter can be sent to potential respondents to explain the importance of participating in the process. A face-to-face interview probably most gives a respondent the feeling that his or her opinion is important. This is also the most costly and time-consuming survey method and must often be supplanted by a self-administered, written questionnaire. A self-administered questionnaire should not take more than thirty minutes to complete, nor should a face-to-face interview exceed an hour. Survey questions should be limited to those that the respondent is capable of answering directly.

Finally, for respondents to feel free to answer questions, confidentiality must be assured in the survey process. An outside, disinterested party administering the survey will help convince respondents that the answers they give to the research questions will be used only for statistical purposes and that their individual answers will not come back to haunt them.

OBJECTIVE ENVIRONMENTAL MEASURES

While survey questions are being formulated during the research design, data collection instruments must be prepared to record and measure the physical attributes of an environment.[16] In order to verify the accuracy and completeness of a research hypothesis, data must be collected from both the people who occupy and use an environment as well as from the environment itself. Hypothesizing that a work area in an office is too small to accommodate a particular set of activities, it would be necessary to measure the attitudes of the workers who use that area and also to measure exactly the permutations of "work-station size." "Size" may have a number of dimensions—floor area, desk-top area, office volume, height of work surface—each of which must be measured during the evaluation process.

Environmental Attributes

The attributes of an environment are the physical characteristics that collectively shape and color the fabric of buildings. A partial list of attributes includes:

- Ambient and task lighting levels and sources
- Comfort levels such as temperature, humidity, and air flow
- Ambient sound levels and noise sources
- Sizes and configuration of functional activity areas
- Density of people and objects in building areas
- Color, texture, and reflective qualities of surfaces
- Flow and movement of people and objects through building areas
- Wear-and-tear qualities of finish surfaces

These attributes will generally be grouped under quantitative data because they are concerned with explicit and uniform building measurements. The floor area of an occupant's work station can be quantified precisely in terms of square feet, while that person's attitudes can only be approximated with survey methods.

While environmental attributes can be measured more precisely than the human perceptions of buildings, the quantification of building attributes is not a simple process. Even in measuring the square footage of a work station, the limits of the work station are subject to a number of interpretations. Does it include the entire area bounded by the person's office walls, or is it the immediate work space around a desk? How is personal work space defined for occupants of open-office environments? Should ambient light be measured with indirect natural lighting conditions, or should lighting levels be measured only under artificial conditions? To collect environmental data that will accurately describe a building's characteristics, the following steps should be taken:

1. Measure the conditions that pertain to a specific research hypothesis. Focus on questions that have been posed to the building users, and limit the number of attributes that will be quantified.
2. Account for fluctuation in attributes due to changes in season, human use, and climate. The measurement of most attributes will depend on a number of time-related variables that will cause the characteristics of buildings to appear dynamic and unpredictable.
3. Isolate the attributes of an environment into as many independent measures as possible. Environments are used by their occupants in highly complex ways. An office cannot be analyzed as if it were a laboratory because of the intricate pattern

of social and physical relationships that exist in real-life situations. Instead of simply measuring the "lighting level" at an occupant's work area, discrete measures—task lighting, morning lighting, cloudy-day lighting, ambient lighting— should be made to provide an accurate picture of the complex meaning of lighting.

Attribute Measurements

Because environmental attributes involve objective descriptions of buildings, they are associated with definitive and universally understood measures. Areas of building activities and size of building fixtures are defined in square-footage and linear dimensions. Noise and ambient sound levels can be recorded with calibrated audiometers and readings can be established in weighted decibel categories. Lighting levels can be measured by either average footcandle readings or by sensitive ESI meters that account for reflectivity and glare conditions. Colors and textures of finished building surfaces can be categorized using standard chromatic and reflectivity charts. Even more subjective building attributes, such as the number and type of objects within a building area, can be recorded and counted using time-lapse photography and video techniques. The key to collecting such information generally lies not in instrumentation but in how the data are collected. If an evaluator were to quantify the whole range of attributes within a building over an extended time, he or she would acquire a comprehensive but probably unmanageable and grossly expensive data set. The objective environmental data collected during an evaluation should be limited to only the information needed to address specific issues.

The accuracy of these data should be such that generalizations about the environmental attributes of a building can be made and an overall picture of the physical conditions within an environment can be constructed. Data can be collected *directly* and *indirectly*. Direct methods require the continuous physical presence of the evaluator in the environment throughout the collection process. The evaluator must perform detailed measurements—such as taking light-meter readings under varying conditions directly in the environment. Indirect methods involve measuring scaled plans or diagrams and do not require the evaluator's physical presence at the building site. Measuring square footage data from furniture plans or counting people in specific building areas using photographic sources are examples of indirect data collection methods. Direct methods will generally yield accurate and detailed data, but are time consuming and disruptive to occupants. Indirect methods, while not as precise, allow the evaluator to study and measure building attributes more rapidly and less obtrusively.

The degree of accuracy of a data collection technique is described as *site-specific* or *zonal*. Site-specific accuracy defines conditions that can be measured at only one specific place in an environment. The measurement of a condition may be so sensitive that major discrepancies in data readings may exist within a very small building area. Fluctuations in readings of task lighting on a desk top, for example, may vary from twenty-five to eighty-five footcandles within the space of a few inches, depending on the direction of the light source, shadow patterns, and surface reflectivities. Zonal measurements of attributes depend less on a constricted area of an environment. Ambient light levels—the general intensity of illumination in a large building area—vary much less from one area to another in comparison with the focused quality of task lights at specific work areas. The same distinction can be made with reference to accurate measurement of the velocity and direction of drafts in an auditorium and the more general recording of ambient temperature and humidity there. Figure 8-9 summarizes how a number of data collection methods might be used to record specific environmental attributes, while figure 8-10 is a checklist of objective measures taken in the computer-center evaluation discussed in chapter 10.

Environmental attributes should be measured in tandem with collection of survey data. Since the purpose is to measure environmental conditions in relation to the perceptions of the people who use that environment, it is important that environmental and survey data be consistent. This means that the data collection from the surveys should be correlated accurately with the measurements of the conditions that affect those perceptions. Attributes that surround the survey population should be measured at the time the survey is administered, especially if those attributes are specifically addressed by the survey questions. Time-dependent and dynamic characteristics of the environment are also considered in data collection in order to account for perceptions that may not be specifically tied to a single measurement of the environment but depend on an "average" or "overall" environmental condition.

Direct	Indirect
Temperature (Z)	Amount of workspace (W)
Relative humidity (Z)	Density of workspace (W)
Light level (W)	Type of workspace (W)
Noise level (Z)	Glare condition (W)
Style of chair (W)	Distance to window (W)
Use of task lighting (W)	Distance to lightwell (W)
Use of extension cords (W)	Distance to entrance (W)
Use of personal objects (W)	Distance to coffee station (W)

Note: Z represents measures made in zones within a building. These measures were then assigned to individual work stations within the respective zone. W represents measures covering individual work stations.

FIGURE 8-9. Types of environmental measures. (Reprinted, by permission, from R. W. Marans and K. F. Spreckelmeyer, *Evaluating Built Environments: A Behavioral Approach* [Ann Arbor: Institute for Social Research, 1981] 17)

DATA ANALYSIS AND DOCUMENTATION

The final step in evaluation is the interpretation of data collected with the survey and environmental attribute instruments. This requires the evaluator to validate each research hypothesis in light of evidence produced during data collection. The initial observations and value judgments made during information gathering are now supported or modified by knowledge of how building users responded to various attributes of that environment. Data analysis methods are used to summarize and manipulate the survey and environmental information and to indicate to the evaluator the trends or generalizations that can be inferred through the data.[17]

Analysis Techniques

Statistical methods are used to analyze the data and to structure how the data are interpreted. Each person surveyed and each building attribute measured is referred to in statistical terms as a *case*, while each question posed in a questionnaire and each dimension describing the characteristics of an attribute is called a *variable*. If a questionnaire containing 87 questions is administered to 200 building occupants and 185 are completed and returned, the survey data would consist of 185 cases each of which addresses 87 variables. Even such a modest survey produces nearly 16,000 pieces of attitu-

Environmental Inventory of Individual Workstations

Floor _Second/north_ Department _Operations_   Recorder _KFS_ Date _7/7/82_

Survey Number _173_

Type of Workstation

- ☐ I   Private conventional office
- ☐ II   Public reception/secretarial
- ☒ III   Open office, modular dividers, regular work surface
- ☐ IV   Open office, modular dividers, CRT
- ☐ V   Pool office, regular work surface
- ☐ VI   Pool office, CRT
- ☐ VII   Work bench
- ☐ VIII Computer room
- ☐ Other _____ Specify

Amount of Workspace

_36_ Square Feet

Area measured in square feet contiguous to main work surface of worker. Include area occupied by desks, chairs, tables, and other furniture/equipment associated with worker. In enclosed spaces with one worker, area is defined by enclosing walls or partitions. In enclosed or open spaces with multiple workers, area is limited to that containing individual worker's furniture/equipment and space 3'-0" beyond it, unless that space infringes on space of neighboring worker, in which case space is defined as half the distance to nearest furniture/equipment.

Density of Workspace

_6_ Persons/400 SF

Number of people who work within a 400 square foot area whose centroid is in the center of the main work surface.

Light Environmental Zone

- ☐ Closed office with no external natural light
- ☐ Closed office with external natural light
- ☒ Open office and within 20 feet of window
- ☐ Open office and more than 20 feet from window

Temperature/Humidity

1st Reading: _75_ ° _42_ rh   Date: _7/7/82_   Time: _9 a.m._
2nd Reading _76_ ° _40_ rh   Date: _7/7/82_   Time: _8:30 p.m._

Lighting

Ill. 994 Lux 92 F.C.
1st Reading: _ESI 227 Lux 26 F.C._ ☒ Sunny ☐ Hazy ☐ Night Date: _7/7_ Time: _10 a.m._
Ill. 995 Lux 92 F.C.
2nd Reading: _ESI 291 Lux 27 F.C._ ☐ Sunny ☐ Hazy ☒ Night Date: _7/7_ Time: _9 p.m._
3rd Reading: _____ ☐ Sunny ☐ Hazy ☐ Night Date: ____ Time: ____

FIGURE 8-10. Environmental data worksheet.

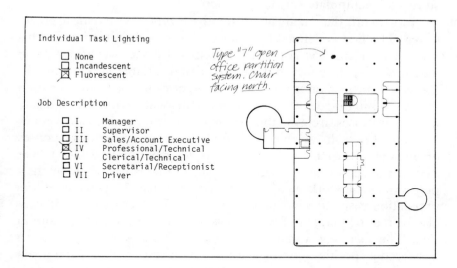

Individual Task Lighting

☐ None
☐ Incandescent
☒ Fluorescent

Job Description

☐ I   Manager
☐ II   Supervisor
☐ III   Sales/Account Executive
☒ IV   Professional/Technical
☐ V   Clerical/Technical
☐ VI   Secretarial/Receptionist
☐ VII   Driver

Type "7" open office partition system. Chair facing *north*.

dinal data. When building attribute measures are added, it becomes apparent that powerful data-processing devices must be employed to store and manipulate this information.

In general, data analysis entails three types of statistical procedures. The first is defined by *frequencies* or *univariate* statistics. This type of data analysis is often referred to by the average or mean measures of each survey and environmental variable. Univariate statistics tell the evaluator the overall content of the data set. For each survey or building attribute variable, statistical frequencies indicate how many cases are available for analysis, the range of answers or measures for each variable, and the aggregate number of responses or measures in each category used to describe the variable. In the case of the survey instrument that asked office workers about their perceptions of work area size, it may be that 27 percent of the population respond that their work areas are "very small." It may also be that 62 percent of work areas are fifty square feet or more in size. The fact that a certain percentage of the survey population answered a specific question with a certain response or that a given number of individual work areas are of a certain size gives the evaluator a general idea of the character of buildings and the perception that people hold in relation to those environments. Univariate analysis techniques rarely suffice to validate the hypotheses of evaluations. If 53 percent of building occupants respond negatively to a particular attribute, does that frequency of response in itself indicate that the attribute is performing poorly? A more detailed analysis is generally necessary before the correctness of the hypothesis can be evaluated.

The second major class of data analysis techniques is *bivariate* statistical methods, which show simple relationships between two research variables. They show simple cause-and-effect relationships. Bivariate analyses also begin to indicate specific trends among variables and variable groupings into larger and more statistically significant patterns. A bivariate analysis might show that, although 53 percent of the total population said that their work areas are too small, the percentage rating this attribute negatively grew to 86 percent among those with fewer than fifty square feet of personal work area. This bivariate analysis, known as a *cross tabulation*, breaks the responses of the research population into categories according to size of respondents' work areas and shows the evaluator the effect that the objective attribute of working area might have on that person's perception of "roominess" or "smallness." A number of specific

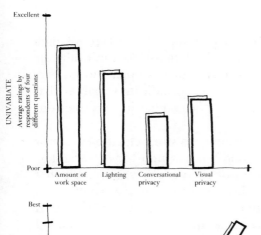

UNIVARIATE

Average ratings by respondents of four different questions

Excellent

Poor

| Amount of work space | Lighting | Conversational privacy | Visual privacy |

Average ratings by an entire population of specific attributes of the environment.

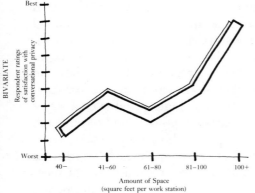

BIVARIATE

Respondent ratings of satisfaction with conversational privacy

Best

Worst

| 40− | 41–60 | 61–80 | 81–100 | 100+ |

Amount of Space
(square feet per work station)

How certain ratings of the environment were matched with the actual conditions that the respondents had at their work stations.

How a number of attributes and ratings by the respondents help to predict overall satisfaction with their work stations (table below)

Satisfaction with Work Station, Predicted by Objective Work Station Attributes and Evaluation of Work Station Attributes (Multiple Classification Analyses; N = 194)

MULTIVARIATE

Predictors	Eta Coefficient	Beta Coefficient[a]			
		Employee Characteristics Only	Employee Characteristics and Attribute Ratings	Employee Characteristics and Objective Attributes	Employee Characteristics, Objective Attributes, and Attribute Ratings
Employee characteristics					
Agency	.28	.34(1)	.17(5)	.20(3)	.39(2)
Job classification	.24	.26(2)	.28(2)	.20(4)	.27(5)
Objective attributes					
Amount of workspace	.39			.49(1)	.50(1)
Chair type	.33			.19(5)	.16(8)
Work station type	.25			.25(2)	.36(3)
Window condition	.26			.14(6)	.31(4)
Attribute ratings					
Aesthetic quality	.38		.18(4)		.15(9)
Space	.33		.29(1)		.26(6)
Conversational privacy	.30		.15(6)		.14(10)
View outside	.21		.19(3)		.17(7)
Percentage of variance explained					
(adjusted multiple R²)		11.2	30.6	25.5	41.1
(unadjusted multiple R²)		15.4	38.3	34.3	52.1

[a] Numbers in parentheses indicate ranking of importance.

FIGURE 8-11. Data analysis examples. (Reprinted, by permission, from R. W. Marans and K. F. Spreckelmeyer, *Evaluating Built Environments: A Behavioral Approach* [Ann Arbor: Institute for Social Research, 1981] 167)

bivariate techniques are available, depending on the type of data available for analysis and the kinds of relationships the evaluator wishes to uncover. A *correlation* analysis, for example, can be performed on certain classes of data in order to indicate variables that are closely related to or correlated with one another in a given evaluation.

Finally, *multivariate* analysis techniques can help the evaluator explain complex relationships among a larger number of variables. In any environment, the responses of the people who inhabit that environment are affected by a wide array of building attributes and social conditions. The investigation of simple bivariate relationships between only a single survey variable and a single environmental measure may not tell the complete story as to why a set of respondents answered as they did. Multivariate analysis provides a deeper understanding of research hypotheses. It allows the evaluator to combine a number of causal variables—known as *independent variables*—to show their collective effect on a single variable or a set of dependent variables. Because multivariate methods tend to be much more powerful than bivariate techniques in how they explain complex relationships in the data set, they are sometimes referred to as *predictive* statistics. An evaluator may use several independent measures of the concept of "size"—actual square footage measurements, density of occupancy, and subjective human ratings of scale—to predict the effect these measures might have on a single dependent indicator of how satisfied respondents are with their work spaces. A multivariate analysis of this data set would begin to indicate which independent variables are significant predictors of how the occupants of a particular environment respond to or perceive their environment.

No single statistical method will provide a definitive answer to an evaluation hypothesis. It is rarely possible for the evaluator to assert with certainty the reasons people respond to environmental conditions in any given situation. The purpose of data analysis is to provide the evaluator with as much information as possible so that an informed decision can be made based on how people perceive and react to their surroundings.

CONCLUSION

Post-occupancy evaluation techniques convert environments into laboratories that provide designers with verifiable information about how people use and perceive those environments. The most important product of an evaluation of an existing environment is objective information that will inform designers about specific decisions to be made in future design problems. The methodology that has been outlined in this chapter is based on the premise that subjective and intuitive observations of existing environments can be reinforced or modified with objective facts and data that answer carefully defined research hypotheses.

Evaluation methodologies and data collection techniques are used throughout the design process, although they are probably best employed during the early stages of the feasibility cycle. They help the designer formulate programmatic information by using existing environmental conditions as design guides and models. In chapter 10, an extensive post-occupancy case study illustrates the use of the above techniques.

NOTES

1. The term "post-occupancy evaluation" is an unfortunate tag for this technique. Although it is commonly understood in the environmental research literature, it misleads the layperson. The term actually defines the research and investigation of *occupied* environments and the study of the ways that buildings are *currently* being used by their occupants. See Davis and Szigeti (1986) for more complete definition.

2. Friedman, Zimring, and Zube (1978) outline a number of historical developments in design evaluation and describe the overall theory of post-occupancy evaluation.

3. Most techniques associated with post-occupancy evaluation have been taken from the social or behavioral sciences. Specific methods outlined in this chapter will be referenced to detailed descriptions or techniques that can be found in Bechtel et al. (1987).

4. The techniques and theories of design evaluation can be found in either the annual proceedings of the EDRA conferences or in *Environment and Behavior*, edited and produced by members of EDRA. The reader's attention is also drawn to evaluation studies that have been recognized in the annual *Progressive Architecture* Research Awards program, especially between the years of 1975 and 1986.

5. See Conway (1973) for a complete description of the conference.

6. The introduction of the "designated services" owner-architect contract by the American Institute of Architects made specialized pre- and post-design services practical within the architectural design process.

7. Refer to *Architectural Record* (1978) for a description of U.S. congressional action in building evaluation. See Law (1984) for a review of evaluation studies in Australia and New Zealand.

8. The Easter Hill Village study by Cooper (1975) is widely regarded as a landmark evaluation that set critical standards for subsequent post-occupancy studies.

9. Manning (1965) is a good source for those interested in studying the early development of building evaluation theories and methodologies.

10. The Marans and Spreckelmeyer study (1981) provides a detailed review of a post-occupancy model and illustrates the model through a single case study. Sample data collection instruments and data analysis methods are included throughout the text.

11. This study is ongoing at the time of this publication. An interim report on the progress of this evaluation can be found in Wineman and Zimring (1986).

12. See Zeisel (1981) and chapter 1 in Bechtel et al. (1987) for further information on observation and archival research methods.

13. Refer to chapter 2 in Bechtel et al. (1987) for a review of interview techniques in design.

14. Spradley (1979) provides a number of ethnographic techniques to aid researchers in the collection of interview data.

15. See chapter 2 by Robert Marans in Bechtel et al. (1987) for an excellent summary of social survey theories and techniques. This material includes detailed guides and formats of questionnaire development and administration in environmental research problems.

16. Marans and Spreckelmeyer (1981) discuss in detail and illustrate a number of the objective environmental measurement techniques outlined in this chapter.

17. Data analysis techniques are closely linked with statistics and are not easily reviewed in a text such as this. The examples given in this chapter are introductory in nature. Refer to Bechtel et al. (1987) for a more complete description of statistical methods.

CHAPTER 9

Communication

THE PURPOSE of communication techniques in the decision-making process is to transmit the nature of a problem to the people who must act during the design process and to make explicit the consequences of actions taken by the design team. This implies that decision makers are able to transmit ideas among themselves and to communicate their decisions to a wide range of clients and building users. Communication techniques set a firm foundation for understanding the nature and content of the problem to be solved.

These techniques also are used to predict the outcomes of a design decision. Decision makers must be able to communicate to one another the important outcomes of each decision made during design in order to measure that decision's validity. Most of the techniques that have been described in this book are concerned with selecting and evaluating design alternatives. Communication techniques are used to insure that all design team members clearly understand the nature and content of those alternatives. Because the consequences of design alternatives are often difficult to envision during early stages of design, communication techniques can be used to simulate those consequences.

Communication techniques create a framework into which the decisions of the design team can be placed. This framework will allow the design team to manipulate the variables of a problem and to predict the effects that changes in those variables may cause.

HISTORY

Communication techniques in architecture and design historically have been concerned with graphic and verbal transmission of design ideas from the designer to a client group. Design decisions have often been communicated from designers to building clients solely through graphic means: perspective drawings, plans, building sections, and building elevations. The impact on decision making has been primarily tied to visual issues; other factors that may be important to the design process often have been overlooked.[1]

To account for the less visual aspects of design projects (costs, the impact of technology on communication patterns in buildings, social and environmental issues, and the historical significance of buildings), new communication techniques have recently been developed in architecture.[2] The designer has sometimes been replaced by communication experts, and clients have viewed these techniques as having little impact on the design process. For example, life-cycle cost analysts and value engineers have developed costing techniques and energy cost models as tools for describing the impact of design decisions on long-term and recurring buildings costs. These techniques, however, do not fit the typical mold of architectural presentations in that the primary means of communication has been numerical and statistical analyses rather than graphics. Because the architect has often been supplanted by the value engineer or the social scientist in explaining the important consequences of design projects, the designer now needs to become fluent in the nongraphic languages of the design process so that the entire range of decisions can be brought under his or her control.[3]

Recent developments in information-processing technologies have made it possible for designers to improve their ability to communicate with complex and nongraphic media. These techniques allow vast quantities of data to be stored, retrieved, and manipulated by the designer and displayed to building users and owners in a variety of formats. The microcomputer, for example, provides the designer with a variety of analytical tools that previously were the province of specialized consultants. New visual media, which allow a design problem to be viewed in a dynamic as well as a static time frame, are also becoming available to architects. Computer-aided design, video reproduction, and animation are new means of utilizing data-processing technologies to increase and expand the designer's ability to communicate complex and dynamic ideas of spatial configurations. Electronic transmission of ideas through telenetworking and conference calling is also making it possible for designers to communicate with larger numbers of decision makers throughout the design process.[4]

It seems likely that designers will rely more heavily on electronic communication techniques in the future. The traditional graphic means of presenting ideas are being replaced by more dynamic and realistic media. The ability of designers to deal with more and varied design solutions through computer-aided design and video techniques will allow designers to expand their role in the decision-making process. This, coupled with data-processing storage capabilities, will enable the designer to expand the number of alternatives that can be presented to client groups and to increase the designer's ability to evaluate those alternatives critically.

THEORY

The concept of modeling is central to the use of communication techniques in design. Modeling involves the representation of realistic alternatives or built environments through the use of symbols. Models enable designers to simulate—cheaply and rapidly—a proposed environment before it is built. The various types of models available to designers will determine, to a large extent, the most appropriate technique for communicating a particular design problem or decision-making situation.[5]

Symbolic Models

The most abstract and general forms of models available to designers are symbolic. Generally associated with mathematical representations of reality, they help designers in problems that require specific, narrow answers to design questions involving limited numbers of independent design variables. Queueing models, which are mathematical representations of the speed with which people and objects move through space, can be used to describe accurately the behavior of people using a waiting line—or queue—at an airport check-out counter or a bank teller position. They provide accurate representations of how spaces are used by people over a specified period of time. Their main disadvantage is that they describe only one activity (that is, the movement of people within a waiting line), not a complex set of behavioral interactions. They do not, for example, tell the designer anything about the area or size of space that people in line occupy.

Symbolic models, therefore, are useful to designers when accurate descriptions of limited types of human behaviors are required. Employing mathematics or other forms of symbolic language, symbolic models are used to communicate design ideas that are limited in scope in situations where the number of design variables are easily quantified or defined. Figure 9-1 illustrates the use of a time chart to represent the progress of work steps in the design process. Here the designer is interested in only one variable—time—and uses the length of a bar chart to represent length of work activities. Other symbolic models might be the simple algebraic equation of a beam formula or the verbal description of an activity area in a program statement.

Analogue Models

Analogue models, which use one symbol or representation to simulate the real object or attribute that is being designed, are less abstract and more closely represent reality than do symbolic models. Better than symbolic models at simulating the behavior of complex concepts, analogue models are appropriate means of communicating concepts in problems with variables that are difficult to manipulate with quantitative mathematical or verbal symbols.

The most common use of analogue models in design communication technique is the two-dimensional drawing of building design products—for example, of topographical features using contour lines on a site plan (fig. 9-2). Analogue models are relatively inexpensive to produce and are useful for communicating graphic ideas. Their primary disadvantage is that, since they use one form of reality to represent the object itself, it is often difficult to simulate concepts such as movement or time.

Analogue models have been successful in communicating ideas that can be readily understood by large numbers of decision makers during early stages of design decisions: for example, site plans and elevation representations of a building project are used to provide general images of the layout of activity spaces and the disposition of functions within building plans. Analogue models are successful at communicating the distribution of spatial configurations throughout a design scheme. Although less accurate than symbolic models in presenting a limited number of environmental dimensions, they are basic tools for communicating graphic and visual ideas in the design process.

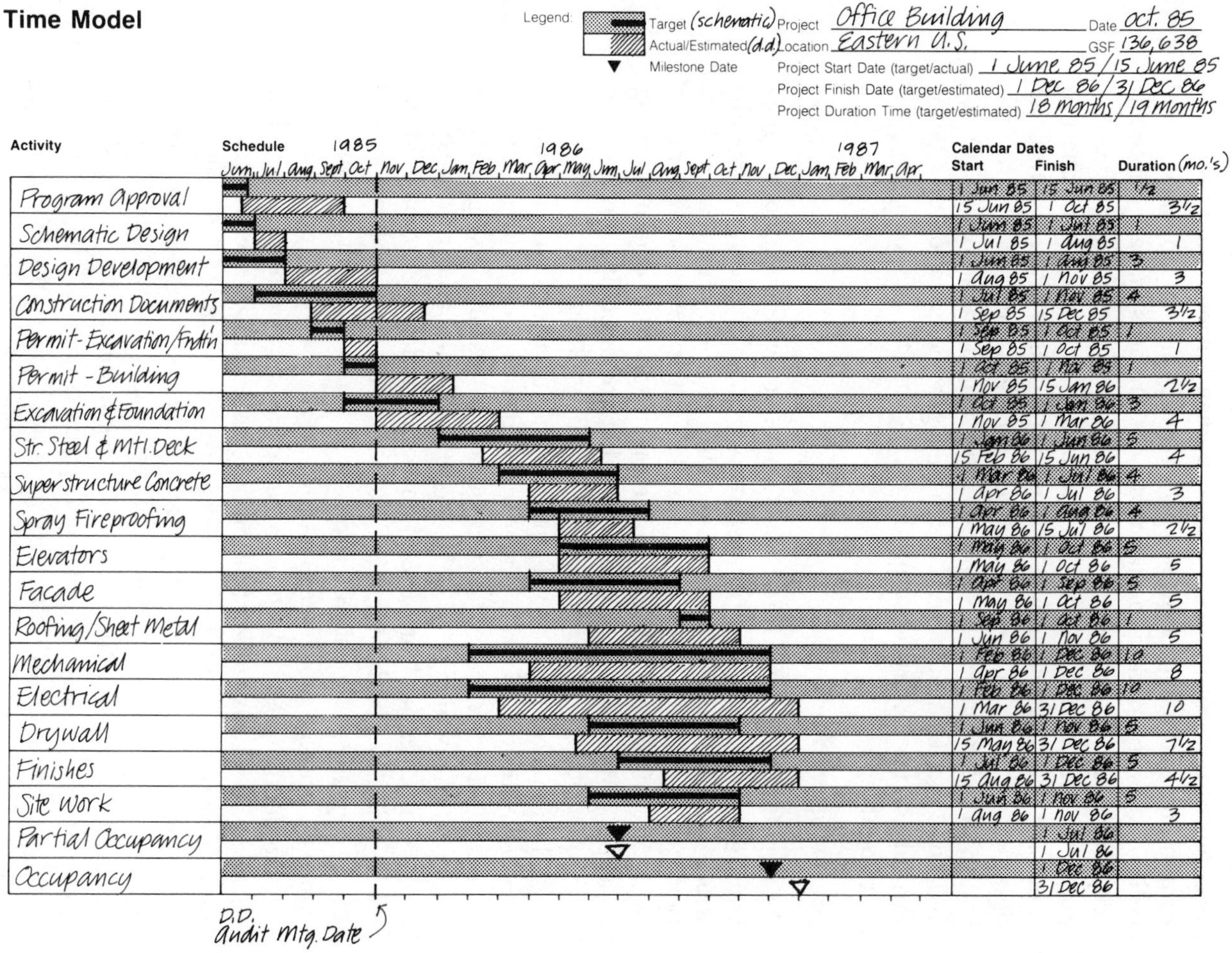

Time Model

FIGURE 9-1. Time model.

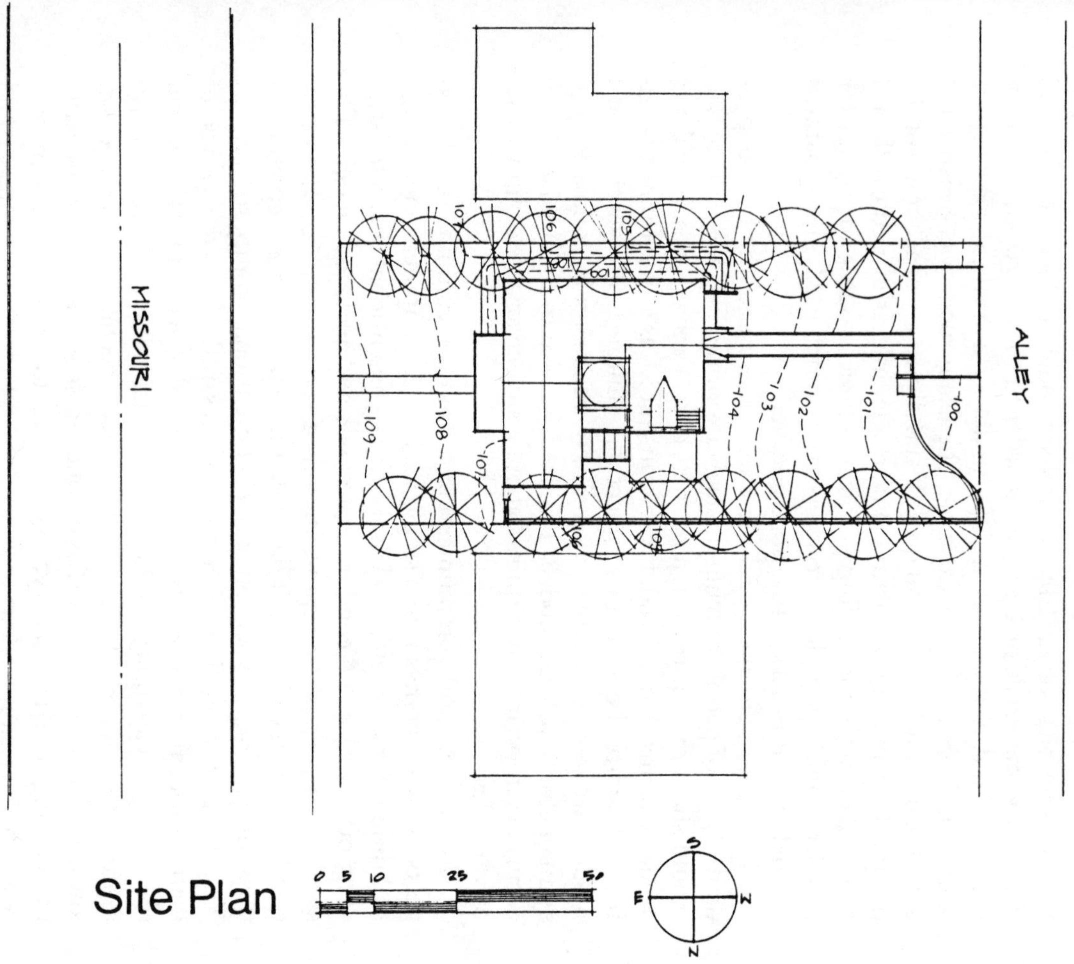
ALLEY
MISSOURI
100
101
102
103
104
105
106
107
108
109
Site Plan
0
5
10
25
50
S
E
W
N

FIGURE 9-2. Site plan drawing.

Iconic Models

Constituting the most concrete and tangible form of architectural communication, iconic models use the characteristics of a real object to represent that object. Iconic scaled models reduce the size and change the materials of a project in order to show three-dimensional character and massing (as in the model of a medical exam room shown in fig. 9-3). In this example, the exam room was constructed at full scale to test the spatial quality and dimensional accuracy of the design. It is an example of an iconic model in that it used cardboard to simulate wall and ceiling surfaces. Iconic models are useful for problems with complex variables that cannot easily be separated or analyzed in isolation from one another.

Where a queueing model accurately represents the time-dependent nature of people moving through a waiting line, an iconic model would show the entire design of an airport waiting lobby in real and accurate terms. Iconic models can transmit ideas that require a tangible link with the designed object or building. However, iconic models are generally more expensive to construct in comparison to symbolic or analogue models and are less easy to manipulate when accurate information is required about a single variable or limited set of variables.

Most successful communication techniques combine several aspects of these models into a single format. A computer-aided design technique, for example, models the three-dimensional characteristics of an office space and combines symbolic and analogue models. The symbolic aspect is the representation of spaces in the computer by numbers and equations. The analogue aspect is the depiction of three-dimensional space on a two-dimensional computer screen. This type of modeling, therefore, successfully uses the power of mathematics to represent three-dimensional space symbolically and the analogue capability of the two-dimensional television screen to represent the physical view of that space. Techniques outlined below combine several types of symbolic, analogue, and iconic models. In deciding on particular types of models to use in the design process, the decision maker will need to weigh the advantages and disadvantages of each model type for given design problems. In the design of a cardiac-care unit in a hospital, for example, the decision may be made to spend a great deal of money and energy in simulating the complete reality of such a room. Cardiac-care rooms must be designed to accommodate critical and dimensionally correct human

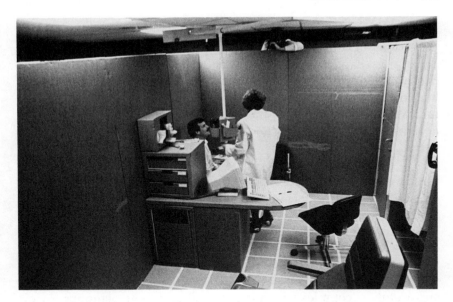

FIGURE 9-3. Full-scale mock-up model of medical examination room. (Reprinted, by permission, from J. Zimmerman, J. Loucks, and S. Polcyn, *Family Practice Facility Examination Room* [Lawrence: The University of Kansas, 1985])

activities. If the client decides that each characteristic of the environment must be studied and viewed in detail, a small-scale iconic model may not be as useful as a full-scale model. On the other hand, it may be found that accurate forms of mathematical models must be used in small parts of a design problem—such as the design of waiting lines in an airport terminal—in order to simulate very narrow and single-objective design problems.

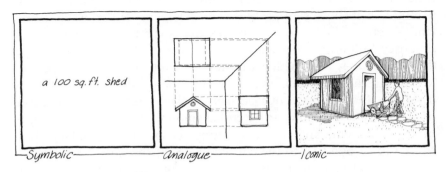

FIGURE 9-4. Model types.

COMMUNICATION TECHNIQUES

Four types of communication techniques are outlined in the remainder of this chapter: group dynamics, scaled models, computer-aided design, and statistical and mathematical analyses. Although they do not encompass all possible communication techniques, they serve to indicate the wide range of methods available to decision makers in design.

Group Dynamics

Group dynamics helps decision makers facilitate the communication of ideas among members of a decision-making group. The purpose is to heighten the definition and understanding of design problems within the team itself. While other communication techniques to be discussed here deal primarily with transmitting ideas to people outside the design team, group dynamics is geared toward persons involved directly with the design problem. Group-dynamic methods are useful to complex committees such as urban planning review boards and large corporations faced with resolving many points of view and conflicting value systems in complex design or planning problems.

Gaming is a group-dynamic technique that simplifies decison making when a large and diverse design team must reach a consensus and select a specific design solution.[6] Gaming was developed to define complex problem statements that contained a number of conflicting design goals and affected many constituent groups. As the title of this technique implies, gaming deals with the concept of playing and assuming roles within a decision-making team. In order to initiate a gaming technique, the members of the design team define a set of rules that describe the primary characteristics and parameters of the design problem. The elements of the design problem—such as the various activities that may be envisioned for a proposed building, the goals and objectives of the client group, and the resources within which the design team must work—are collected together in much the same way as a "Monopoly" game is designed. Once the various decision makers understand and agree on the rules of the game, an extended amount of time is spent simply playing the game and thus simulating the process of making decisions and responding to the consequences of those decisions.

A central concept in gaming is that of role reversal. A major difficulty presented by large, complex design problems is the lack of

FIGURE 9-5. Group dynamics.

understanding that each decision maker possesses with respect to the values and ideas held by the other members of the design team. Role reversal allows the opportunity for the various members of the design team to see and appreciate other points of view. In the design of a corporate headquarters building, for example, which may involve as many as twenty decision makers, the president of the corporation may assume the role of the comptroller of that corporation while the comptroller may assume the role of a user representative. Role reversal helps to uncover the values of each decision maker and communicate them to other design team members. As the game progresses, the various members—many of whom are in the position of making decisions for people who may hold radically different opinions of the design—begin to understand the complexity and the values of decisions to be made.

An advantage of gaming is that once the rules have been established in a design game, the situation can be replayed again and again. Team members can assume different roles and new situations can be posed as the game progresses. The conclusion is a clearer definition of the design problem and a heightened awareness among decision makers of its complexity. Because a situation has been played out and various team members have simulated decisions that result in specific environmental outcomes, decisions can be made or avoided based on a deeper understanding of the nature of a problem. As decision makers see and appreciate the consequences of decisions in the game, they can more confidently distribute resources available in the real-world situation. Just as the board game "Monopoly" helps people understand the consequences of investing money in real estate and appreciate the concept of informed risk-taking, a gaming situation in design will help decision makers understand the implications of arranging activities and allocating construction budgets in design problems.

Other group-dynamic communications methods—such as brainstorming and Delphi techniques—were reviewed in chapter 5. Those techniques are also methods that improve the exchange of ideas and information within the decision-making team. They are designed to facilitate social interaction among decision makers and to help design team members reach a consensus on the definition of design problems. Most group-dynamic techniques are based on symbolic models in that the primary methods of understanding the nature of a problem come through the use of logic and verbal communication.

Scaled Models

Scaled-model communication techniques are closely related to the iconic models associated with architectural design. Architects have long used scaled models to communicate visual and three-dimensional aspects of designs. With video and photographic technologies, the ability of architects to simulate complex and dynamic human interactions in built environments is enhanced.[7] Scaled models help the decision-making group to appreciate three-dimensional consequences of design solutions and to communicate those consequences to a visually unsophisticated group of people. Whereas group-dynamic techniques are of use primarily within the decision-making team, scaled-model techniques help designers express their ideas to a wider audience. Because scaled-model techniques use iconic representations of a design problem, they are useful for realistically showing the outcome of design decisions.

Full-size models have come to be used in design projects to

explain in detail the critical consequences of complex design alternatives. Whereas most scaled models in architecture have been focused on small-scale representations of space, full-scale mock-ups of proposed environments help people appreciate directly the feeling and scale of design decisions. In projects such as hospitals, family-practice clinics, and research facilities that require a great deal of attention on the part of the designer in terms of equipment layouts and the minute details of human behavior, it is important for the decision maker to appreciate in detail the effects that spatial configurations have on people. In a large hospital replacement project, a decision-making team constructed three critical-care patient rooms at full scale in order to simulate the behavior of people within tight space constrictions. The designer believed that spatial configurations of these rooms were critical to the successful operation of the entire facility; decisions dealing in inches and feet were crucial to the decision-making process. Designs were mocked up at full scale, and physicians and hospital staff performed critical activities in the rooms in order to simulate how the placement of walls, doors, windows, and medical equipment enhanced or limited critical medical procedures. Approximately twenty-five scenarios were simulated in the mock-ups and recorded in video and photographs. The designer was thus able to see where the rooms required major design changes to accommodate specific activities.[8]

The obvious drawback to full-scale modeling is its high cost. New video techniques have now made it possible for designers to construct small-scale mock-ups of environments and, using sophisticated lenses and optic fibers, move people visually through a proposed environment. The miniaturization of video recorders makes it possible for designers to walk people through a simulated environment on a small scale and avoid the necessity of actually building the environment to experience it. This allows decision makers rapidly to reconfigure design alternatives and visually reintroduce people into the space.[9]

Video taping's most important contribution to scaled models is to introduce the element of time into the design process. Whereas traditional architectural models and modeling techniques have been static representations of design solutions, the use of full-scale modeling and video makes it possible for people to experience the dynamic and changeable characteristics of environments. The ability for people actually to walk through or to experience visually the effects of walking through design alternatives adds an important dimension of realism to decision making. Not only can models simulate three-dimensional representations of space, they also allow the users and clients of designs to appreciate the "feel" of those spaces. Full-scale mock-ups have been used in the later stages of design, for example, to allow clients to select material finishes, colors, and textures in the context of actual spatial configurations of the proposed environment. Whereas many decisions at this stage in design have been made using color boards or color chips, now owners and users of buildings are able to see how these finish selections will come across in reality. Material selections can now be simulated with a great deal of accuracy using scaled models, and potential problems in the selection process can be spotted and corrected before construction begins.

Scaled-model techniques bring the reality of a completed environment into focus during the early stages of design. In the past, many decisions about design details were often made during construction. By doing this earlier, changes can be effected with far less cost and disruption.

Computer-aided Design

Advances in data-processing technologies in the form of computer graphics and computer-aided design programs have enhanced the designer's abilities to manipulate and understand the consequences of complex design solutions. Using symbolic models to represent three-dimensional spaces and using analogue techniques to display these spaces on two-dimensional video screens, computer-aided design allows designers to simulate three-dimensional design solutions electronically. Geometric configurations of designs can be put into computer programs so that a three-dimensional representation is achieved. An important advantage of this technique is its speed.[10]

High-speed computers and the miniaturization of computer hardware allow designers to construct computer models of design solutions cheaply and rapidly. Since 1980, the microcomputer has allowed even the smallest firm to simulate design solutions using computer graphic techniques. Larger architectural firms have begun to use computer simulation models as marketing tools and as an aid in explaining to their clients the consequences of life-cycle, energy, and budgetary decisions. Animation allows the designer to "walk" a client group through a building solution and to simulate the dynamic character of that environment. Although a large amount of time is

FIGURE 9-6. Computer-aided design.

required to input geometric data into computer programs, the time saved is great when many different configurations must be hypothesized during design. Once a geometric data base has been established for a design solution, the designer can make changes to that solution quickly and can easily alter the configuration of the design.

Computer-aided techniques have seen some of the most interesting and productive uses in energy design.[11] By simulating the sun's movement and position at a given site, for example, the designer can see the consequences of building configurations and site orientations during the course of an entire solar year. When graphic techniques of solar design are combined with analytic programs to calculate heat loss and gain, the consequences of designs can be simulated rapidly and the designer can make significant modifications in design solutions.

The computer's ability to combine analytic techniques with graphic output allows the designer to see not only a single consequence of design solutions but complex relationships in the decision-making process. Whereas scaled-model techniques promote understanding of the visual and tactile consequences of environments, computer-aided design uses the visual characteristics of design problems to explain the analytic and abstract dimensions in a medium designers can understand. Because computer-aided design techniques are symbolic in nature, the power of mathematical simulation can be brought to bear on many interrelated problems in design.

The use of computer-aided design in architecture has increased rapidly during the last decade and has the potential to change radically how architects practice. With miniaturized computer hardware and reduced software costs, many new programs are becoming available that allow designers to simulate a wide range of design consequences and to expand the scope of design services. A recent development in microcomputer technology, for example, combines scaled-model techniques and computer-aided design programs. Using video-imaging hardware, a scaled model can be videotaped and put into the memory of a microcomputer; that image can then be manipulated in much the same way that a designer might use overlays and transparencies. The combination of communication techniques using the microcomputer has let designers transmit visual ideas in a new and powerful language.[12]

Statistics and Mathematical Analysis

The use of statistics in design was discussed in chapter 8 and its use demonstrated in post-occupancy evaluation. Statistics is also useful in design problems characterized by uncertainty. Because statistics is concerned with probabilities and chance, it can be used to predict weather patterns, population growth, and social behavior. Architects traditionally have relied on statistical analyses in large-scale planning projects where accurate climatic and demographic information has been required.

Mathematical analysis is an ancient mode of architectural communication. The reduction of building forms to precise geometric diagrams has always been a powerful tool for architects, both to quickly communicate complex ideas to their clients, as well as to structure the physical elements of design. With the introduction of analytic models of mechanics, designers were able to calculate the behavior of structural components of buildings and the thermal performance of mechanical systems.[13]

Recently, a number of analytic tools have been made available to architects in energy and cost analyses. Computer-aided simulation

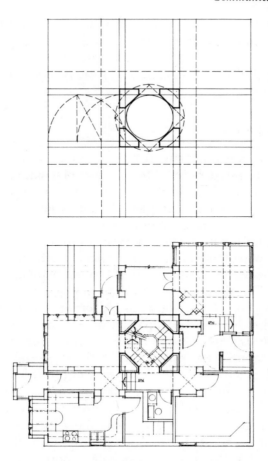

FIGURE 9-7. Mathematics and design.

models predict the thermal performance of buildings and how specific changes might affect thermal properties design alternatives. Life-cycle cost models assess the long-term economic impact of design decisions on buildings, not only during the later stages of design but as feedback throughout the building cycle.

Some of the most useful mathematical applications in architecture are those that have been used to model and analyze complex medical facilities. Because the functions of hospitals must be understood in minute detail by designers, accurate predictive models are essential design tools. The flow of people and material into and out of a suite of surgery rooms, for example, can be modeled in much the same way as an industrial process. Mathematical simulation models of these environmental processes have been incorporated into a number of hospital programming practices and have been used to measure the physical and economic implications of alternative hospital designs.[14]

CONCLUSION

Each design problem benefits from the entire set of communication techniques discussed here. The process of communicating ideas within the design team probably demands that a range of these tools be called on in even the simplest design project. The key is the ability to select the most appropriate form of communication for transmitting information at every point in the decision-making process. This is where the differences between symbolic, analogue, and iconic models become critical; the ability to distinguish the relative strengths and weaknesses of each is an important asset.

The following chapter outlines a decision-making process from feasibility through the occupancy of a single design project. Throughout this process, attempts were made to incorporate a range of communication techniques. One of the most difficult problems facing the decision maker in design is the breadth and volume of information that must be sorted, analyzed, and stored for later reference. Communication techniques serve two critical functions in this respect. First, they provide ways that allow the decision maker to simplify a large and complex data set into a form that quickly enlightens a specific aspect of the design. An enormous amount of life-cycle cost information, for example, is condensed into a simple cost model; a direct application of a symbolic (mathematical) model allows the design team to analyze rapidly a single component of the problem. Second, these techniques provide a mechanism to document design decisions. Photographic documentation of the client's original work environment, for example, became not just a static representation for the architectural programmer, but a vehicle through which succeeding decisions concerning furniture layouts, building image, and space budgeting could be compared and evaluated. The effective use of communication techniques plays an essential part not only in transmitting design concepts, but also in mapping the decision process.

The following case study does not include the full range of communication techniques available to designers. In fact, the techniques that are illustrated will be quite familiar to designers. Using the case study as a skeletal outline, the reader is encouraged to draw on material from the preceding chapters that will contribute to the decision-making process in his or her own design projects.

NOTES

1. This discussion does not intend to imply that graphic communication techniques are not, and should not, be the designer's primary concern. This topic has been well documented and reference is made to the journal *Representation* (1984) for review of the theoretical development of traditional graphic skills in architectural education.

2. Refer to the recent editions of *Architectural Technology* (AIA) for specific examples of computer-aided design, mathematical modeling, life-cycle cost, and simulation techniques as applied in architectural practice.

3. See Pressman and Tennsyon (1983) for a discussion of how the need to incorporate new forms of communication techniques in design has affected design education.

4. The most fundamental changes in how designers deal with information have been a direct result of the microprocessor revolution. A general discussion of how this revolution will affect modern communication techniques can be found in Naisbitt (1982).

5. See Ackoff (1967) and Ackoff and Sasieni (1968, 60–74) for detailed reviews of the use of models in decision making.

6. See Greenblat and Duke (1981) and Hasell and Taylor (1981) for a review of gaming theories and design applications.

7. Refer to Burden (1985) for a review of new photographic and video techniques in architectural illustration.

8. A complete description of this modeling technique can be found in King et al. (1982). A simulation that used many of the research methods developed in this study was performed in the design of a family-practice clinic and reported in Zimmerman et al. (1985).

9. See Burden (1985, 68–90) and Joedicke and Mayer (1982) for examples of video simulation techniques.

10. Cross (1977) details a number of the consequences of introducing the computer into the design process, and Kemper (1985) reviews the use of CAD Systems in architectural offices and schools.

11. A listing of computer software for energy analyses is compiled in the *AIA Energy Professional Development Program* (1983) and DAEDALUS (1986).

12. A good review of computer uses in architectural design can be found in Doubilet and Fisher (1986).

13. The use of geometry as a design determinant has been documented extensively and will not be covered in detail in this discussion. The reader is encouraged to consult Clark and Pause (1985) for an excellent review of this topic.

14. Frank Zilm (1980) describes the use of queueing models in hospital programming and sets forth a number of useful guidelines for incorporating analytic methods in architectural practice.

CHAPTER 10

Case Study Examples

THE APPROACH to decision making outlined in this book is a combination of theories and data collection techniques from a variety of disciplines and professions. The practice of architecture, however, is a complex and creative activity that cannot be reduced to a simple set of procedures. Architects and engineers should view the methodology of decision making described in chapter 3 as a framework in which information is referenced and design team members monitor the progress of the solution. Each design project requires a unique application of the methodology, not a rote implementation of the five-step process. Some projects may require the design team to devote a large amount of time searching out programmatic solutions and very little time evaluating them. Others may be concerned almost exclusively with data collection for a post-occupancy evaluation. The application of the techniques presented in chapters 4 through 9 should be tailored to the nature of the design problem and should not become a formulaic response to the methodology. The methodology should be viewed as a conceptual template for decision making.

The case study presented in this chapter shows how the decision techniques are used in a single design project. The project is the design of a data-processing center, conducted over a three-year period. This case study, which was provided by Mr. Frank Jennings of Automatic Data Processing, is a project in which both authors participated between 1979 and 1982. In order to condense the narrative, a number of examples from the study have been modified. The decision process covered an initial feasibility analysis to define the goals and objectives of the building client and users; a design analysis of building systems and costs; and a post-occupancy evaluation to

213

measure the degree to which those goals and objectives were met in the final building solution. The project addressed a wide range of user and client perspectives, from capital and life-cycle costs to occupant perceptions of space utilization and comfort. It employed a number of decision techniques, including function analysis, cost and energy modeling, observation, objective environmental measurements, interviews, surveys, group creativity, and decision analysis. The decision-making team had two goals: first, to establish a procedure by which the client could conduct building evaluations and provide program data for future projects; second, to measure how well a single building satisfied the needs of the people who use, maintain, and manage the facility. Data were collected through management, customer and contractor interviews, employee questionnaires, site observations and photography, Delphi sessions, and evaluation workshops. Conclusions were based on comparisons with data collected in a number of similar building-evaluation studies. The major finding was that increased client and user participation in the design process, as well as a high level of design quality in the building itself, generated very positive responses from people who work in, visit, and manage the facility.

FEASIBILITY

A large data-processing company was contemplating the design of a computer facility in a major city in the eastern United States. This was to be one of a number of such centers in various parts of the country and would be a regional headquarters and central receiving station for a large portion of the state in which it was located. It was to house the same functions as a number of similar facilities in other geographic locations. As a part of early planning, the client had established a concise statement of these functions and had used the function-analysis technique to record the primary activities and processes that would occur in the building (fig. 10-1). The information contained in the FAST diagram was used as a guide not only for programming this facility but also as a basis for comparing other data-processing centers as to the functions contained in a single building program.

The client defined a space budget of 44,000 gross square feet, and the facility manager expressed a need for rapid, nondisruptive

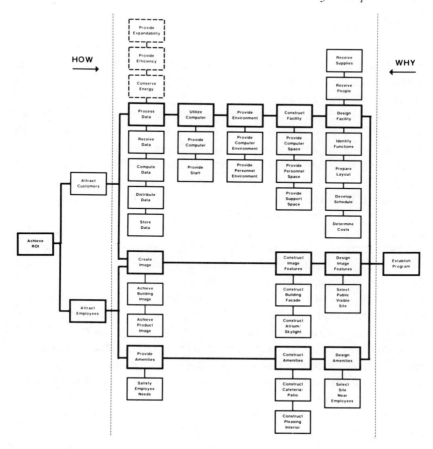

FIGURE 10-1. FAST diagram: data processing center.

growth in the facility due to anticipated changes in computer technology. A monetary budget of approximately fifty dollars per gross
square foot was established. During the early project phases, a design team was assembled and charged with planning, designing,
constructing, and operating the building.

Owner decisions were made by facility representatives of the
corporation and members of the local management staff. The project
architect and design engineers were involved in all phases of the
project, as was an evaluation team composed of cost and value analysts, lighting specialists, and construction managers.

Project Goals

The primary decisions the design team faced during the early phases of programming concerned the strategic issues of building function, exterior massing, and resource allocation. The first task was to define precisely the owner's and users' project goals. The most important objective of decision making during the feasibility phase of a project tends to center on problem definition. In order to structure the problem in such a way as to make it possible to monitor design progress, the design team concentrated on collecting and analyzing two distinct kinds of information. The first was design concepts that began to address the functional, visual, and technical concerns of the building type being considered. A data-processing center has by nature certain characteristics that can be isolated and defined in general terms. In this case study, a Delphi process helped the team focus on these characteristics and categorize the attributes necessary for successful completion of the project. Figure 10-2 is a sample Delphi sheet generated by the design team to describe the basic design assumptions to be considered in the architectural layout of activity areas within the building. Similar Delphi exercises were conducted for the building's structural, architectural, mechanical, and electrical systems. In essence, this information began to sketch for the design team the broad outline of feasible project boundaries. Generation of these early, abstract design concepts hinted at the most critical issues that would need to be addressed and the economic and functional consequences of the future design solutions.

Simultaneously the design team also began to seek out careful definitions of client and building-user goals. Whereas the Delphi sessions expanded the range of feasible design concepts, the process of defining goals restricted and narrowed the problem statement. The design goals were to be precise statements of what the project should accomplish and how the success of future design solutions would be evaluated. Six design goals were defined in this case study: *flexibility, capital costs, owning and operating costs, expansion capabilities, energy conservation,* and *external building image.* These are broad categories and, except for cost-related goals, there is no common measurement system to compare one with another. It was difficult, for example, for the design team to conceive of a uniform scale that could measure—from positive to negative—the concepts of flexibility and image. Using the scaling techniques of decision analysis, however, the design team was able to construct such measurement systems and formulate six rating scales. Five-point rating scales were used, each point defined by a verbal description arrived at by the design team.

After each scale was constructed, the team asked, "What relative degrees of importance exist among these six objectives?" Using a number of trade-off techniques, the team was able to rank the six objectives from most to least important and to assign a numeric value to each. This procedure was useful not only to weight the objectives but also as a way of evaluating and rethinking the original objectives. The team discovered during this exercise, for example, that the ranking changed during trade-off exercises as various team members exchanged information and collectively generated new knowledge and ideas. Figure 10-3 lists the original six design goals.

Evaluation

By this point in the project, a number of preliminary design concepts had been generated (fig. 10-2) and a well-defined set of design goals stated (fig. 10-3). Each of these concepts satisfied the basic requirements of the project, and each was unique in how it addressed the design goals. One alternative was strong in economic terms but did not perform well with respect to expansion potential. Specific evaluations of each alternative were conducted to measure objectively its exact consequences against a single design goal. Life-cycle cost analyses were conducted to determine long-term economic consequences of each concept, and capital cost estimates were established as measures of the immediate consequences of construction. One analysis is shown for three programmatic alternatives developed by the design team during the latter stages of the feasibility phase (fig. 10-4). Delphi sessions were used to evaluate the more subjective goals of image and function.

In the Delphi sessions, the team organized the group's thoughts and opinions and focused its collective expertise on evaluating the more subjective criteria. The facility manager drew on his experience from other data-processing facilities to evaluate the potential success of the functional characteristics of the three proposed solutions. The client organization also employed post-occupancy evaluation techniques to test the detailed functional criteria of alternatives. Because the proposed building would probably be a multi-story facility and existing building activities were being housed in a single-story structure, the building manager decided to test the effects of

Cost Control

The Delphi Method

Layout	Element Description	Project	Computer Center	Cycle	1
$2,456,000	Target Cost	Location	Eastern U.S.	Sheet	3
	Estimated Cost	Bldg. Type	Office	Date	
		Const. Type	Steel Frame	Phase	Concept

Functions (Verb/Noun)

Process	Data
Create	Image
Provide	amenities

Components

	Cost (budget)
01 Foundations	$30,800
02 Substructure	110,000
03 Superstructure	308,000
04 Exterior Closure	220,000
05 Roofing	66,000
06 Interior Construction	286,000
07 Conveying Systems	28,600
08 Mechanical	449,600
09 Electrical	264,000
10 General Conditions	286,000
11 Equipment	11,000
12 Site	396,000
Total Construction	2,456,000

Alternatives

One Level, Front Expansion
    (see sketch 1)
One Level, Side Expansion
    (see sketch 2)
One Level, Rear Expansion
    (see sketch 3)
Two Levels, Front Expansion
    (see sketch 4)
Two Levels, Side Expansion
    (see sketch 5)
Two Levels, Rear Expansion
    (see sketch 6)
Three Levels (incl. bsmt.), Front Exp.
    (see sketch 7)
Three Levels (incl. bsmt.), Side Exp.
    (see sketch 8)
Three Levels (incl. bsmt.), Rear Exp.
    (see sketch 9)

Rational & Assumptions

1. Building size approx. 44,000 sf
2. Facility must provide expansion for operations, sales
   and computer spaces.
3. Site will accommodate a one, two, or three level facility.

FIGURE 10-2. Delphi summary and concept alternatives.

added travel time and visual separation of building activities. A building across the street from the existing data-processing structure was rented briefly and a group from a specific department was moved into this facility for three months. In this way, building activities were tested in a setting similar to that envisioned for the new facility; in-depth interviews evaluated specific environmental

Building Expansion

	Front Expansion	Side Expansion	Rear Expansion
ONE LEVEL	① W O M / A S O C / E	② C W / E O M / S A	③ E / W C O S / M A
TWO LEVELS — 1st fl.	④ A S W← / E	⑤ E S A W←	⑥ E / S M W← / A
TWO LEVELS — 2nd fl.	M D C / E (Alt. #2)	E C O M	E / C O
THREE LEVELS — 1st fl. (or bsmt.)	⑦ M W←	⑧ W←	⑨ M W←
THREE LEVELS — 2nd fl.	A S C / E	E C S A / S	E / O
THREE LEVELS — 3rd fl.	O / E (Alt. #3)	E O M (Alt. #1)	E / C S A

Legend: O – Operations S – Sales W – Warehouse
E – Expansion A – Administration C – Computer M – Mechanical

effects of certain functional arrangements on the affected building users.

Synthesis

After the various concepts had been evaluated with respect to each design goal, the design team compared each alternative to the others in terms of the combined goal statements. A system of weighted-

Project ___Data Processing Center___   Date ___8/80___

Objective Name ___Capital Costs___   Objective No. ___1___

Objective Descriptions

Low Value	
1	$60.00/SF
2	$56.25/SF
3	$52.50/SF
4	$48.75/SF
5	$45.00/SF
High Value	

Project ___Data Processing Center___   Date ___8/80___

Objective Name ___Owning and Operating Costs___
___(Energy, Maint., Tax, Repair)___   Objective No. ___2___

Objective Descriptions

Low Value	
1	$5.00/SF/year
2	$4.50/SF/year
3	$4.00/SF/year
4	$3.50/SF/year
5	$3.00/SF/year
High Value	

Objective Descriptions

Low Value

1   Very little perceived image and a minimum amount of public visibility.

2   Very little perceived image in a site that has a moderate degree of public visibility.

3   A distinct image (not necessarily companys) is apparent in a moderately visible site location.

4   An image associated with company is moderately visible in a public site.

5   Prestigious image with a recognizable company visual image and message. Highly visible site utilization.

High Value

Objective Descriptions

Low Value

1   50% (25,000 SF) expansion with some disruption of functional activities and facility destruction.

2   50% expansion without destruction of facilities but some functional inconveniences.

3   50% expansion without destruction of facilities and no major functional disruptions.

4   100% (50,000 SF) expansion with significant increase in facility and operating costs and a moderate amount of functional inconvenience.

5   100% expansion without destruction of facilities or significant cost increases. No functional disruption.

High Value

FIGURE 10-3. Preliminary design objectives.

Decision Analysis
Scaling Objectives

Project _Data Processing Center_   Date _8/80_

Objective Name _Energy Conservation_   Objective No. _5_

Objective Descriptions

Low Value	
1	50 watts/sf
2	45 watts/sf
3	40 watts/sf
4	35 watts/sf
5	30 watts/sf
High Value	

Decision Analysis
Scaling Objectives

Project _Data Processing Center_   Date _8/80_

Objective Name _Flexibility of Space_   Objective No. _6_

Objective Descriptions

Low Value	
1	Moderate structural changes necessary and moderate functional disruption to achieve change in internal activities.
2	Minor structural and moderate architectural change with moderate functional disruption.
3	Moderate architectural change with moderate functional disruption. No structural change.
4	Minor architectural change with minor functional disruption. No structural change.
5	Furniture and equipment change in open office planning arrangement with little functional disruption.
High Value	

FIG. 10-3. (*Continued*)

Life-Cycle Cost Analysis
Using Present-Worth Costs

Life-Cycle Costing Estimate
General Purpose Work Sheet

Study Title: Building Layout
Discount Rate: 10% Date:
Economic Life: 25 years (constant dollars)

	Year	PW Factor	Diff. Escal. Rate	PWA W/Escal.	Alt 1 (Sketch #6) Est. Costs	Alt 1 Present Worth	Alt 2 (Sketch #4) Est. Costs	Alt 2 Present Worth	Alt 3 (Sketch #7) Est. Costs	Alt 3 Present Worth	Alt 4 Est. Costs	Alt 4 Present Worth
Initial/Collateral Costs												
A. Structural					10.74/sf	$472,600	9.30/sf	$409,200	10.74/sf	$472,600		
B. Architectural					16.10/sf	708,400	15.20/sf	668,800	15.26/sf	671,400		
C. Mechanical					12.40/sf	545,600	12.02/sf	528,900	12.40/sf	545,600		
D. Electrical					6.50/sf	286,000	6.50/sf	286,000	6.50/sf	286,000		
E. Equipment					0.25/sf	11,000	0.25/sf	11,000	0.25/sf	11,000		
F. General Conditions					6.82/sf	300,000	6.42/sf	282,500	6.70/sf	292,800		
G. Site					9.00/sf	396,000	9.80/sf	387,200	9.00/sf	396,000		
Total Initial/Collateral Costs						2,719,600		2,573,600		2,677,400		
Replacement/Salvage (Single Expenditure)												
A. Carpeting/Interiors	8	0.466			177,100	82,500	167,200	77,900	167,900	78,200		
B. Lighting System	10	0.385			50,600	19,500	50,600	19,500	50,600	19,500		
C. HVAC System	12	0.319			193,000	61,600	184,000	58,900	193,000	61,600		
D. Carpeting/Interiors	16	0.218			177,100	38,600	167,200	36,400	167,900	36,600		
E. Lighting	20	0.149			50,600	7,500	50,600	7,500	50,600	7,500		
F. Roofing	20	0.149			58,500	8,700	63,100	9,400	58,500	8,700		
G.												
H.												
Salvage (Resale Value)	25	0.092				NIC		NIC		NIC		
Total Replacement/Salvage Costs						218,400		209,600		212,100		
Annual Costs												
A. Energy-Elect. (carpenter)			1%	9.894	71,500	707,400	69,000	682,700	68,000	672,800		
B. Energy-Nat.Gas (heat)			2%	10.819	15,000	162,300	13,000	140,600	13,500	146,100		
C. Maint.-Custodial			0%	9.077	35,000	317,700	30,000	272,300	33,000	299,500		
D. Maint.-Architectural			0%	9.077	11,000	99,800	10,500	95,300	11,000	99,800		
E. Maint.-Mechanical			0%	9.077	15,400	139,800	14,500	131,600	15,000	136,200		
F. Maint.-Electrical			0%	9.077	8,800	79,900	8,800	79,900	8,800	79,900		
G. Maint.-Site			0%	9.077	4,400	39,900	4,200	38,100	4,400	39,900		
Total Annual Costs						1,546,800		1,440,500		1,474,200		
Total Present-Worth Life-Cycle Costs						4,484,800		4,223,700		4,363,700		
Life-Cycle Present-Worth Dollar Savings						—		261,100		121,100		

(1) Note: Staffing, Insurance, Taxes, etc. are the same for all schemes.

PW – Present Worth   PWA – Present Worth Of Annuity

FIGURE 10-4. Evaluation of building layout costs.

average evaluation was used. In order to implement this evaluation procedure, the team members familiarized themselves with the measuring scales of the design goals and then rated each concept in light of these goals. Figure 10-5 shows the combined results of the team's evaluations, indicating that the third solution was the preferred scheme. Synthesis and analysis of this information turned up a solution combining the ideas and goals generated during feasibility studies. The decision-making techniques described above were used during the early stages of the project to measure the effectiveness of building layout choices. These techniques provided a uniform system of evaluation by a diverse design team. Each team member had a different assessment of the problem and a different attitude toward each design objective. Predesign evaluation techniques, however, provided a common point of departure and standard vocabulary for the team and helped to focus its attention during the crucial phase of problem definition. Standardized measurement scales created a framework within which participants could reach a degree of consensus concerning design strategy.

Recommendations

The focus of building evaluation at the feasibility phase was to balance client goals with the most appropriate program alternative. The choices available to the designer and client during this phase were numerous. The task was to narrow these choices and define precisely the problem to be solved during design. The decision methods used in this phase were not expected to produce a single answer, but were rather a means to set the parameters and context of the problem.

The products of this stage were the set of client and building-user goal statements, general ideas concerning the cost and functional constraints of the proposed building, and synthesis of a number of programming and schematic design alternatives. Evaluation techniques had analyzed the effectiveness of a range of design concepts, and the design team selected a specific solution for development during design. The design team had transformed the problem from a loosely defined statement of client and user needs to a precisely worded building program. The decision-making process helped the team determine the economic and functional feasibility of the proposed facility and yielded a programming document that would be the context of the early stages of design.

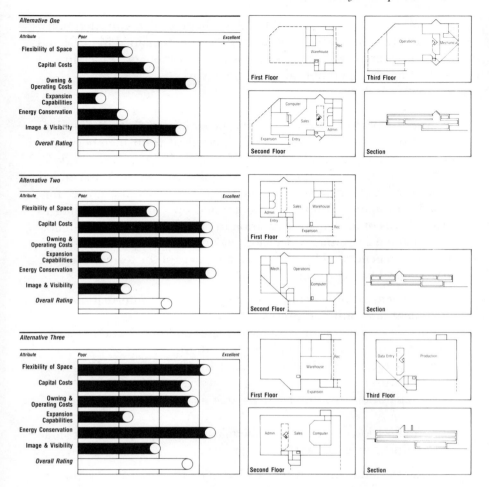

FIGURE 10-5. Building layout evaluation and team synthesis.

DESIGN

During the design stage of the data-processing center project, it was the design team's goal to refine the range of programming alternatives, analyze cost and functional objectives, and develop a strategy for monitoring and improving the design as it progressed toward construction. Although the decision-making team was composed of the same members who participated in the feasibility study, the project designer now assumed a leading role because decisions were more concerned with technical and aesthetic design considerations. The format of the decision process, however, remained in place and the project architect again assumed the position of leadership in conducting the operation of the team's work.

Context

Because the project's basic goals and programmatic alternatives had been resolved by the design team, individual team members conducted much of the detailed work in the early design phase. Working within their areas of expertise, they collected data and assembled ideas to refine the problem statement. The designer and owner furnished information from the program and documents pertaining to various areas of design specialization in order to prepare team members for the next round of decision-making workshops. Examples of information generated by individual members of the team during the early stages of design were:

- Refinement of functional and organizational information from client and building users
- Review of preliminary cost estimates and preparation of a cost model by the value engineer (fig. 10-6)
- Preparation of an energy model by the mechanical engineer (fig. 10-7)
- Preparation of a net-to-gross area analysis by the project designer
- Finalization of decisions to be taken by the project architect at the next meeting of the design team

After design team members had studied the program documents and assembled information in their respective areas of expertise, the project architect organized a three-day work session. The process of decision making was similar to that outlined in the feasibility stage and the description of activities contained in the case study found in chapter 3. To illustrate the team's tasks during the design workshop, the following brief summary of activities is offered.

Information

The team analyzed the latest project documents submitted by the project designer and reviewed the most recent changes in the client's enclosure, structural, and mechanical and electrical systems for the building. Figure 10-8 is the function analysis of the lighting and

Cost Model

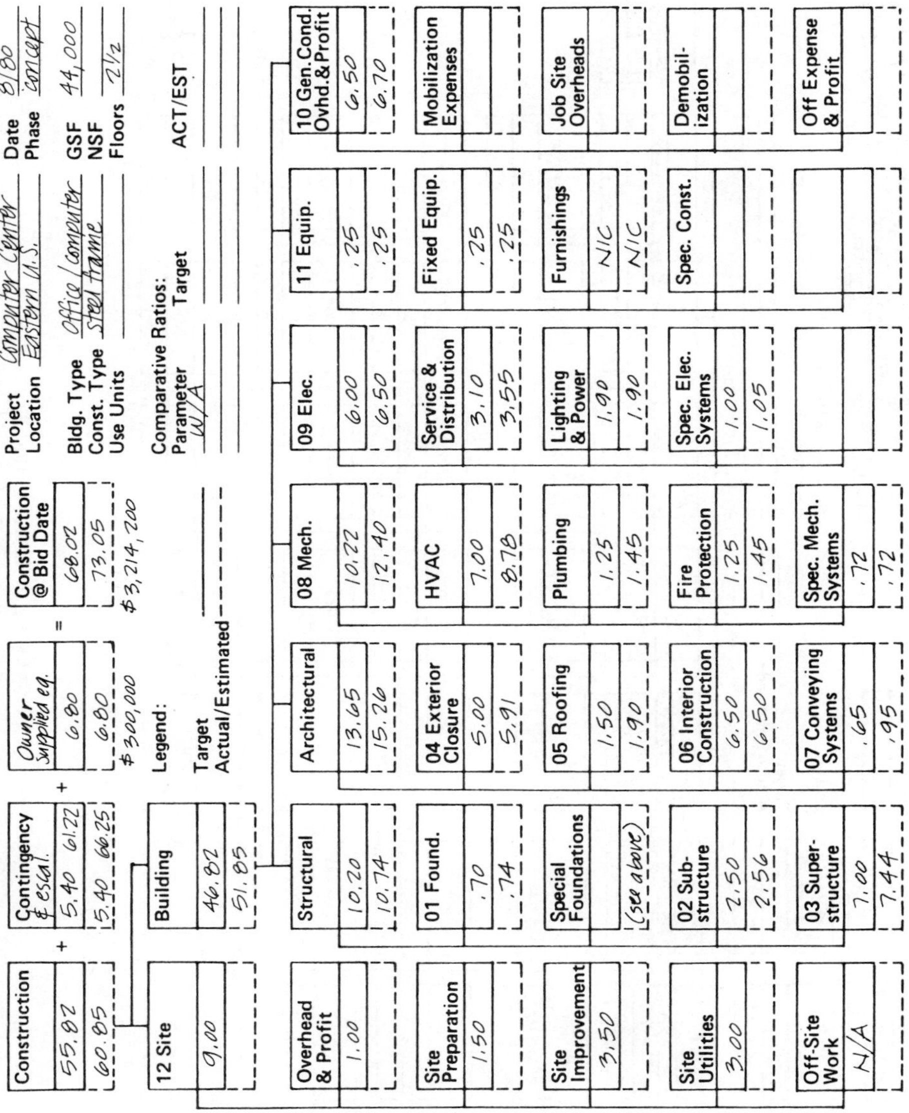

Project Computer Center
Location Eastern U.S.
Bldg. Type Office Computer
Const. Type Steel Frame
Use Units _____
Date 8/80
Phase Concept
GSF 44,000
NSF _____
Floors 2½

Comparative Ratios:
Parameter N/A
Target _____
ACT/EST _____

Construction 55.82 / 60.05 + Contingency & escal. 5.40 61.22 / 5.40 66.25 + Owner supplied eq. 6.80 / 6.80 $300,000 = Construction @ Bid Date 68.02 / 73.05 $3,214,700

Legend:
Target _____
Actual/Estimated ------

12 Site 9.00

Building 46.82 / 51.85

	Structural	Architectural	08 Mech.	09 Elec.	11 Equip.	10 Gen. Cond. Ovhd. & Profit
Target	10.20	13.05	10.22	6.00	.25	6.50
Act/Est	10.74	15.26	12.40	6.50	.25	6.70

	01 Found.	04 Exterior Closure	HVAC	Service & Distribution	Fixed Equip.	Mobilization Expenses
Target	.70	5.00	7.00	3.10	.25	
Act/Est	.74	5.91	8.78	3.55	.25	

	Special Foundations	05 Roofing	Plumbing	Lighting & Power	Furnishings	Job Site Overheads
Target	(see above)	1.50	1.25	1.90	NIC	
Act/Est		1.90	1.45	1.90	NIC	

	02 Sub-structure	06 Interior Construction	Fire Protection	Spec. Elec. Systems	Spec. Const.	Demobilization
Target	2.50	6.50	1.25	1.00		
Act/Est	2.56	6.50	1.45	1.05		

	03 Super-structure	07 Conveying Systems	Spec. Mech. Systems			Off Expense & Profit
Target	7.00	.65	.72			
Act/Est	7.44	.95	.72			

Overhead & Profit 1.00
Site Preparation 1.50
Site Improvement 3.50
Site Utilities 3.00
Off-Site Work N/A

FIGURE 10-6. Cost model.

Worksheet 2

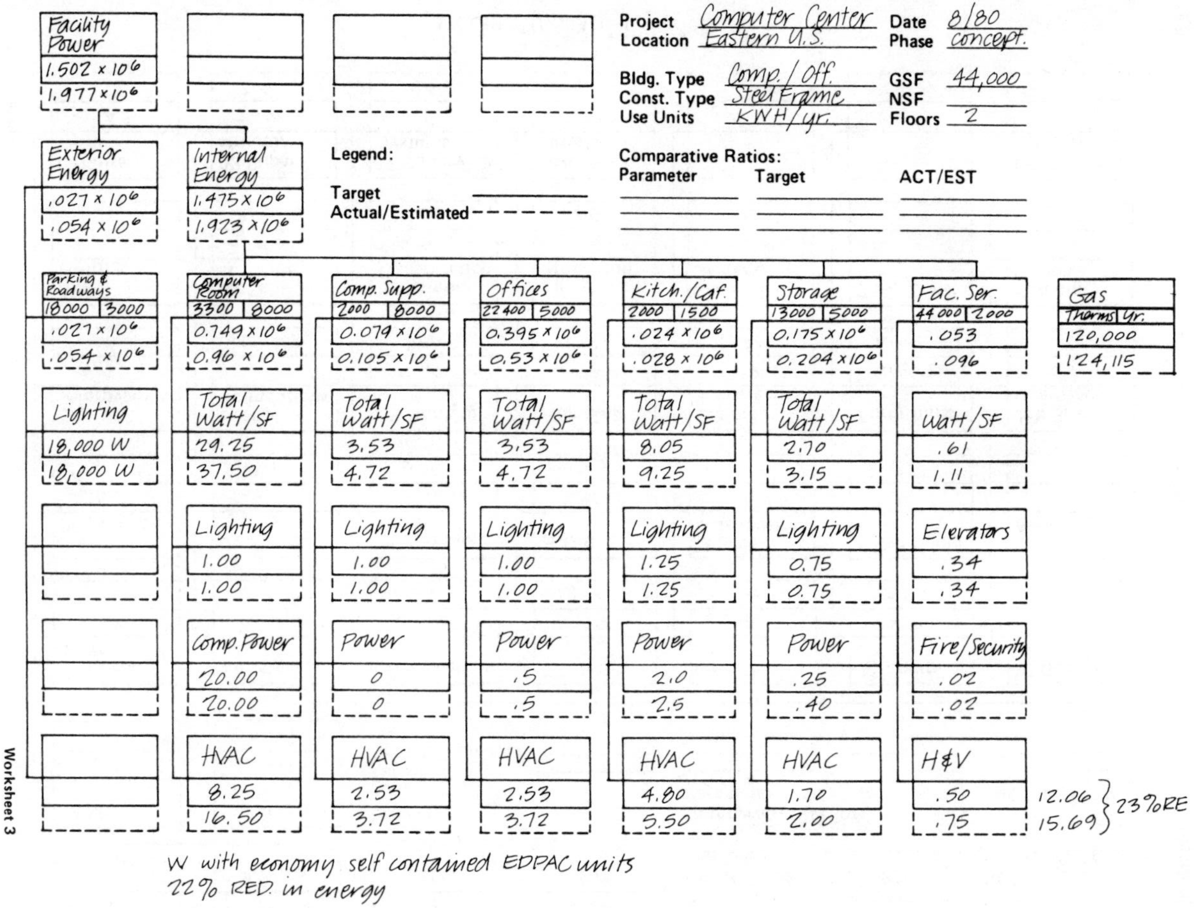

FIGURE 10-7. Energy model.

Function Analysis

Project: Computer Processing Center Item: 092 Lighting & Power Basic Function: Illuminate Objects / Distribute Power Date: _____

Quantity	Unit	Component	Function Verb	Noun	Kind *	Explanation	Original Cost	Worth
30,750	LNFT	Copper Wire	distribute	power	U/B		5,000	4,000
10,570	LNFT	Unsul. Copper Ground Wire	distribute	power	"		1,800	1,800
6,020	LNFT	EMT Conduit	protect	wire	U/S		6,200	2,000
1,300	LN FT	EMT Conduit Fittings	connect	conduit	U/S		4,500	1,000
380	Each	Office Lighting Fixtures	illuminate	objects	U/B	2×4, 2 Lamp, Recessed	42,500	32,500
			improve	interior image	A/B			10,000
40	Each	Corridor Lighting Fixtures	illuminate	objects	U/B	1×4, 2 Lamp, Recessed	4,200	3,200
			improve	interior image	A/B			1,000
22	Each	Lobby Lighting Fixtures	illuminate	objects	U/B	Wall Mounted, 2 Lamp	2,300	500
			improve	interior image	A/B			1,800
9	Each	Entry Lighting Fixtures	illuminate	objects	U/B	Incand. Drum Light, Recessed	900	200
			improve	interior image	A/B			700
12	Each	Exit Lighting	identify	exit	U/B		700	500
8	Each	Lighting & Recept Panels	divide	power	U/S		6,000	6,000
230	Each	Recept. & Switch Boxes	house	connections	U/S		3,400	2,000
183	Each	Receptacles	connect	appliance	U/B		1,400	1,400
50	Each	Switches	control	lighting	U/S		300	200
264	Each	Recept. Cover Plates	conceal	wiring	A/S		2,300	1,100
120	Each	Telephone Cover Plates	conceal	wiring	A/S		2,000	1,000
50	Each	Switch Cover Plates	conceal	wiring	A/S		100	500
							83,600	71,400

Total $\dfrac{Cost}{Worth} = \dfrac{83,600}{71,400} = 1.17$

* Function Type: Use or Aesthetic / Basic or Secondary

FIGURE 10-8. Lighting systems function analysis.

power system. The functions of any given building system controlled the overall approach to the building design. This procedure forced participants to think in terms of specialized functions and the costs associated with these functions. By preparing function-analysis diagrams, team members clearly communicated the purposes of the building systems within their own areas of specialization in a format comprehensible to other design participants.

Speculation

Speculation involved the generation of design alternatives addressing various building components. In a number of Delphi sessions, the team created a range of system alternatives and design options. The original project goals guided the team to focus on cost control, system flexibility, and design quality. An effort was made not to restrict creative solutions to the problem or to reject any design idea as infeasible. The team was seeking as many approaches to the problem as possible, and free association of ideas was encouraged. The team identified more than one hundred ideas during the Delphi session and began to assemble a range of alternatives for further consideration. Figure 10-9 is the Delphi sheet for the lighting system.

Evaluation

The design team next began to assess the merits of various system alternatives generated during the Delphi sessions. Advantages and disadvantages were listed for each alternative. Detailed life-cycle cost and capital cost estimates were made for each alternative and solutions with the greatest potential for cost savings were developed further. The system alternatives were ranked and the most promising reviewed by the design team (according to the project goals); changes were then made in the set of feasible design solutions (fig. 10-10).

Synthesis

During synthesis, each building system alternative was combined into complete design proposals and evaluated against the project goal statements. Decision analysis techniques were used to synthesize design ideas, and weighted-evaluation comparisons were conducted for each building system (fig. 10-11). Because it was important that the team convey the general concept of its recommendations to the project designer, each building system alternative was accompanied

Cost Control
The Delphi Method

Lighting	Element Description	Project	*Computer Center*	**Cycle**	*#1*
		Location	*Eastern U.S.*	Sheet	*3*
	Target Cost	Bldg. Type	*Office*	Date	
50,600	Estimated Cost	Const. Type	*Steel Frame*	Phase	*Schematic*

Functions (Verb/Noun)

Illuminate	*Objects*
Identify	*Exit*
Provide	*(emergency) Lighting*

Components | **Cost**
Office Lighting	*$42,500*
Corridor Lighting	*4,200*
Lobby Lighting	*2,300*
Entry Lighting	*900*
Exit Lighting	*700*

Total	*$50,600*

Alternatives

Direct Ceiling Mounted Fluorescent
Recessed Ceiling Mounted Fluorescent
Indirect Floor Mounted Fluorescent
Indirect Floor Mounted Metal Halide
Indirect Floor Mounted High Pressure Sodium
Ceiling Fluorescent, Parabolic Louvers
Ceiling Fluorescent, Polarized Lenses
Ceiling Fluorescent, K-12 Lenses
Indirect Furniture Mounted Fluorescent
Indirect Column Mounted Fluorescent
Indirect Ceiling Mounted Fluorescent
Three Lamp Parabolic Fluorescent

Rationale & Assumptions

FIGURE 10-9. Delphi worksheet for lighting systems.

Life-Cycle Cost Analysis
Using Present-Worth Costs

Life-Cycle Costing Estimate
General Purpose Work Sheet

Study Title: Lighting Systems
Discount Rate: 10%   Date: _____
Economic Life: 25 years

Section	Item	Year / Diff. Escal. Rate	PW Factor / PWA W/Escal.	Alt 1 Est. Costs	Alt 1 Present Worth	Alt 2 Est. Costs	Alt 2 Present Worth	Alt 3 Est. Costs	Alt 3 Present Worth	Alt 4 Est. Costs	Alt 4 Present Worth
Describe				2'x4' 2 lamp fluorescent, K-12 lens		2'x4' 2 lamp fluorescent, parabolic louver		indirect ceiling/column mounted, 2 lamp fluorescent		indirect floor/furniture mntd, metal halide (250 w)	
Initial/Collateral Costs	A. 2'x4' 2-lamp fluorescent, k-12 lens			380 fixtures $42,500	42,500						
	B. 2'x4' 2-lamp fluorescent parabolic					380 fixtures $46,400	46,400				
	C. indirect ceiling col mnt:4 2-lamp fluor.							560 fixtures $100,800	100,800		
	D. indirect floor/furn. mnt:4 metal halide									150 fixtures $60,000	60,000
	E.										
	F.										
	G.										
	Total Initial/Collateral Costs			42,500	42,500	46,400	46,400	100,800	100,800	60,000	60,000
Replacement/Salvage (Single Expenditure)	A. Lighting System	10	0.386	42,500	16,400	46,400	17,900	100,800	38,900	60,000	23,200
	B. Lighting System	20	0.149	42,500	6,300	46,400	6,900	100,800	15,000	60,000	8,900
	C.										
	D.										
	E.										
	F.										
	G.										
	H.										
	Salvage (Resale Value)	25	0.092	NIC		NIC		NIC		NIC	
	Total Replacement/Salvage Costs				22,700		24,800		53,900		32,100
Annual Costs	A. Electrical Energy	1%	9.894	14,500	143,500	14,500	143,500	21,400	211,700	17,400	172,200
	B. Maintenance	0%	9.077	1,400	12,700	1,400	12,700	2,100	19,100	3,200	29,000
	C. Employee Productivity (assume 2% improvmnt. for indirect systems)	0%	9.077	40,000	363,100	40,000	363,100	0	0	0	0
	D.										
	E.										
	F.										
	G.										
	Total Annual Costs				519,300		519,300		230,800		201,200
LCC	**Total Present-Worth Life-Cycle Costs**				584,500		590,500		385,500		293,300
	Life-Cycle Present-Worth Dollar Savings				—		(6,000)		199,000		291,200

PW — Present Worth   PWA — Present Worth Of Annuity   ( ) Additional Cost

Project Title __Computer Processing Center__
Installation & Location __Eastern U.S.__
Design Feature __Lighting System__

Parameter Studied	Representative Values	Alternative 1		Alternative 2		Alternative 3		Alternative 4	
		Parameter Value	Net PW on ABC	Parameter Value	Net PW on ABC	Parameter Value	Net PW on ABC	Parameter Value	Net PW on ABC
Employee Productivity (% less with direct lighting)	Low	0%	221.4	0%	227.4	0%	385.5	0%	293.3
	Intermediate								
	Best Estimate	-2%	584.5	-2%	590.5	0%	385.5	0%	293.3
	Intermediate								
	High	-4%	947.6	-4%	953.6	0%	385.5	0%	293.3
Energy Escalation Rates – Electrical	Low	0%	512.7	0%	578.7	0%	368.0	0%	279.1
	Intermediate								
	Best Estimate	1%	584.5	1%	590.5	1%	385.5	1%	293.3
	Intermediate								
	High	2%	597.9	2%	603.9	2%	405.3	2%	309.4

Notes (Sensitivity Test 1) / Notes (Sensitivity Test 2)

☒ $ x 10³ ☐ $ x 10⁴

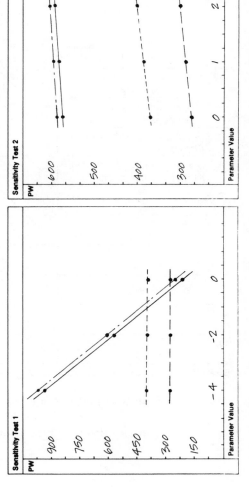

FIGURE 10-10. Lighting systems cost evaluation.

Analysis Matrix

<u>Design Development</u>
Analytical Phase

<u>Lighting System - Open Offices</u>
Basic Function

List the best ideas from ranking and comparison techniques. Determine which one stacks up the best against the desired criteria.

Desired Criteria:
a. Initial Cost
b. Energy Efficiency
c. Task Visibility (greater productivity)
d. Occupant Visual Comfort (greater productivity)
e. Maintainability
f. Appearance (image)
g. Flexibility (change)

	Weight of Importance	a .10	b .18	c .30	d .24	e .06	f .09	g .03	Total 1.00
1.	2×4, 2-lamp Fluorescent K-12 lens	.5/5	.72/4	.9/3	.72/3	.24/4	.27/3	.06/2	3.41
2.	2×4, 2-lamp Fluorescent Parabolic	.4/4	.72/4	1.2/4	.72/3	.24/4	.36/4	.06/2	3.70
3.	Indirect Ceiling/Column Mounted 2-lamp Fluor.	.1/1	.36/2	1.5/5	.96/4	.18/3	.36/4	.09/3	3.55
4.	Indirect Floor/Furniture Mounted Metal Halide	.2/2	.54/3	1.5/5	.96/4	.18/3	.45/5	.12/4	3.95
5.									
6.									
7.									
8.									
9.									
10.									

Excellent - 5   Very Good - 4   Good - 3   Fair - 2   Poor - 1

Note: All fixtures assumed to use energy efficient ballasts and lamps.

FIGURE 10-11. Synthesis of lighting systems.

by a brief narrative comparing the original set of feasible alternatives to the list of preferred solutions and options. Sketches and design calculations, where appropriate, were prepared by the team members with responsibilities in particular areas of expertise.

Recommendations

The last step of the workshop was to present the design recommendations to be implemented in succeeding stages of design. The recommendations were listed as information sources that the project designer could use to develop and expand the building design. This information, consisting of detailed analyses and evaluations of various building components, was used by the project designer to continue refining design documents. A summary of workshop results was presented at a group meeting of the design team so the client could initiate a review of the project and direct the designer to undertake further studies. The design team was issued a new set of detailed design data, and work began anew on design development.

During the design phase, a series of decision-making workshops was held to review the latest developments in the construction documents. As the design moved to a higher level of detail, the study team varied in size from as few as three to as many as six members in each area of expertise. The decision workshops took from a few days to a week to review particular aspects of design adequately. Normally, the project architect developed a list of study areas and a budgeted amount of time in which to complete the decision-making process. The team in turn placed priorities on study areas based on the complexities of design tasks at that point in the process. Decisions concerning final selection of structural systems in the design, for example, were made rather quickly, while a longer study and group discussion were required for such topics as material handling systems and environmental controls.

Design workshops were conducted in such a way as to allow the maximum necessary time for all members of the design team to participate in discussions by the entire group. In order to achieve this, the larger design team was generally broken down into at least two small groups that concentrated on specialized areas of the design. The project architect oversaw the operation of the team as a whole and coordinated information exchange among team members. Typical design teams were composed of the following members:

Layout/Site/Structural/Architectural

Project Architect (Team Leader)
Project Designer
Structural Engineer
Site Planner
Civil Engineer
Owner Representative
User Representative

Energy/Mechanical/Electrical

Mechanical Engineer (Team Leader)
Designer
Energy Engineer
Electrical Engineer
Lighting Engineer
Owner Representative
User Representative

Design Products

At the completion of the design phase, the team had arrived at a consensus as to how the proposed building should respond to the original client and user goals. A major product to emerge from the decision process during the latter stages of design was a seventh project goal addressing the need to improve the quality of the work environment and ambient working conditions for building users. It was also found during analysis of the building layout that in order to maximize the visibility of the building's exterior image, a three-story solution was probably required. Because the building also had to house functions requiring a high degree of social interaction and interpersonal communication, the added travel distance and office separation in a multi-story facility had to be ameliorated. For this reason, a goal called "employee satisfaction" was incorporated into the original analysis, and the designer paid special attention to increasing the ambient quality of the work environment. The final design solution included a major social gathering space and a well-lighted atrium core as the major point of vertical movement through the building (fig. 10-12). Although this design philosophy produced negative results in the control of capital expenditures, the design

FIGURE 10-12. Interior atrium with central stairways and employee lounge.

team felt strongly about the incorporation of such a level of design quality in the final building documents.

CONSTRUCTION

Although the case study was not formally evaluated during the construction stage, decision methodology is an important management tool here also. Since the 1960s construction management has been a widely used professional service. Its principal functions are the review, evaluation, and implementation of ways to reduce time and cost in order to improve construction quality. This approach to design decision-making is now accepted by the American Institute of Architects as a professional service that may be offered by specially trained architects.

One of the first construction issues (arising sometimes even before design begins) is the construction procurement method a client will use. A design team might perform a constructability review during the 95 percent construction document stage. This would include drawing coordination, quality and sufficiency of detailing, adequacy of specifications, ease of construction, simplification of on-site construction, and minimization of the number of building trades involved. Methods of competitive procurement of materials and equipment might also be explored. This would include study of the proper lead time for procuring material and equipment. A review of the general conditions of the contract helps identify whether proper care will be taken regarding site records, inspections, temporary utilities, and insurance. A breakdown of costs by trades allows the designer to make cost-saving suggestions before construction begins. These suggestions are sometimes known as value engineering change proposals (VECPs). Just as costs might be examined, so the construction schedule can be revised to reduce the total construction time. Identifying the major project risks, or liability issues, and exploring how to minimize them is another important issue. These risks might be strikes, labor shortages, inflation, late delivery of materials, and adverse weather. Proper management procedures will also take account of site security, construction safety practices, environmental issues, and management information reporting systems that keep all data readily available for review during construction.

Once the project has entered the construction phase, the form of decision making changes from reviewing proposed approaches to inspecting and monitoring actual field activities. A routine duty is the monitoring of construction progress against the contractor's schedule. Likewise, the contractor's costs are compared with performance indicators and the original design estimate. Inspection of work, including materials used, for conformity to the design and specifications, is also a normal part of construction evaluation. Testing can be done to ensure that the contractor quality control program is followed. Security provisions, contractor safety procedures, and labor relations practices can be monitored. A final area of evaluation during construction is the review and validation of proposed change orders.

At the completion of construction, further follow-up is appropriate to evaluate overall contractor performance: comparisons of estimated and actual costs, preliminary schedules and actual completion dates, and quality levels established by the design team compared with the final product. Interviews are often conducted with the subcontractor to judge the management abilities of the prime contractor and construction manager. Craftspeople responsible for constructing specific components of the building should be interviewed to assess working conditions, safety practices, security provisions, management-labor relations, and design flaws. A review of the number and type of change orders to the contract will yield a better understanding of how to modify certain design practices in future projects. Finally, it is appropriate to review and evaluate facility testing and start-up operations. This might include studying move-in coordination efforts to make sure they are timely and effective.

There are many opportunities for continued decision processes during the construction stage. The techniques presented earlier in this text—especially creativity, life-cycle costing, and decision analysis—are productive in making decisions for the concerns raised during construction.

OCCUPANCY

Continuing decision making into the occupancy phase of the facility cycle serves two primary purposes in the design process. First, it helps the designer and client identify how building components and space arrangements are performing under real environmental and social conditions. Second, it serves as a feedback mechanism to indicate how the facility has addressed the original client goals. The first purpose provides information to the client and building users that is immediately applicable in helping them fine tune and improve their environment. The second purpose is more a long-term one in that it generates new knowledge for architects and clients and helps to improve the process of defining design problems and establishing feasible design objectives. In effect, the examination of the occupied building completes the decision-making cycle in that it measures the effectiveness of a building in satisfying the needs the owner articulated during the project feasibility stage.

Context

Using the six original design goals and the seventh additional goal regarding employee satisfaction, a post-occupancy evaluation was conducted to measure the effects of the completed building on workers, managers, owners, and customers. Information was obtained through observations of activity patterns in the facility, measurements of ambient conditions in the building, interviews with department supervisors, employee questionnaires, telephone interviews with the builders, and analyses of energy and construction records. Because the original design goals were themselves diverse measures of the building's performance, the methods used to evaluate these goals had to address a wide range of environmental, economic, and social issues. It would not have been feasible, for example, to test the effectiveness of the building in terms of how it satisfied the needs of office workers without also measuring the economic costs associated with that level of satisfaction. The evaluation methods employed during occupancy therefore reflected the diversity and complexity of building functions and the goals of all the people associated with the facility.

Information

In order to carry out the evaluation, the original design team members were reassembled six months after the building users had occupied the building. Project goals were reviewed and a series of quick on-site inspections was made to familiarize the team with any changes that had occurred in the design since completion of construction. Photographs of critical work areas were taken during the course of the work day and detailed observations were made to record how specific spaces were being used. The team also interviewed department supervisors to uncover major problem areas and acquire general assessments of the work environment (fig. 10–13). These initial observations and interviews indicated that the building had performed above the expectations of the owners and managers in terms of image and functional goals and was viewed as a key ingredient in promoting a positive image for the company.

Speculation

At the completion of the initial information gathering, the team met to discuss the relative strengths and weaknesses of the building in satisfying client and user group needs. Brainstorming sessions flushed out major problems that appeared to exist in the building and put in perspective issues raised during interviews with department supervisors. These ideas were grouped into categories, and hypotheses were established concerning the effectiveness of building attributes. A major issue that evolved from preliminary evaluation of the building was the additional travel time a multi-story building design required. Another was the amount and type of lighting at each work area and how employees responded to lighting conditions during the work day. In all, fifteen specific evaluative topics were established by the team, and data collection instruments were designed to measure the social and physical conditions of the building.

INTERVIEW NO. 8

DEPARTMENT Technical/Operations

XYZ BUILDING MANAGEMENT INTERVIEW

Overview: We are asking management personnel specific questions to help us in our evaluation of the new XYZ Company building. Your comments will be treated confidentially and will only be used as a representative sample of management feelings about the facility. We will ask you both your response and your employee's responses to each of the following topics.

1. a) How do you feel about the location of the building in terms of its parking and transportation facilities?

No problem with location, even though 15 min.'s more travel time required. Public transportation not available, but no noticeable effects on travel time.
Parking is somewhat far from building, but only minor concern. Would prefer more secure parking at night (maybe fence or guard for those who work night shift.)

b) How do your employees and/or customers feel about the new location?

Originally, some concern with extra travel, but no major problems after first 3 months. Anticipated losing some employees when company cars were removed. So far, this has not happened. No comments heard from customers.

c) Have you heard any comments from other employees about the new location?

Some concern about ice and snow removal because new location is on top of a steep hill. Very good for view and image, bad for access in bad weather.

FIGURE 10-13. Interview worksheets.

2. a) What are your thoughts on the new building in terms of its external appearance?

Like the prominance of the hill location, but the company logo is not visible in its present position.
Stair towers (especially the color) are a constant source of comment. Overall design is o.k. People are curious about "modern, slick" appearance.

b) What comments have you heard from your employees concerning the external appearance of the new building?

Same as above, especially about the color and shape of the stair towers.

c) How do you think the new building fits into the landscape of its site?

Very positive comments, especially considering the number of trees and amount of turf area. Much more green space than most commercial parks. Parking area is well landscaped and is obscured from the public access area. Suburban setting is good. Horizontal emphasis of design fits well with site.

3. a) What has the building done for the image of XYZ?

Very positive response in comparison with old facility. Has not attracted new customers, but the unique design has established an "XYZ" image. The color of the stair towers is the most unique feature. The atrium is a very positive entry for clients.

b) What has the building done for the sales and business of XYZ?

There seem to be more people in the building, some just to see the atrium. Excellent client exposure. Certainly, new environment hasn't "hurt" the sales or corporate image.

FIG. 10-13. (Continued)

4. a) What do <u>you</u> think about the public spaces -- such as the entry lobby, the lounges, the atrium, and the training area -- in the new building?

Nice amenities, especially view from hilltop. Ability to go outside on patio is good. Atrium creates a feeling of openess. Staircase in atrium is a major "public space". Crowding in entry lobby somewhat a problem.

b) What comments have you heard from <u>your employees and/or customers</u> about the public spaces?

Havn't heard complaints about cafeteria location, although counters in vending area aren't functional for eating. No comments on food vending service. Very positive comments about atrium space.

5. a) What do <u>you</u> think about the arrangement of spaces within the new building?

Had to hire one extra employee because of multistory design. Would be better to move operations closer to computer room. No objective measures on loss or gain in productivity. Should change design guidelines to put computer room on same floor and close to operations.

b) What comments have you heard from <u>your employees</u> with regard to the arrangement of spaces in the building?

Negative comments concerning use of dumbwaiter. Not a big problem ; can live with the multistory design, but not optimum situation.

c) Is the building arranged so that it is easy or difficult to perform the job in your department?

Data entry and accounting are close to each other, which is the most critical functional criterion. Work stations need more space ; very tight.

FIG. 10-13. (*Continued*)

6. a) What do you think of the way the space looks in your department?

   Data entry is good, especially the windows and views. Main problem is the small work stations. Nice overall aesthetics. Light levels are OK, especially with ambient natural light.

   b) What comments have you heard from your employees on the way the space in the department looks?

   Overall, good comments. Public areas are especially pleasing. Doesn't look like an "average" office space. People either like or hate the art work selected by the designers.

   c) Is there anything especially pleasing or displeasing about the space that you have heard from the people in your department?

   Most positive comments concerned the open and clear process which allowed user inputs during design. Atrium and plantings emphasize the open and light quality of the building. Most negative aspect is the fact that the building is three stories. Computer is remote from operations. Work stations are too small.

7. a) What are the functions that are performed in your department?

   Manage production units in data entry, accounts applications, and payroll.

   b) How many employees do you have and what are their hours?

   Approximately 65 employees, split between day and night shifts.

FIG. 10-13. (Continued)

Evaluation

In order to measure the degree of employee satisfaction, a question-naire was prepared and administered to the 150-person work force (see fig. 10-14). This revealed to the owner an aspect of design that had not been defined during the feasibility phase of the decision-making process. Employee satisfaction had been added to the list of design goals when it became apparent during the design phase that this would have a major impact on the facility's functional success. In fact, employee response was so positive that it became apparent that this design goal needed to be thoroughly investigated and un-derstood in future building programs. In order to collect attitudinal data that could place employees' opinions in the context of a larger population, the questionnaire was modeled after one used in a na-tionwide survey of office workers and an evaluation of a federal office building. A sampling of responses from these surveys (fig. 10-15) indicated that the case-study employees were significantly happier with their environment in a wide range of categories than occupants surveyed in previous studies. These findings quantified the positive assessments of the client group and reinforced feelings uncovered in the earlier interviews.

While the questionnaires were being administered, a series of objective environmental measures was being collected. Light-meter readings were taken at selected locations throughout the day and night to test the degrees to which the lighting design successfully provided specified levels of illumination (fig. 10-16). Construction costs were tallied from data supplied by contractor and client to compare against cost models prepared during the design phase. Util-ity bills and energy audits were assembled to begin the long-term process of measuring the building's life-cycle costs and the energy-conservation capabilities (fig. 10-17). Finally, interviews were con-ducted with the contractors and subcontractors to uncover problems encountered during construction and to highlight decisions made during design that had positive or adverse effects on construction. These data were collected by the team and compiled into a report that was circulated to the client and the design team.

Synthesis and Recommendations

The final meeting of the design team occurred three years after the first feasibility study began. With the aid of information collected during the post-occupancy evaluation, a synthesis of various compo-

XYZ BUILDING OCCUPANTS QUESTIONNAIRE

August 1982

Dear XYZ Building   Occupants:

This is the questionnaire we told you about several days ago. As you may recall, it is designed to help us in our evaluation of the new XYZ Company   building. Please fill it out as completely as possible and return it to the collection box at the reception desk.

If there is any question that you are unable to answer or don't want to answer, just skip it and go on to the next one. As mentioned before, your responses to the questions will remain anonymous. Thank you for your cooperation.

Sincerely,

Stephen J. Kirk, AIA, CVS
Project Manager
XYZ Building Evaluation Team

1. How long have you worked for the XYZ Company?
   ☐ LESS THAN 6 MONTHS
   ☐ MORE THAN 6 MONTHS, BUT LESS THAN 2 YEARS
   ☐ 2 YEARS OR MORE, BUT LESS THAN 5 YEARS
   ☐ 5 - 10 YEARS
   ☐ MORE THAN 10 YEARS

2. How do you usually get to and from work? (Choose One)
   ☐ OWN CAR
   ☐ COMPANY CAR
   ☐ SHARE RIDE OR CAR POOL
   ☐ OTHER: _____
                    Specify

1

FIGURE 10-14. Questionnaire samples.

3. Compared to where you parked before you worked in the new XYZ building, is your current parking:

☐ MORE CONVENIENTLY LOCATED
☐ LESS CONVENIENTLY LOCATED
☐ ABOUT THE SAME
☐ DID NOT DRIVE BEFORE

4. Before you began working in this building, how did you usually get to and from work?

☐ OWN CAR
☐ COMPANY CAR
☐ SHARE RIDE OR CAR POOL
☐ BUS
☐ WALK
☐ BICYCLE
☐ OTHER:_____
                    Specify
☐ WASN'T EMPLOYED

5. How would you rate the location of the new XYZ building as a place to work?

☐ EXCELLENT
☐ PRETTY GOOD
☐ FAIR
☐ POOR

6. Overall, compared to where you worked before, is the location of the new building:

☐ BETTER ⟹ 7a. How is it better?_____
                    _____
                    _____

☐ WORSE ⟹ 7b. How is it worse?_____
                    _____
                    _____

☐ SAME
☐ WASN'T EMPLOYED

2

FIG. 10-14. (*Continued*)

7. Here are some words used to describe office buildings. Please rate each of the following by placing an X in the box that best describes your feelings about the new building. For example, if you think the building is "attractive", put an X next to the word "attractive", and if you think it is "unattractive", put an X right next to the word "unattractive", and if you think it is somewhere in between, please put an X where you think it belongs.

ATTRACTIVE	☐	☐	☐	☐	☐	☐	☐ UNATTRACTIVE
WELL KEPT UP INTERIORS	☐	☐	☐	☐	☐	☐	☐ POORLY KEPT UP INTERIORS
WELL KEPT UP ON OUTSIDE	☐	☐	☐	☐	☐	☐	☐ POORLY KEPT UP ON OUTSIDE
GOOD ARCHITECTURAL QUALITY	☐	☐	☐	☐	☐	☐	☐ POOR ARCHITECTURAL QUALITY
EASY TO FIND WAY AROUND	☐	☐	☐	☐	☐	☐	☐ DIFFICULT TO FIND WAY AROUND
PLEASANT	☐	☐	☐	☐	☐	☐	☐ UNPLEASANT
GOOD OVERALL DESIGN	☐	☐	☐	☐	☐	☐	☐ POOR OVERALL DESIGN
STIMULATING SPACES	☐	☐	☐	☐	☐	☐	☐ UNSTIMULATING SPACES
GOOD PERSONAL SAFETY	☐	☐	☐	☐	☐	☐	☐ POOR PERSONAL SAFETY

8. During the past month, how many times have you:

		NONE	1-2 TIMES	3-10 TIMES	11-20 TIMES	MORE OFTEN
a.	BEEN TO A CONFERENCE ROOM	☐	☐	☐	☐	☐
b.	USED THE VENDING MACHINES	☐	☐	☐	☐	☐
c.	USED THE INDOOR LOUNGE AREA	☐	☐	☐	☐	☐
d.	USED THE OUTDOOR PATIO AREA	☐	☐	☐	☐	☐

9. Overall, how would you rate the building as a place to work?
☐ EXCELLENT
☐ PRETTY GOOD
☐ FAIR
☐ POOR

10. The way offices and other work spaces in my department are arranged in terms of making it easier for employees to get their jobs done well is:
☐ EXCELLENT
☐ PRETTY GOOD
☐ FAIR
☐ POOR

11. The way the overall space in my department looks is:
☐ EXCELLENT
☐ PRETTY GOOD
☐ FAIR
☐ POOR

3

FIG. 10-14. (Continued)

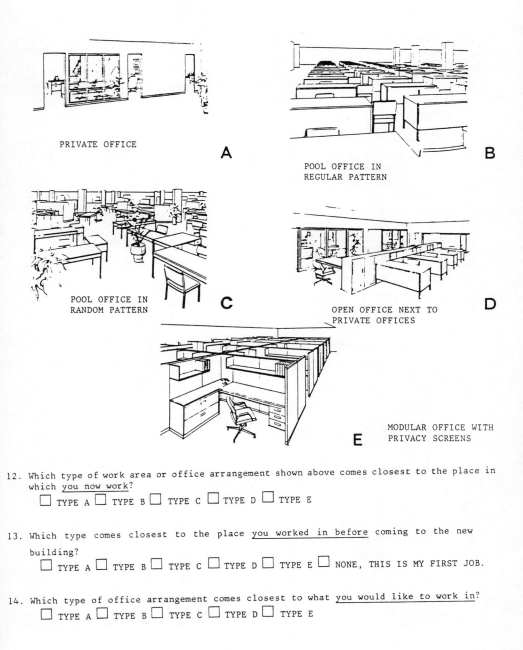

PRIVATE OFFICE

A

POOL OFFICE IN
REGULAR PATTERN

B

POOL OFFICE IN
RANDOM PATTERN

C

OPEN OFFICE NEXT TO
PRIVATE OFFICES

D

MODULAR OFFICE WITH
PRIVACY SCREENS

E

12. Which type of work area or office arrangement shown above comes closest to the place in which <u>you now work</u>?

☐ TYPE A ☐ TYPE B ☐ TYPE C ☐ TYPE D ☐ TYPE E

13. Which type comes closest to the place <u>you worked in before</u> coming to the new building?

☐ TYPE A ☐ TYPE B ☐ TYPE C ☐ TYPE D ☐ TYPE E ☐ NONE, THIS IS MY FIRST JOB.

14. Which type of office arrangement comes closest to what <u>you would like to work in</u>?

☐ TYPE A ☐ TYPE B ☐ TYPE C ☐ TYPE D ☐ TYPE E

4

FIG. 10-14. (*Continued*)

15. Sometimes the arrangement of offices and work stations can be distracting to people working in an office building. Please indicate how bothersome each of the following is to your work at the new XYZ building.

NOISE	NOT AT ALL BOTHERSOME	NOT VERY BOTHERSOME	FAIRLY BOTHERSOME	VERY BOTHERSOME
a. RINGING TELEPHONES IN MY OWN DEPARTMENT	☐	☐	☐	☐
b. RINGING TELEPHONES IN OTHER DEPARTMENTS	☐	☐	☐	☐
c. NOISE FROM OTHER EQUIPMENT IN MY OWN DEPARTMENT	☐	☐	☐	☐
d. NOISE FROM EQUIPMENT IN OTHER DEPARTMENTS	☐	☐	☐	☐
e. CONVERSATIONS OF OTHERS IN MY DEPARTMENT	☐	☐	☐	☐
f. CONVERSATIONS OF OTHERS FROM OTHER DEPARTMENTS	☐	☐	☐	☐
g. NOISE FROM LOBBY/CORRIDORS	☐	☐	☐	
h. NOISE FROM VENTILATING SYSTEM	☐	☐	☐	☐
i. NOISE FROM OUTSIDE SOURCES	☐	☐	☐	☐
j. MUSIC SYSTEM	☐	☐	☐	☐
LIGHTING				
k. GLARE FROM NATURAL SUNLIGHT	☐	☐	☐	☐
l. GLARE FROM ARTIFICIAL LIGHTS	☐	☐	☐	☐
HEATING AND VENTILATING				
m. TOO HOT IN SUMMER	☐	☐	☐	☐
n. TOO COLD IN SUMMER	☐	☐	☐	☐
o. TOO COLD IN WINTER	☐	☐	☐	☐
p. TOO HOT IN WINTER	☐	☐	☐	☐
q. DRAFTS	☐	☐	☐	☐
r. HEAT FROM NATURAL SUNLIGHT	☐	☐	☐	☐
s. STUFFY AIR	☐	☐	☐	☐
OTHER DISTRACTIONS				
t. PEOPLE WALKING AROUND	☐	☐	☐	☐
u. REARRANGING OF FURNITURE	☐	☐	☐	☐
v. WALKING UP STAIRS TOO OFTEN	☐	☐	☐	☐
w. WALKING TOO FAR TO GET TO OTHER DEPARTMENTS	☐	☐	☐	☐
x. FOOD ODORS	☐	☐	☐	☐
y. WORKING OUTSIDE MY WORK STATION BECAUSE OF LACK OF SPACE	☐	☐	☐	☐

5

FIG. 10-14. (*Continued*)

16. On an <u>average working day</u>, about how much of your time is spent at your desk or work station?

- [ ] ALL OR 100 PER CENT
- [ ] 76 - 99 PER CENT
- [ ] 51 - 75 PER CENT
- [ ] 26 - 50 PER CENT
- [ ] 1 - 25 PER CENT
- [ ] NONE

17. On an <u>average working day</u>, how often does someone from outside the building come to see you on business?

- [ ] NEVER
- [ ] 1 - 2 TIMES
- [ ] 3 - 4 TIMES
- [ ] 5 - 10 TIMES
- [ ] MORE THAN 10 TIMES

18. On an <u>average working day</u>, how many times do you meet with fellow workers at your desk/work station to discuss or perform work?

- [ ] NEVER
- [ ] 1 - 2 TIMES
- [ ] 3 - 4 TIMES
- [ ] 5 - 10 TIMES
- [ ] MORE THAN 10 TIMES

19. On an <u>average working day</u>, about how much of the time is spent talking on the telephone?

- [ ] 76 - 100 PER CENT
- [ ] 51 - 75 PER CENT
- [ ] 26 - 50 PER CENT
- [ ] 11 - 25 PER CENT
- [ ] 1 - 10 PER CENT
- [ ] NONE; WORK DOESN'T REQUIRE PHONE CONVERSATIONS

6

FIG. 10-14. (*Continued*)

20. On an <u>average working day</u>, about how many phone conversations do you have?

☐   NONE
☐   1 - 2
☐   3 - 4
☐   5 - 10
☐   MORE THAN 10

21. Please rate your personal work station on each of these characteristics:

	EXCELLENT	GOOD	FAIR	POOR
a. AMOUNT OF SPACE AVAILABLE TO YOU	☐	☐	☐	☐
b. MATERIALS USED FOR DESKS, TABLES AND CHAIRS	☐	☐	☐	☐
c. LIGHTING FOR THE WORK YOU DO	☐	☐	☐	☐
d. LOCATION OF CEILING LIGHTS IN RELATION TO WORK AREA	☐	☐	☐	☐
e. COLOR OF WALLS AND PARTITIONS	☐	☐	☐	☐
f. AMOUNT OF SPACE FOR STORING THINGS	☐	☐	☐	☐
g. ATTRACTIVENESS	☐	☐	☐	☐
h. CONVERSATIONAL PRIVACY	☐	☐	☐	☐
i. TYPE OF FLOOR COVERING	☐	☐	☐	☐
j. YOUR VIEW OUTSIDE	☐	☐	☐	☐
k. ACCESS TO OTHER PEOPLE YOU HAVE TO WORK WITH	☐	☐	☐	☐
l. WALL AREA FOR HANGING THINGS (E.G., PICTURES)	☐	☐	☐	☐
m. STYLE OF YOUR FURNITURE	☐	☐	☐	☐
n. NUMBER OF ELECTRICAL OUTLETS	☐	☐	☐	☐
o. LOCATION OF ELECTRICAL OUTLETS	☐	☐	☐	☐
p. VISUAL PRIVACY	☐	☐	☐	☐
q. AMOUNT OF SURFACE AREA FOR WORK	☐	☐	☐	☐
r. COMFORT OF YOUR CHAIR	☐	☐	☐	☐
s. OVERALL AESTHETIC QUALITY	☐	☐	☐	☐
t. VENTILATION AND AIR CIRCULATION	☐	☐	☐	☐
u. HEATING	☐	☐	☐	☐
v. AIR QUALITY	☐	☐	☐	☐
w. HEIGHT OF WORK SURFACE	☐	☐	☐	☐
x. SIZE OF WORK SURFACE	☐	☐	☐	☐

FIG. 10-14. (*Continued*)

22. Compared to where you worked before coming to the new building, is your present work station:

☐ BETTER ⟹ 22a. How is it better _____

_____

☐ WORSE ⟹ 22b. How is it worse? _____

_____

☐ SAME
☐ WASN'T EMPLOYED

23. Here are some statements about peoples' jobs. Please indicate how true each is in your job.

	VERY TRUE	SOMEWHAT TRUE	NOT VERY TRUE	NOT AT ALL TRUE
TRAVEL TO AND FROM WORK IS CONVENIENT	☐	☐	☐	☐
WHENEVER I TALK TO CO-WORKERS, OTHERS CAN HEAR OUR CONVERSATION	☐	☐	☐	☐
WHENEVER I TALK ON THE TELEPHONE OTHERS AROUND ME CAN HEAR MY CONVERSATION	☐	☐	☐	☐
I HAVE ACCESS TO THE EQUIPMENT AND MATERIAL I NEED TO GET THE JOB DONE WELL	☐	☐	☐	☐
THE PHYSICAL SURROUNDINGS ARE PLEASANT	☐	☐	☐	☐
MY WORK SURFACE, STORAGE SPACE, CHAIR AND OTHER FURNITURE ARE WHAT I NEED TO GET THE JOB DONE WELL	☐	☐	☐	☐
I FEEL TOO VISIBLE IN MY WORK SPACE	☐	☐	☐	☐
MY JOB IS BEST DONE IN AN AREA AWAY FROM OTHER PEOPLE	☐	☐	☐	☐
TO DO MY JOB WELL REQUIRES A QUIET PLACE	☐	☐	☐	☐
THE WORK IS INTERESTING	☐	☐	☐	☐
COMPARED TO WHERE I WORKED BEFORE COMING TO THIS BUILDING, I DO MORE WORK NOW	☐	☐	☐	☐

24. Overall, how satisfied are you with your work station?

☐ VERY SATISFIED   ☐ FAIRLY SATISFIED   ☐ NOT VERY SATISFIED   ☐ NOT AT ALL SATISFIED

8

FIG. 10-14. (*Continued*)

25. Below are some characteristics of offices. Please rank them as they relate to <u>how important</u> each is in terms of <u>doing your job well</u>. Rank them from 1 to 18, with the most important as "1" and the least important as "18".

RANK

a. LIGHTING FOR THE WORK YOU DO ____

b. COMFORT OF YOUR CHAIR ____

c. AMOUNT OF SURFACE AREA FOR WORK ____

d. AMOUNT OF SPACE FOR STORING THINGS ____

e. SIZE OF WORK AREA ____

f. LOCATION OF WORK AREA IN BUILDING ____

g. ACCESS TO FELLOW WORKERS ____

h. CONVERSATIONAL PRIVACY ____

i. AIR CIRCULATION ____

j. VISUAL PRIVACY ____

k. A VIEW TO THE OUTSIDE ____

l. ARRANGEMENT OF YOUR WORK AREA ____

m. ATTRACTIVENESS OF YOUR WORK AREA ____

n. QUIET OFFICE AREA ____

o. DISTANCE FROM HOME TO OFFICE ____

p. CLOSENESS OF SHOPPING OR EATING FACILITIES FROM YOUR OFFICE ____

q. LOUNGE AREA IN BUILDING ____

r. CAFETERIA SERVICES IN BUILDING ____

26. How many days during the week are you usually at work in the new building?

☐ 2 DAYS OR LESS PER WEEK

☐ 3 - 4 DAYS PER WEEK

☐ 5 DAYS PER WEEK

☐ MORE THAN 5 DAYS PER WEEK

27. During your average working day, how many times do you leave the building in connectiⓘ with your work?

☐ NONE, NEVER LEAVE BUILDING

☐ 1 - 2 TIMES

☐ 3 - 4 TIMES

☐ 5 OR MORE TIMES

9

FIG. 10-14. (*Continued*)

28. About how long does it take you to get to work?

☐ LESS THAN 15 MINUTES
☐ 15 - 29 MINUTES
☐ 30 - 44 MINUTES
☐ 45 - 59 MINUTES
☐ ONE HOUR OR MORE

29. Are you:
☐ FEMALE ☐ MALE

30. Do you work for XYZ:
☐ FULL TIME ☐ PART TIME

31. Please indicate your age:
☐ UNDER 30
☐ 30 - 40
☐ 41 - 55
☐ 56 OR OVER

This completes the questionnaire. Thank you for your cooperation. If you have any additional comments about the building, please feel free to write them down on the back of this page.

Please return this questionnaire to the collection box at the reception desk.

FIG. 10-14. (*Continued*)

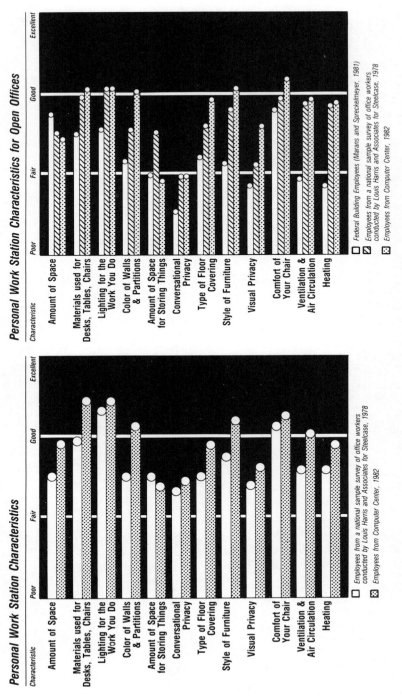

FIGURE 10-15. Questionnaire responses and comparisons.

FIGURE 10-16. Lighting evaluation. (Photograph courtesy of Elliot Rappaport)

nents of the completed building was begun, to match the original design goals against how the building was being used. Although economic consequences of the design were not in line with the original project budget, the higher quality of construction and environmental amenities bought by the higher capital costs were found to be directly responsible for employee satisfaction. The original design goals were used to measure the building's effectiveness as a work place and, more important, formed the basis for recommendations for revisions in the client's design process. The evaluation generated a large amount of performance data for the design team and the client, and established a new knowledge base for subsequent facilities of this type. Data collected verified the benefits of investing in higher quality spatial arrangements and materials than planned during the feasibility stage. The architect now had specific information

Computer Processing Center, Annual Energy/Fuel Consumption

| Month | Electricity | | Natural Gas | | Total Cost |
	Kwh	Cost[1]	mcf	Cost[2]	
January	64,138	$4111	517	$2856	$6967
February	86,152	5522	238	1313	6835
March	82,688	5300	215	1187	6487
April	98,477	6312	189	1045	7357
May	100,833	6463	49	273	6736
June	113,501	7275	118	650	7925
July	106,200	6807	6	35	6842
August	94,545	6060	18	97	6157
September	99,684	6347	50	278	6625
October	95,684	6133	212	1173	7306
November	79,349	5086	234	1291	6377
December	82,797	5307	609	3364	8671
Totals	1,103,400	$70,723	2455	$13,562	$84,285 ($1.81/ GSF)[3]
Equivalent Kwh	1,103,400	+	719,310	=	1,822,710 kwh

1. Electrical cost/Kwh = $0.064
2. Natural gas cost/mcf = $5.524
3. Gross square footage = 46,540

FIGURE 10-17. Annual energy consumption.

about how certain environments affect building occupants; the owner could now accurately determine levels of capital and life-cycle expenditures that would be required in future building projects. The results of the building evaluation are summarized in figure 10-18.

CONCLUSION

The approach to decision making outlined in this case study allows the design and client actors to participate in all stages of the building process. Although this methodology has been developed for use in a variety of project contexts and is supported by a number of theoretical frameworks, the basic elements are straightforward. Any number of facility requirements can be met with a wide range of design

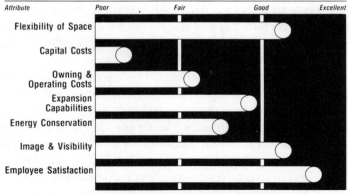

FIGURE 10-18. Overall building evaluation.

alternatives. These alternatives may involve a new building, or they may call for reorganization of an existing facility.

The premise of this decision-making process is the design team's recognition and definition of all the factors that might affect the feasibility, design, construction, and occupancy of a building solution. During decision making these concerns will take on added meaning and importance. In some instances, the economic factors associated with the reduction of capital cost, minimization of life-cycle costs, and energy conservation can best be addressed by a person trained in life-cycle implications of building systems. The functional and operational concerns of a building program—such as the need for flexibility, pedestrian circulation, ambient environmental conditions, and building image—may best be articulated by those who will occupy the completed facility and the designer who will assemble the building components. The decision-making process outlined here assumes that modern design problems are composed of complex and conflicting design objectives and must be addressed from a wide range of client, user, design, and technical viewpoints.

Finally, the decision-making process outlined in the five-step methodology was applied to the case study project in a cyclical and flexible manner. The methodology provided a template that could be understood by all members of the design team and was useful to the project architect as a means of moving the project from one phase of decision making to the next. Although certain techniques were often concentrated in certain steps of the methodology—for example, the Delphi technique usually applied during the speculation phase—rigid adherence to a regimen of methods usage is not required or useful to the decision-making process. During the feasibility stage of the facility cycle, for example, the design team seemed more concerned with information collection and creativity searches for programming alternatives. The activities of the design stage, however, were more centered on the introduction of evaluation and synthesis methods in order to sift through a large amount of building system information and arrive at specific design recommendations.

The key to the use of this decision-making approach is the recognition that the design process is a fluid and dynamic set of technical and creative activities. The facility cycle itself has been defined as an iterative rather than a linear process; architects often reenter the cycle during occupancy in order to collect the necessary data required for a project feasibility study. In the same way, the five-step methodology should be viewed by the design team as a way of mapping and planning the process of decision making, not as a prescriptive formula for arriving at an "optimal" solution. The most pressing problem outlined in chapter 1 of this text was the removal of the architect as the central decision maker in contemporary design projects. The growing complexity of modern environmental projects and increased specialization in the design field, the diffuse character of client and user groups, and the pressures of running a competitive design practice were presented as historical backdrops to this problem. The introduction of a systematic approach to decision making and the use of a variety of decision techniques by the architect is seen as a way to manage and coordinate the act of design. In the past creativity has been associated primarily with the visual and spatial characteristics of design. We would suggest that the act of design must also include the ability of the architect to create a social environment in which the design team can effectively interact and communicate throughout the course of a project. The creative act of design therefore should be as much concerned with the *process* of architectural decisions as with the visual and physical *products* of those decisions.

Bibliography

CHAPTER 1

Amara, Roy. 1981. "The Futures Field: Which Direction Now?" *The Futurist* 6:42–46.

Blau, Judith R. 1984. *Architects and Firms: A Sociological Perspective on Architectural Practice*. Cambridge: The MIT Press.

Browne, Malcolm W. 1980. "Is Problem-Solving America's Lost Art?" *The New York Times*, July 29, III, 1:1.

Domer, Dennis E., J. William Carswell, and Kent F. Spreckelmeyer. 1983. *A Survey of Architectural Education for the Kansas Society of Architects*. Lawrence: The University of Kansas.

Hoesli, Bernhard. 1970. *Alvar Aalto Synopsis*. Basel: Birkhauser Verlag.

Hubbard, Barbara Marx. 1981. "Critical Path to an All-Win World." *The Futurist* 6:31–41.

Jacobs, Jane. 1961. *The Death and Life of Great American Cities*. New York: Vintage Books.

Jencks, Charles. 1984. *The Language of Post-Modern Architecture*. 4th edition. New York: Rizzoli.

Kostof, Spiro, ed. 1977. *The Architect: Chapters in the History of the Profession*. New York: Oxford University Press.

Lapidus, Morris. 1967. *Architecture: A Profession and a Business*. New York: Van Nostrand Reinhold.

Lerup, Lars. 1977. *Building the Unfinished: Architecture and Human Action*. Beverly Hills: Sage.

Orr, Frank. 1982. *Professional Practice in Architecture*. New York: Van Nostrand Reinhold.

Patton, Phil. 1981. "The Madcap Buildings of Best Products." *Mainliner* 2:77–84.

Ray, Keith. 1976. *This Business of Building Design*. Matteson, Ill.: Greatlakes Living Press.

Rudofsky, Bernard. 1964. *Architecture Without Architects*. New York: Museum of Modern Art.

Ruusuvuori, Aarno. 1978. *Alvar Aalto*. Helsinki: Museum of Finnish Architecture.

Saint, Andrew. 1983. *The Image of the Architect*. New Haven: Yale University Press.

Schön, Donald. 1983. *The Reflective Practitioner: How Professionals Think in Action*. New York: Basic Books.

Schumacher, E. F. 1973. *Small is Beautiful: Economics as if People Mattered*. New York: Harper and Row.

Toffler, Alvin. 1980. *The Third Wave*. New York: Morrow.

Venturi, Robert. 1966. *Complexity and Contradiction in Architecture*. New York: The Museum of Modern Art.

Wolfe, Tom. 1981. *From Bauhaus to Our House*. New York: Farrar Straus Giroux.

CHAPTER 2

American Institute of Architects (AIA). 1973. *Architect's Handbook of Professional Practice*. Washington, D.C.: AIA.

Bechtel, Robert, Robert W. Marans, and William Michelson, eds. 1987. *Methods in Environmental and Behavioral Research*. New York: Van Nostrand Reinhold.

Brandon, P. S., and J. A. Powell, eds. 1984. *Quality and Profit in Building Design*. London: E. & F. Spon.

Burstein, David. 1982. *Project Management for the Design Professional*. New York: Whitney Library of Design.

Coxe, Weld. 1980. *Managing Architectural and Engineering Practice*. New York: Wiley.

DeVido, Alfredo. 1984. *Innovative Management Techniques for Architectural Design and Construction*. New York: Whitney Library of Design.

Haviland, David S. 1981. *Managing Architectural Projects: The Effective Project Manager*. Washington, D.C.: American Institute of Architects.

Mitchell, William J. 1977. *Computer Aided Architectural Design*. New York: Van Nostrand Reinhold.

Palmer, Mickey. 1981. *The Architect's Guide to Facility Programming*. Washington, D.C.: American Institute of Architects.

Preiser, Wolfgang F. E., ed. 1978. *Facility Programming*. Stroudsburg, Pa.: Dowden, Hutchinson & Ross.

Wade, John W. 1977. *Architecture Problems and Purposes*. New York: Wiley.

Willis, Arthur James. 1981. *The Architect in Practice*. 6th ed. London: Granada.

CHAPTER 3

Ackoff, Russell L., and Maurice Sasieni. 1968. *Fundamentals of Operations Research*. New York: Wiley.

American Institute of Architects (AIA). 1977. *Owner-Architect Agreement, AIA Documents B141 and B161*. Washington, D.C.: AIA.

Bronowski, Jacob. 1955. *The Common Sense of Science*. Cambridge: Harvard University Press.

Cross, Nigel, ed. 1984. *Developments in Design Methodology*. New York: Wiley.

Greene, Herb. 1981. *Building to Last: Architecture as Ongoing Art*. New York: Architectural Book Publishing.

Jones, J. Christopher. 1981. *Design Methods: Seeds of Human Futures*. New York: Wiley.

Mackinder, Margaret. 1982. *Design Decision Making in Architectural Practice*. York, England: Institute of Advanced Architectural Studies.

Marshall, Lane L. 1983. *Action by Design: Facilitating Design Decisions into the 21st Century*. Washington, D.C.: American Society of Landscape Architects.

Page, Clint. 1984. *The Public Sector Designs*. Washington, D.C.: Partners for Livable Places.

Peña, William. 1977. *Problem Seeking: An Architectural Programming Primer*. Boston: Cahners.

Spreckelmeyer, Kent F. 1982. "Architectural Programming as an Evaluation Tool in Design." *Proceedings of the 13th Annual Conference of the Environmental Design Research Association*, 289–296. College Park, Md.

CHAPTER 4

Bytheway, Charles W. 1965. "Basic Function Determination Technique." *Proceedings of the Fifth National Meeting of the Society of American Value Engineers* 2:21–23.

Clawson, Robert H. 1970. *Value Engineering for Management*. Princeton: Auerbach.

Dell'Isola, Alphonse J. 1982. *Value Engineering in the Construction Industry*. New York: Van Nostrand Reinhold.

Dell'Isola, Alphonse J., and Stephen J. Kirk. 1981. *Life Cycle Costing for Design Professionals*. New York: McGraw-Hill.

Fallon, Carlos. 1971. *Value Analysis to Improve Productivity*. New York: Wiley-Interscience.

Fasal, John H. 1972. *Practical Value Analysis Methods*. New York: Hayden.

Miles, Lawrence D. 1972. *Techniques in Value Analysis and Engineering*. New York: McGraw-Hill.

O'Brien, James J. 1976. *Value Analysis in Design and Construction*. New York: McGraw-Hill.

Oughton, Frederick. 1969. *Value Analysis and Value Engineering*. London: Pitman.

Parker, Donald. 1977. *Value Engineering Theory*. Washington, D.C.: Society of American Value Engineers.

United States Environmental Protection Agency (EPA). 1976. *Value Engineering Workbook for Construction Projects*. Washington, D.C.: EPA. 43019-76-008, July.

U.S. General Services Administration (GSA). 1978. *Value Management Handbook*. Washington, D.C.: GSA. PBS-P-8000.1A, October 31.

CHAPTER 5

Adams, James L. 1979. *Conceptual Blockbusting: A Guide to Better Ideas*. 2d ed. New York: Norton.

Alexander, Christopher, S. Ishikawa, and M. Silverstein. 1977. *A Pattern Language*. New York: Oxford University Press.

Arieti, Silvano. 1976. *Creativity: The Magic Synthesis*. New York: Basic Books.

Australia Department of Defense. 1983. *Value Analysis*. Canberra: Department of Defense.

Broadbent, Geoffrey. 1973. *Design in Architecture*. New York: Wiley.

Clark, Charles H. 1958. *Brainstorming*. New York: Doubleday.

Clark, Roger H., and Michael Pause. 1985. *Precedents in Architecture*. New York: Van Nostrand Reinhold.

Crowe, Norman, and Paul Laseau. 1984. *Visual Notes for Architects and Designers*. New York: Van Nostrand Reinhold.

DeBono, Edward. 1970. *Lateral Thinking: Creativity Step by Step*. New York: Harper & Row.

Dell'Isola, Alphonse J. 1982. *Value Engineering in the Construction Industry*. New York: Van Nostrand Reinhold.

Edwards, Betty. 1979. *Drawing on the Right Side of the Brain*. Los Angeles: Tarcher.

Feldman, Edwin B. 1975. *Building Design for Maintainability*. New York: McGraw-Hill.

Gordon, William J. J. 1961. *Synectics: The Development of Creative Capacity*. New York: Harper.

Judson, Horace Freeland. 1980. *The Search for Solutions*. New York: Holt, Rinehart & Winston.

Kirk, Stephen J. 1980. "Delphi: An Aid in Project Cost Control." *Architectural Record* 12:51–55.

Koestler, Arthur. 1967. *The Act of Creation: A Study of the Conscious and Unconscious in Science and Art*. New York: Dell.

Laseau, Paul. 1980. *Graphic Thinking for Architects and Designers.* New York: Van Nostrand Reinhold.

Linstone, H. A., and M. Turoof, eds. 1975. *The Delphi Method: Techniques and Applications.* New York: Addison-Wesley.

Maslow, Abraham. 1976. *The Farther Reaches of Human Nature.* New York: Penguin.

Miles, Lawrence D. 1972. *Techniques in Value Analysis and Engineering.* New York: McGraw-Hill.

Osborn, Alex F. 1957. *Applied Imagination: Principles and Procedures of Creative Thinking.* New York: Scribner's.

Parnes, Sidney J., Ruth B. Noller, and Angelo M. Biondi, eds. 1977. *Guide to Creative Action.* New York: Scribner's.

Raudsepp, Eugene, and George P. Hough. 1977. *Creative Growth Games.* New York: Harcourt Brace Jovanovich.

Rose, Steward. 1975. *The Delphi Method: Self-Help Mini Guide.* Washington, D.C.: American Institute of Architects.

Taylor, Calvin W., and F. Barron, eds. 1963. *Scientific Creativity: It's Recognition and Development.* New York: Wiley.

U.S. General Services Administration (GSA). 1978. *Value Management Handbook.* Washington, D.C.: GSA. PBS-P-80001A, October 31.

Whiting, Charles. 1958. *Creative Thinking.* New York: Reinhold.

Zimmerman, Larry, and Glen Hart. 1982. *Value Engineering: A Practical Approach for Owners, Designers, and Contractors.* New York: Van Nostrand Reinhold.

CHAPTER 6

American Institute of Architects (AIA). 1977. *Life Cycle Cost Analysis: A Guide for Architects.* Washington, D.C.: AIA.

American Society for Testing and Materials (ASTM). 1983. *Measuring Life-Cycle Costs of Buildings and Building Systems.* ASTM E917-83. Philadelphia: ASTM.

Brown, Robert J., and Rudolph R. Yanick. 1980. *Life Cycle Costing: A Practical Guide for Energy Managers.* Atlanta: Fairmount.

Dell'Isola, Alphonse J. 1982. *Value Engineering in the Construction Industry.* New York: Van Nostrand Reinhold.

Dell'Isola, Alphonse J., and Stephen J. Kirk. 1981. *Life Cycle Costing for Design Professionals.* New York: McGraw-Hill.

――――. 1983. *Life Cycle Cost Data.* New York: McGraw-Hill.

Grant, Eugene L., W. Grant Ireson, and Richard Levenworth. 1976. *Principles of Engineering Economy.* New York: Ronald.

Griffith, Edwin B. 1975. *Life Cycle Cost-Benefit Analysis: A Basic Course in*

Economic Decision Making. Document PB-251848/LK. Springfield, Va.: National Technical Information Center.

Haviland, David S. 1978. *Life Cycle Cost Analysis 2: Using It in Practice.* Washington, D.C.: American Institute of Architects.

Kirk, Stephen J. 1979–80. "Life Cycle Costing: Increasingly Popular Route to Design Value." *Architectural Record* (2-part article) 12:63–67, and 1:59–63.

Miles, Lawrence D. 1972. *Techniques in Value Analysis and Engineering.* New York: McGraw-Hill.

Nielsen, Kris R. 1973. "Tax Consideration in Building Design." *AIA Journal* 9:28–31.

Rugg, Rosalie T. 1975. *Solar Heating and Cooling in Buildings: Methods of Economic Evaluation.* NBSIR75-712. Washington, D.C.: National Bureau of Standards, July.

Samuelson, Paul A. 1980. *Economics.* 9th ed. New York: McGraw-Hill.

Sizemore, M. M., H. O. Clark, and W. S. Ostrander. 1979. *Energy Planning for Buildings.* Washington, D.C.: American Institute of Architects.

Stone, P. A. 1975. *Building Design Evaluation: Costs-in-Use.* 2d ed. New York: Wiley.

Terotechnology: An Introduction to the Management of Physical Resources. 1976. Leatherhead, Surrey: National Terotechnology Center.

U.S. Comptroller General, 1972. "Study of Health Care Facilities Construction Costs." Washington, D.C.: U.S. Congress, November.

U.S. Department of Defense (DoD). 1970. *LCC-1: Life Cycle Costing Procurement Guide.* Washington, D.C.: DoD, July.

———. 1970. *LCC-2: Casebook of Life Cycle Costing in Equipment Procurement.* Washington, D.C.: DoD, July.

———. 1973. *LCC-3: Life Cycle Costing Guide for System Acquisition.* Washington, D.C.: DoD, January.

U.S. Department of Health, Education, and Welfare (HEW). 1973. *Evaluation of the Health Facilities Process.* Vol. 4. *Evaluation of Life Cycle Costs.* Washington, D.C.: HEW, March 31.

———. 1973. *Life Cycle Budgeting as an Aid to Decision Making.* Building Information Circular (draft). Washington, D.C.: HEW, Office of Facilities Engineering and Property Management.

U.S. General Services Administration (GSA). 1972. *Life Cycle Management Model for Project Management of Buildings.* Washington, D.C.: GSA, July.

———. 1976. *Life Cycle Costing in the Public Buildings Service.* Washington, D.C.: GSA.

———. 1977. *Life Cycle Costing Workbook: A Guide for the Implementation of Life Cycle Costing in the Federal Supply Service.* Washington, D.C.: GSA.

CHAPTER 7

Bechtel, Robert, Robert W. Marans, and William Michelson, eds. 1987. *Methods in Environmental and Behavioral Research.* New York: Van Nostrand Reinhold.

Behn, Robert D., and James W. Vaupee. 1982. *Quick Analysis for Busy Decision Makers.* New York: Basic Books.

Coombs, Clyde H. 1976. *A Theory of Data.* Ann Arbor: Mathesis.

Coombs, Clyde H., and James Bowen. 1971. "Additivity of Risk in Portfolios." *Perception and Psychophysics* 10, no. 1:43–46.

Hwang, Ching-Lai. 1981. *Multiple Attribute Decision Making: A State-of-the-Art Survey.* Berlin: Springer-Verlag.

Jones, J. Christopher. 1981. *Design Methods: Seeds of Human Features.* New York: Wiley.

Keeney, Ralph L. 1977. "The Art of Assessing Multiattribute Utility Functions." *Organizational Behavior and Human Performance* 19:267–310.

Keeney, Ralph L., and Howard Raiffa. 1976. *Decisions with Multiple Objectives.* New York: Wiley.

Kirk, Stephen J. 1980. "Delphi: An Aid in Project Cost Control." *Architectural Record* 12:51–55.

———. 1981. "Value Assessment in Facilities Design: Multi-Value Indices." *Proceedings of the Society of American Value Engineers,* 58–64.

Mattar, Samir, W. Bitterlich, P. Manning, and P. Fazio. 1978. "A Decision Model for the Design of Building Enclosures." *Building and Environment* 13:201–16.

Parshall, Steven A., and William M. Peña. 1983. *Evaluating Facilities: A Practical Approach to Post-Occupancy Evaluation.* Houston: Candill, Rowlett, Scott.

Peña, William. 1977. *Problem Seeking: An Architectural Primer.* Boston: Cahners.

Raiffa, Howard. 1970. *Decision Analysis.* Reading, Mass.: Addison-Wesley.

Rubinstein, Moshe F. 1980. *Concepts in Problem-Solving.* Englewood Cliffs, N.J.: Prentice-Hall.

Runkel, Philip J., and Joseph E. McGrath. 1972. *Research on Human Behavior: A Systematic Guide to Method.* New York: Holt, Rinehart & Winston.

Seaton, Richard. 1978. "Modeling Architectural Problems." *Design Methods and Theories* 12, no. 1:46–52.

Spetzler, Carl S., and Axel S. S. von Holstein. 1975. "Probability Encoding in Decision Analysis." *Management Science* 22:340–58.

Spreckelmeyer, Kent F. 1981. "Application of a Computer-Aided Decision Technique in Architectural Programming." D. Arch. diss. University of Michigan, Ann Arbor.

———. 1982. "Architectural Programming as an Evaluation Tool in Design." *Proceedings of the 13th Annual Conference of the Environmental Design Research Association*, 289–96. College Park, Md.

Starr, Chauncey. 1969. "Social Benefit Versus Technological Risk." *Science* 165:1232–38.

Thompson, Michael. 1977. "The Architect's Dilemma." *Design Methods and Theories* 11, no. 1:11–16.

Wright, George, ed. 1985. *Behavioral Decision Making*. New York: Plenum.

CHAPTER 8

Ankerl, Geza. 1981. *Experimental Sociology of Architecture: A Guide to Theory, Research, and Literature*. New York: Mouton.

Architectural Record. 1978. "The New Buildings: Those Guiding Principles." 12:110–11.

Banham, Reyner. 1984. *The Architecture of the Well-Tempered Environment*. 2d ed. Chicago: University of Chicago Press.

Bechtel, Robert B. 1977. *Enclosing Behavior*. Stroudsburg, Pa.: Dowden, Hutchinson & Ross.

Bechtel, Robert, Robert W. Marans, and William Michelson, eds. 1987. *Methods in Environmental and Behavioral Research*. New York: Van Nostrand Reinhold.

Bennett, Corwin. 1977. *Spaces for People: Human Factors in Design*. Englewood Cliffs, N.J.: Prentice-Hall.

Brebner, John. 1982. *Environmental Psychology in Building Design*. London: Applied Science.

Broadbent, Geoffrey, R. Bunt, and T. Llorens, eds. 1980. *Meaning and Behavior in the Built Environment*. New York: Wiley.

Conway, Donald. 1973. *Architectural Design and the Social Sciences*. Washington, D.C.: American Institute of Architects.

Cooper, Claire C. 1975. *Easter Hill Village: Some Social Implications of Design*. New York: Free Press.

Davis, Gerald, ed. 1986. *Building Performance: Function, Preservation, and Rehabilitation*. Philadelphia: American Society of Testing and Materials.

Davis, Gerald, and Françoise Szigeti. 1986. "Planning and Programming Offices: Determining User Requirements." In *Behavioral Issues in Office Design*, ed. Jean D. Wineman, 23–41. New York: Van Nostrand Reinhold.

Deasy, C. M. 1985. *Designing Places for People: A Handbook on Human Behavior for Architects, Designers, and Facility Managers*. New York: Whitney Library of Design.

Farbstein, Jay. 1984. "Using the Program: Applications to Design, Occupancy, and Evaluation." *Proceedings of the 15th Annual Conference of the*

Environmental Design Research Association. San Luis Obispo, Cal., 240–51.

Farbstein, Jay, and Min Kantrowitz. 1978. *People in Places*. Englewood Cliffs, N.J.: Prentice-Hall.

Friedman, Arnold, Craig Zimring, and Ervin Zube. 1978. *Environmental Design Evaluation*. New York: Plenum.

Groat, Linda. 1984. "Public Opinions of Contextual Fit: A Lay Panel Reacts to Some Notable Efforts." *Architecture* 11:72–75.

Harris, Louis, and Associates. 1978. *The Steelcase National Survey of Office Environments: Do They Work?* Grand Rapids: Steelcase, Inc.

Hillier, Bill, and Julienne Hanson. 1984. *The Social Logic of Space*. New York: Cambridge University Press.

Kraemer, Sieverts & Partners. 1977. Translated by James L. Ritchie. *Open-Plan Offices: New Ideas, Experience, and Improvements*. London: Mc-Graw-Hill.

Lang, Jon, Charles Burnette, Walter Moleski, and D. Vachon, eds. 1974. *Design for Human Behavior*. Stroudsburg, Pa.: Dowden, Hutchinson & Ross.

Law, Noel. 1984. "Post-Occupancy Evaluation within DHC: A Review of Four Pilot Studies." Canberra, Australia: Department of Housing and Construction, March.

Manning, Peter. 1965. *Office Design: A Study of Environment*. Liverpool: University of Liverpool, Dept. of Building Science.

Marans, Robert W., and Kent F. Spreckelmeyer. 1981. *Evaluating Built Environments: A Behavioral Approach*. Ann Arbor: Institute for Social Research.

———. 1986. "A Conceptual Model for Evaluating Work Environments." In *Behavioral Issues in Office Design*, ed. Jean D. Wineman, 67–84. New York: Van Nostrand Reinhold.

Sanoff, Henry. 1977. *Methods of Architectural Programming*. Stroudsburg, Pa.: Dowden, Hutchinson & Ross.

Shibley, Robert G. 1982. "Building Evaluation Services." *Progressive Architecture* 12:64–66.

Sommer, Robert. 1983. *Social Design: Creating Buildings with People in Mind*. Englewood Cliffs, N.J.: Prentice-Hall.

Spradley, James P. 1979. *The Ethnographic Interview*. New York: Holt, Rinehart & Winston.

Wilson, Forrest, 1984. *A Graphic Survey of Perception and Behavior for the Design Professions*. New York: Van Nostrand Reinhold.

Wineman, Jean D., ed. 1986. *Behavioral Issues in Office Design*. New York: Van Nostrand Reinhold.

Wineman, Jean, and Craig Zimring. 1986. "Energy Past and Future." *Progressive Architecture* 4:114–17.

Zeisel, John. 1981. *Inquiry by Design*. Monterey, Cal.: Brooks/Cole.
Zimring, Craig M., and Janet E. Reizenstin. "A Primer on Post-Occupancy Evaluation." *AIA Journal* 11:52–58.

CHAPTER 9

Ackoff, Russell L. 1967. *The Design of Social Research*. Chicago: The University of Chicago Press.
Ackoff, Russell L., and Maurice W. Sasieni. 1968. *Fundamentals of Operations Research*. New York: Wiley.
American Institute of Architects (AIA). 1983. "Microcomputer-based Energy Analysis." In *AIA Energy Professional Development Program*. Washington, D.C.: AIA.
Burden, Ernest. 1985. *Design Simulation*. New York: Wiley.
Clark, Roger H., and Michael Pause. 1985. *Precedents in Architecture*. New York: Van Nostrand Reinhold.
Clipson, Colin W., and Joseph J. Wehrer. 1973. *Planning for Cardiac Care*. Ann Arbor: Health Administration Press, University of Michigan.
Cross, Nigel. 1977. *The Automated Architect*. London: Pion.
Data-base for Engineers and Architects to Locate and Utilize Software (DAEDALUS). 1986. *HVAC/Energy Analysis Software Directory*. Washington, D.C.: American Consulting Engineers Council.
Doubilet, Susan, and Thomas Fisher. 1986. "Intelligent Computers." *Progressive Architecture* 6:104–13.
Greenblat, C. S., and R. D. Duke. 1981. *Principles and Practices of Gaming-Simulation*. Beverly Hills: Sage.
Hasell, Jo, and John L. Taylor. 1981. "Gaming/Simulation: An Approach to the Study of Environmental Change and Development." *Proceedings of the 12th Annual Conference of the Environmental Design Research Association*, Ames, Iowa, 119–32.
Joedicke, Jurgen, and Walter Mayer. 1982. "The Hospital Ward from the Bed Perspective." *German Research* 2:26–28.
Kemper, Alfred M. 1985. *Pioneers in CAD in Architecture*. Pacifica, Cal.: Hurland/Swenson.
King, Jonathan, Robert W. Marans, and Lois Solomon. 1982. *Pre-Construction Evaluation*. Ann Arbor: Architectural Research Laboratory.
Naisbitt, John. 1982. *Megatrends: Ten New Directions Transforming Our Lives*. New York: Warner Communications.
Pressman, Norman, and June Tennsyon. 1983. "Dilemmas Facing Social Scientists and Designers." *Journal of Architectural Education* (Summer):16–21.
Representation, Journal of Graphic Education. 1984. "Teaching Graphics and the Role of the Journal: An Interview of JGE Editors" 1:2–3, 17–18.

Zilm, Frank S. 1980. *Computer Modeling in Hospital Planning: Three Case Studies*. Ann Arbor: Architectural Research Laboratory.

Zimmerman, Jane, James Loucks, and Stephen Polcyn. 1985. *Family Practice Medical Facility Examination Room*. Lawrence: University of Kansas.

Index

Pages in *italic* contain figures.